Reshaping Social Work Series

Series Editors: **Robert Adams, Lena Dominelli and Malcolm Payne**

The **Reshaping Social Work** series aims to develop the knowledge base for critical, reflective practitioners. Each book is designed to support students on qualifying social work programmes and update practitioners on crucial issues in today's social work, strengthening research knowledge, critical analysis and skilled practice to shape social work to meet future challenges.

Published titles

Anti-Racist Practice in Social Work Kish Bhatti-Sinclair
Social Work and Spirituality Margaret Holloway and Bernard Moss
Social Work Research for Social Justice Beth Humphries
Social Care Practice in Context Malcolm Payne
Critical Issues in Social Work with Older People Mo Ray, Miriam Bernard and
    Judith Phillips
Social Work and Power Roger Smith

Invitation to authors

The Series Editors welcome proposals for new books within the *Reshaping Social Work* series. Please contact one of the series editors for an initial discussion:

- Robert Adams at rvadams@rvadams.karoo.co.uk
- Lena Dominelli at lena.dominelli@durham.ac.uk
- Malcolm Payne at M.Payne@stchristophers.org.uk

Reshaping Social Work
Series Editors: **Robert Adams, Lena Dominelli and Malcolm Payne**
Series Standing Order ISBN 1–4039–4878–X
(outside North America only)

You can receive future titles in this series as they are published by placing a standing order. Please contact your bookseller or, in the case of difficulty, write to us at the address below with your name and address, the title of the series and the ISBN quoted above.

Customer Services Department
Macmillan Distribution Ltd
Houndmills
Basingstoke
Hampshire
RG21 6XS
England

Anti-Racist Practice in Social Work

Kish Bhatti-Sinclair

palgrave
macmillan

First published 2011 by
PALGRAVE MACMILLAN

Palgrave Macmillan in the UK is an imprint of Macmillan Publishers Limited, registered in England, company number 785998, of Houndmills, Basingstoke, Hampshire RG21 6XS

Palgrave Macmillan in the US is a division of St Martin's Press LLC, 175 Fifth Avenue, New York, NY 10010.

Palgrave Macmillan is the global academic imprint of the above companies and has companies and representatives throughout the world.

Palgrave® and Macmillan® are registered trademarks in the United States, the United Kingdom, Europe and other countries.

ISBN: 978–0–230–01307–0

This book is printed on paper suitable for recycling and made from fully managed and sustained forest sources. Logging, pulping and manufacturing processes are expected to conform to the environmental regulations of the country of origin.

A catalogue record for this book is available from the British Library.

A catalog record for this book is available from the Library of Congress.

10 9 8 7 6 5 4 3 2 1
20 19 18 17 16 15 14 13 12 11

Printed and bound in Great Britain by
CPI Antony Rowe, Chippenham and Eastbourne

Contents

List of figures and tables

Figures

Tables

List of practice examples and exercises

Practice examples

Exercises

Acknowledgements

A special thank you to Lena Dominelli for many years of support for this and other work.

Particular gratitude to PACs (People who Access Care Services) group for their contribution to service user participation and involvement in social work education.

Many thanks to past and present students and practice teachers in the Division of Social Work Studies, University of Southampton.

Introduction

The debate on 'race' and racism has a substantial history in social work, and social welfare in Britain has contributed greatly to the development of fundamental ideas on human rights, equality of opportunity, anti-discriminatory practice, empowerment, identity, diversity and difference. The attention given to 'race' and racism has been both sustained and casual at different times, and students and social workers may wonder, therefore, why anti-racist practice continues to be important to contemporary professional practice. The answer lies partly in the idea that social workers remain committed to human rights, ethics and values (Dominelli, 1997) and continuously seek a sharper understanding of how to apply theoretical concepts found in:

- universal humanitarian principles
- professional ethics (Banks, 2004) and codes of conduct
- national law, policy and procedure.

There are many other more philosophical reasons, including the premise that advantages such as money and other material resources are better shared, and that this is likely to result in a happier and more equal society (Hugman, 2005).

This chapter sets out some of the key messages from the relevant literature and introduces the arguments for anti-racist practice to those seeking broader knowledge and understanding, such as students, social workers, managers and allied professional groups. The contribution made by social work service users is incorporated throughout the book.

BME (black and minority ethnic) will be used as an acronym to depict people seen as different on the basis of colour, culture, religion, tradition, custom and country of birth or origin. A glossary of terms can be found at the end of this book, and terminology and the understanding of words are further examined in Chapters 1 and 2. Although models and exercises are provided, the book is not a manual on how to work with cultural, religious or ethnic differences. Some attention is paid to issues of identity and social cohesion, but other areas of serious concern to society, such as Islamaphobia, extremism and secularism, are beyond the parameters of this book.

The book is more concerned to engage readers in examining personal prejudice, checking assumptions and avoiding approaches which may be discriminatory. It also sets out the legal and policy duties of all public employees as well as social work students in relation to 'race' and racism.

Why anti-racist practice?

Social work training includes components on ethics and values primarily because practitioners deal with the poorest and most deprived individuals and groups in society. As a result, professionals are aware that most people accessing their services are likely to be disadvantaged and that some groups face greater hardship than others. This is confirmed by statistical information. For example, there are 1.6 million British Muslims in the UK, of which 46% were born in the UK and 38% reside in London (Khan, 2008). Of the 46% born in the UK, 62% are Pakistani or Bangladeshi, and 39% have no qualifications (compared to 29% for the population as a whole). Data such as this is interesting for social workers seeking to provide services informed by evidence. Deeper analysis of the figures may lead to better targeted work with, for example, Pakistani and Bangladeshi children (living with one earning BME adult) who face an approximately 50% chance of poverty. This is compared to 15% for white children in similar situations. BME children in general also live in larger than average family groups (Khan, 2008).

The age profile of Pakistani and Bangladeshi people is typically younger than other groups (Khan, 2008), and it is possible that future social workers will be involved more in the lives of such families. To illustrate this, Practice example 0.1 offers a snapshot of one family living in relative poverty – an area of concern for welfare more generally but not necessarily a priority area for social work intervention. It is an amalgamation of anecdotal information on similar families, offered by teachers and health visitors concerned to highlight the importance of child wellbeing at the bottom end of need.

practice example 0.1

A BME family living in relative poverty

A Bangladeshi family, consisting of two adults and four children, is living in a three-bedroom council flat in an inner London borough. The mother was born and grew up in London, and the father arrived from Bangladesh after their marriage. Both parents receive welfare benefits but appear to do occasional low-income, home-based work (such as tailoring). Neighbours report excessive crying and banging on the walls, which they claim is coming from one child, aged three, believed to have unassessed learning difficulties. Another child aged four is due to begin school shortly but appears not to be at a nursery and is at home with the parents. The other children, a seven-year-old daughter and a nine-year-old son, are at the local primary school. They often come to school late in a tired state and are away for longer than normal holiday periods, which are not explained to, or authorized by, the school. The school teachers have expressed concern to the education welfare and health services who have visited the family but the parents have both been politely unresponsive to their concerns about the children. They state clearly that they love their children, work hard and provide a good home for the family.

The relevant teachers, health visitors and education welfare officers agree that the parents are genuine but are still concerned that their understanding of child wellbeing may be different from that expected within wider society. The agencies have sought social work input, but thus far this has not been forthcoming from the authorities because the case is not deemed sufficiently serious to warrant intervention.

This example may be seen to perpetuate stereotypes, but it is based on real families and there is some truth in the situation faced by the parents and children, surviving with minimal contact with children's services beyond school. Ethnicity, language and cultural differences may compound disadvantages in such cases because the family may not understand welfare rights or wish to seek public services. It may also be that teachers and health visitors see the family as self-isolating and blame the adults without sufficient understanding of the facts of the situation.

It is easier to jump to immediate conclusions than to check on the strength, resilience and child-rearing skills of the family members. Anti-racist practice suggests that the family's capacity to cope with the welfare needs of the four children requires a well-planned, coordinated investigation by all the professional groups involved. Public sector organizations across the board have a responsibility to maximize the chances available to such families and to break the cycle of deprivation faced by one generation after another (Chapter 1).

However, there are challenges facing the professionals working with such families and these include:

■ how best to allay the fears of the neighbours expressing concerns about the children within relevant confidentiality and data protection frameworks
■ how to communicate child welfare standards sensitively but firmly to the parents
■ how to create organizational awareness of the needs of British-born children being brought up by parents following Bangladeshi norms and values
■ how to guide the parents to take an interest in and seek advice from authorities on the services available for learning difficulties.

Ways forward may include:

■ referral by the school to the local social work children and families team

- training and supervision provided by the manager/team/organization on the knowledge and skills needed by the professional taking the lead on the case
- a meeting between the lead professional and the parents to explain procedures and inform them that concerns for the children have been expressed which have to be responded to
- assessment of the needs of the whole family as well as each individual child
- a confident, well-informed exchange with the parents on their norms and values on child welfare
- clarification of the services available for relevant members
- assurances that the family's cultural and religious differences will be respected by all professionals.

The family may require initial contact and assessment from social workers, but need continuous multi-agency support rather than crisis intervention. Professionals may wish to discuss the ethical content of their work and apply the agreed principles sensitively when engaging with the parents. This is particularly important if the standards of child-care are different and have to be negotiated to fit in with law and policy.

The book's argument and organization

The multiracial profile of Britain is largely based on the numbers residing in urban areas. For example, 80% of Muslims reside in the five large conurbations of the UK (Khan, 2008). There is a good argument for legally driven anti-racist social work practice (Dominelli, 2008) in these areas (Chapter 1), but there is also a need to consider how services are delivered to BME groups in rural settings. Strategic planning based on government and other data is seen to be critical to anti-racist practice in all parts of the UK; for example, the Commission for Racial Equality (CRE, 2002) sought evidence from public authorities on the use of the 2001 census in public services.

Social workers functioning in suburban, semi-rural and rural settings may particularly benefit from understanding and using research evidence on individuals and communities in their locality and region. Knowledge such as this is likely to produce a finer definition of marginalized groups and sharper, more efficient services. For example, the ethnicity of service user groups in large parts of Britain is white, but in many areas, small community groups, such as Gypsies and Travellers, need services which are particular to their cultural needs and familial patterns of care. Difference is often conceptualized beyond skin colour and can have serious consequences for groups such as Gypsies and Travellers (Chapter 2). This is illustrated by the experience of 100 Roma immigrants in Belfast in 2009, who were forced to return to Romania as a result of racist intimidation by Northern Irish citizens. The analysis in media reports (*The Guardian*, 27 June 2009) suggested that the Roma people face similar discrimination in other countries and that the deportation of Roma people is on the rise across Europe. In cases such as this, newer immigrants appear to be intimidated as much by white people as other more established Roma or Gypsies.

Services based on local demographic information as well as research evidence will be equally responsive to Bangladeshi and Roma families. However, social workers intervening in their lives also need time and resources to develop long-term, trusting relationships. Participative approaches which promote the norms and values of the relevant group need to be developed through, for example, seeking community volunteers who can be consulted on child wellbeing and kinship patterns of care.

A key aim of this book is to consider ways forward which are meaningful and useful for students, social workers and service users. Another task is to examine professional knowledge, provide an opportunity to engage with 'race' as a social construct and make the process of learning helpful and inclusive (Chapters 3 and 4). A greater, more ambitious goal is to offer the profession an opportunity to develop the knowledge and skills to confidently defend anti-racist practice in the 21st century.

A great deal of the work on issues of 'race' and racism took place in the 1970s and 80s. Social workers were aware that the focus on anti-racism often led to the development of good practice for all service users (Chapter 5). Although significant, anti-racist activity occurred in a compressed, compact manner over a short period of time. It did, however, perform a number of important functions:

1 It informed social workers about their ethical and legal duties.
2 For many committed practitioners, it provided a place where principles of justice and equality could be promoted.
3 It allowed the expression of personal ideology based on ethnic, cultural and religious background and the exploration of individual identity at a number of levels.
4 It examined how racism was understood, expressed and transmitted more widely in society as well as through social work education (Chapter 6).

Developments such as this illustrate the relevance of recent history to contemporary practice. Ideas and theories from the past offer examples of what worked and what did not, highlight gaps and offer an opportunity to maximize learning. A great many outcomes from this period can be further explored and developed in order that anti-racist social work practice can survive the rapid global changes of the new millennium.

The structure of the book is set out below. The chapter summaries offer a snapshot of the arguments, highlight specific content and introduce the key concerns.

Chapter summaries

The imperative for a well-informed workforce grows greater as social workers (as a group) increasingly represent the profession to other occupations and (individually) maintain their positions with regulatory bodies such as the General Social Care Council (GSCC) or the Health Professions Council (HPC) and the proposed College of Social Work (Social Work Task Force, 2009).

Within their own professional settings, social workers are aware that services are provided to legally defined groups and know how to interpret statutory responsibilities on a daily basis. Professional practice is deemed to follow principles of equality and fairness, and the overarching aim of the legally informed social worker is to ensure equal access to benefits and facilities, and to consult service users on needs, quality and standards. In relation to anti-racist practice, however, social workers continue to seek knowledge and guidance on finer ethical interventions.

Chapter 1 introduces the key influences and debates on anti-racist practice and sets out key laws on 'race' and racism in relation to social work practice. It also provides the backdrop to the Equality Act 2006 and its overseeing body, the Equality and Human Rights Commission (EHRC). The Equality Act 2006 brings together important equality functions in relation to 'race', religion or belief, gender (including gender identity), disability and sexual orientation. It links ideas, such as how 'race' intersects with other equality areas, and suggests that multiple discrimination and institutional racism need to be incorporated into law, policy and practice. The chapter also examines the relevance of social activism, identity and identification to anti-racist social work practice.

Professionals in welfare organizations are increasingly challenged by technological and communication change and, in order to keep up with this, they have to maintain their knowledge, skills and values. The argument in Chapter 2 is that globalization and internationalization impact on the everyday concerns of those delivering welfare services, for example in relation to groups such as unaccompanied asylum seekers. Social workers are aware that globalization, a term principally linked to trade and economic integration, requires some attention but often struggle to make sense of its meaning within everyday work. International events, however, directly influence welfare provision. For example, the newly elected British government announced stringent public expenditure cuts in 2010 in response to the financial mismanagement by international banks which took place in previous years.

Within a scenario where welfare is squeezed by financial pressures fuelled elsewhere, Britain continues to assist its citizens, as well as visitors from other European countries. Within this context and despite tighter budgets, social workers, along with other service providers, have to confidently meet their legal and policy obligations, both to those who have just arrived as well as to those who are better established.

In order to meet their obligations, social workers are looking for examples of good practice and new ideas from other parts of the world, which can be applied within different regions of the UK. Chapter 2 seeks to examine the impact of global forces on anti-racist social work practice and introduces words, ideas and principles on globalization which relate to 'race' and racism. There is an argument for a better understanding of the relationship between global events and the everyday concerns of social work professionals.

The need for better professional standards, underpinned by knowledge-based education, was reinforced in 2009 by the Social Work Task Force Report. This report recommended a Social Work Reform Board, which was then set up in January 2010, to oversee the setting up of a national College of Social Work, a further confirmation of the need for a sharper focus on practice informed by evidence.

Chapter 3 examines the links between universal, professional and personal knowledge in relation to the development of capacity and identity. The overarching aim is to question ideology, in order to maintain commitment to personal and professional development and change built on common historical threads. This examination is informed by the thinking of selected BME activists and writers who have had a significant influence on the development of anti-racist social work practice. Chapter 3 evaluates how and where knowledge is produced, who uses it and who benefits from it. This is supported by exercises to enable readers to explore the multidimensional nature of identity and how individuals identify and relate to others, while building professional and interdisciplinary knowledge.

One of the outcomes of modernization is that social workers are working with constant change, both in their operational duties and in the way they are defined and regulated (Social Work Task Force, 2009). Roles, tasks and responsibilities are at the same time fixed, for example in relation to the probationary and higher licensed status recommended by the Social Work Task Force, and fluid, for example in a multidisciplinary team. Payne (2009, p. 59) suggests that social workers are increasingly undertaking 'hybrid' duties, supported by a range of funding sources. Within this context, professionals are required to adapt methods and approaches to suit the multiprofessional nature of the workplace, while promoting core professional values on issues such as 'race' and racism.

The overarching aim of Chapter 4 is to offer ideas which can inform employers and employees seeking to enhance existing practice, as well as to promote new thinking on 'race' and racism. There is an imperative to acquire specific knowledge which supports the development of policy and research and so the argument for good practice is supported by models and exercises which promote individual and group understanding.

Chapter 5 compares the experience of BME and other service user groups in relation to anti-racist practice. The two perspectives are pertinent and relevant to social work both for professional and ethical reasons (Forbat, 2004). The role of service users and BME groups within consultative and participatory social care processes is considered in a manner which suggests that the two groups share a number of features as public sector stakeholders who use and inform the development of services.

Service user feedback on improving practice, both generally and in relation to BME needs, is long-standing, and such groups have regularly highlighted barriers which impede change and development. As a result, the involvement and empowerment of service users in welfare provision is considered widely in the social work literature (Cree and Davis, 2007), particularly in relation to consultation, participation and direct input on organizational policies and procedures (Leach, 1996).

BME service users have attempted to change the planning and delivery of public services, but found superficial rather than substantive responses from organizational leaders, as well as from professionals (SCIE, 2006). Chapter 5 evaluates the background to service user involvement, considers approaches which empower service users and examines the relevant laws, policies and practices.

The move from the focus on 'race' and racism in the 1980s and 90s towards the more universal principles set out in the degree in social work in 2003 has resulted in less teaching and assessment of anti-racist practice. Evidence suggests that educational processes, which examine students' knowledge, understanding and strategies relating to 'race' and racism, have diminished over time (Singh, 2006). This has meant that social work students may not be knowledgeable about their legal and policy duties in relation to the Race Relations (Amendment) Act 2000. Overall, the change has not been critiqued by the academic and practice community in the social work literature. However, the Social Work Task Force Report (2009) recommends structural changes to the programmes of study and, therefore, offers a new opportunity to incorporate 'race' and racism within emerging thinking on social work training and education.

Chapter 6 aims to examine anti-racist practice within the context of the new professional regulatory frameworks on social work roles and tasks (Higham, 2009). It also considers how students and newly qualified social workers may progress from entry into the profession to gaining a licence to practise at the end of the probationary year. The need to develop learning organizations is supported by the Social Work Task Force Report (2009), which recommends the advanced teaching organization status, a move which is likely to enhance workplace learning and embed support for social work staff into training.

Finally, Chapter 7 seeks to summarize the contents of the book and introduces the rationale for the development of anti-racist practice to students, social workers and managers. The aim is to offer a snapshot of the perspectives included in the book and to invite discussion with service users, related professionals, policy makers and social work educators on creative ways to improve services affected by racism and discrimination.

1 Influences on anti-racist social work practice

Introduction

This chapter introduces the relevant legal frameworks and considers the impact of social activism on 'race' and racism in relation to professional social work and social care.

Statutory provisions have a significant influence on professional practice in the UK, and as a result social workers are skilful users of laws, policies and procedures, particularly those which support direct interventions. Regulation and registration systems stipulate that public sector workers continuously update their knowledge and skills, as well as seek guidance on, for example, how the gap between personal values and professional practice can be met. Despite this, social workers do not always see the necessity of understanding broader legal provisions on human rights, equality, discrimination and racism.

Ongoing training and support are necessary because developmental change is a significant feature of contemporary social policy. Legal provisions on 'race' and racism are not integral to social work laws, and professionals need well-planned opportunities to incorporate anti-racist laws into the procedures and guidance they follow on an everyday basis. This can be undertaken as part of regular supervision sessions with managers who have the relevant experience, and/or within continuous professional development personal plans, and/or specialist anti-racist training provided by employers.

The justification to employers for investment in this lies in the argument that a reasonable understanding of legal frameworks allows social workers and students to:

- practise as trainees, employees and representatives of government and non-governmental organizations
- provide services to defined service user groups
- interpret and integrate statute into organizational guidance
- base practice on the principles of equality and fairness.

Regular and constant change within social policy is illustrated by the 1997–2010 Labour government review of equal opportunity laws in the early 2000s, which resulted in the Equality Act 2006, an overarching legal framework which covers a number of anti-discriminatory areas including 'race' and racism.

Conscious of the changing landscape, this chapter will also reflect on how words and definitions link language to legal and moral meanings. The Glossary introduces relevant terminology and defines, for example, racism and racial discrimination, two terms which are often used interchangeably but each holding a distinctive legal meaning. Racial discrimination, if proven, is a criminal act, whereas racism is an ideology and/or a belief system. The Race Relations (Amendment) Act 2000 and the Equality Act 2006 (see Table 1.1 below) allow for a clear differentiation between racism as an act and racism as a belief. So an association or political group, such as the British National Party (BNP), would be proceeding unlawfully by actively excluding membership of the party on the grounds of racial difference. This may be seen as a racist act. If the BNP was also suggesting that the multiracial profile of London meant that the capital city did not represent British people, this would be seen as a belief.

Laws on 'race', racism and equality

The Race Relations (Amendment) Act 2000 provides important additions to the Race Relations Act 1976 and other predecessor laws, such as the 1965 and 1968 Race Relations Acts. The 2000 Act outlaws discrimination in all public authority functions and, in particular, empowers the inspection of children's services by organizations such as Ofsted (Office for Standards in Education), and requires social services and social care agencies to consult and report on:

- measurable outcomes – how equal treatment is defined and measured
- targeted services – which services are specifically meeting the needs of the local BME populations
- information – the means by which the public is informed of such services
- complaints procedures – how these are received and responded to.

Legislation on 'race', racism and equality, based on the Race Relations Act 1965 and the Race Relations Act 1968, has been incorporated in the frameworks set out in Table 1.1. The basic principle is that amended laws, codes and guidance incorporate past provisions, and so, for example, the 1984 Code of Practice for the Elimination of Racial Discrimination and the Promotion of Equality of Opportunity in Employment remains in force today and may be included in subsequent laws.

Table 1.1 Primary laws on 'race' and racism

Law	Overseeing government body	Main provisions
Race Relations Act 1965	The Race Relations Board	Outlawed racism in public places and transportation
Race Relations Act 1968	The Race Relations Board	Incorporated housing and employment as arenas where racism may take place
Race Relations Act 1976	The Commission for Racial Equality (CRE)	Differentiated between direct and indirect discrimination, set out public sector duties and incorporated the following key principles: ▪ Defined direct and indirect discrimination and made it unlawful ▪ Outlawed unfair treatment and victimization in training and employment ▪ Covered the provision of goods, facilities, services, education, housing and other activities ▪ Individuals are allowed to bring proceedings and claim damages (but the original provisions excluded government departments)
Race Relations (Amendment) Act 2000	The Commission for Racial Equality (CRE)	Amendments to the above. Power to issue a statutory Code of Practice on the Duty to Promote Race Equality. The Code applies to public authorities in England and Wales. The Code of Practice for Scotland applies to devolved authorities in Scotland
Equality Act 2006	The Equality and Human Rights Commission (EHRC), combining the remit of the outgoing CRE, the Equal Opportunities Commission and the Disability Rights Commission and covering England, Northern Ireland, Wales and Scotland	Absorbed important equality functions in relation to 'race', religion or belief, gender (including gender identity), disability and sexual orientation. Defined and outlawed discrimination on the grounds of race, gender, disability, sexual orientation, transgender, religion/belief and age. Placed a general duty on public bodies to promote race equality and good race relations

In relation to the responsibilities of social workers, the overarching aim of the law is to ensure equal access to benefits and facilities and to consult service users on needs, quality and standards. For employers of public sector staff (including students), the laws relate to equal treatment within, for example, recruitment, retention and promotion processes, as well as more general worker rights (GSCC, 2002a).

The bringing together of equality legislation under the umbrella of the Equality Act 2006 has made life easier for students, social workers and employers, but the relevance of this Act to social work laws requires clarification. The Equality Act 2006 assembles important statutory duties for public sector workers and is overseen by one overarching body, the Equality and Human Rights Commission (EHRC). In practical terms, this means that most of the information for complying with this Act is signposted or provided by the EHRC, and challenges to the relevant laws can be filtered through the EHRC for England, Scotland and Wales (http://www.equalityhumanrights.com/).

The amalgamation of equality functions has a number of critics, however, including the Race Equality Foundation (previously the Race Equality Unit of the National Institute for Social Work), which expressed particular concern about the dilution of 'race'-related provisions under a single equality law (Race Equality Foundation, 2008). This suggests that the relationship between and across equality areas needs to be taken into account if structural and institutional racism, for example in children's services, is to be addressed properly.

In order to maintain focus, the Race Equality Foundation (2008) recommended greater attention be paid to the following areas:

- how 'race' intersects with and incorporates other equality areas, such as age-related children's rights
- multiple discrimination, for example the combined impact of sex/disability/age on a service user from a BME background
- compliance measures which address anti-racism in the same way as other anti-discriminatory areas, such as sex discrimination
- weak or unenforced laws, such as those which leave people frustrated or angry
- the disproportionate focus on costs and administrative burdens, for example within resource-led organizational systems
- effective enforcement tools, such as performance indicators, reports and inspections.

The Race Equality Foundation suggests that such issues are critical to the development of anti-racist policies, and that they have not been sufficiently incorporated into the modernization of laws on equality and human rights.

Participation and consultation are also areas of concern for the Race

Equality Foundation (2008, p. 17), which commented on the poor recognition given to black perspectives within law and public policy:

> Certainly, there has been a raft of legislation developed over the years but each legislative development has been the subject of a struggle carried out by pressure groups and activists. This fact is nowhere reflected in the pages of the review.

Social justice and social work

The review of equality laws, leading to the Equality Act 2006, included discussion on anti-racist principles, duties and responsibilities in the White Paper *Fairness for All: A New Commission for Equality and Human Rights* (DTI, 2004; McGhee, 2008). Subsequent work by the Equalities and Human Rights Commission (Equalities Review, 2007b) was driven by the need to produce data (particularly in areas such as sexual orientation and religion) based on defined and measurable outcomes. The EHRC sought evidence of economic, educational and social achievement, and why, for example, some BME groups and individuals accomplished more than others. In relation to 'race', the EHRC focused on the poor representation of ethnic minorities in the following sectors: Parliament, business and the media (Equalities Review, 2007a). More broadly, the EHRC looked for indicators of success and how the opening and closing of opportunities impacts on individual achievement. So, for example, the commission looked to find out more about factors such as environment, working conditions and general image to enable professionals to work better with BME service users, and for organizations to have a higher representation of BME workers (CRE, 2002).

Despite what may look like positive messages, the underlying motivation for these ideas is questioned by critics. They suggest that successive governments, in response to the changing nature of society and the demographic profile of the population, promote strategies, such as better integration of BME workers, which aim to assimilate immigrants within the host society, rather than promote multiculturalism, difference and diversity:

> it is in the promise to better manage post-entry integration of migrant communities where the government's assimilationist strategy is revealed ... this is dedicated to scouring away the surface of cultural distinctiveness in migrant communities to break down the cultural barriers to their full integration that is antithetical to a multicultural project dedicated to respecting diversity. (McGhee, 2005, p. 74)

There is little doubt, however, that the multiracial profile of the country requires that some thought be given to cohesion, commonality and fusion by those delivering services within statutory and independent sectors. Adherence to central government provisions is complicated (as demonstrated by Practice example 1.1 below) by the sheer number of legal provisions, for example on wellbeing and age, and this may result in incoherent rather than focused strategic responses. It is likely that a unitary local authority serving approximately 500,000 residents, of which 8% are from BME communities, will fail to employ a unified approach to equality within all services. Laws may be implemented differently across, as well as inside, the same department or division. For example, education may be applying assimilationist models within its schools, while children and families workers, following social work laws, may be more concerned to ensure that the rights of the child are defined clearly within protection and safeguarding processes. It may be that assimilation approaches are appropriate in schools, while upholding rights for looked after children is relevant to social justice and the improvement of life chances. Both strategies may be equally valuable, but teachers and social workers need time together to examine the operational strategies used to apply the law in everyday work.

Practice example 1.1 illustrates the complexities of applying anti-racist laws which relate to education, children's rights, equality and discrimination.

Using anti-racist law in practice

practice example 1.1

A family has been referred to the children and families service for assessment. A young man of Somalian background (aged 15) has been referred by his school because he is demonstrating signs of extreme anger and frustration towards teachers and other pupils. The school believes that the young man may have an undiagnosed learning difficulty as well as behavioural problems. Other parents have reported to the school that he has been violent towards members of his own family (including younger siblings), but attempts to talk to his parents have not been successful. The young man's wellbeing as well as future prospects are at risk and the teachers are concerned that he will leave school without any qualifications or ways to gain further training and skills.

The children and families service responds by saying that the age of the young man means that he is likely to be transferred to adult services within the coming months. The social workers also informally suggest to the head teacher that addressing poor behaviour and attainment is not within the remit of a service with limited resources and overwhelming child protection duties.

Practice example 1.1 suggests that the rights of the young person may not be entirely taken into account, and that he may be discriminated against on a number of grounds including his age, (dis)ability and ethnic origin. It appears that there is insufficient consideration of cultural and religious issues as required by the Children Act 1989. There is a hint of dismissal by the children and families service because he may be too old to be assessed for future (children's) services. His possible needs as a disabled Somali young person are not specified or referred for further assessment, and this may be seen as indirect discrimination on the grounds of age and disability.

It is unclear whether the Code of Practice on the Duty to Promote Race Equality (Race Relations (Amendment) Act 2000) has been considered by the children and families service in relation to Somali families more generally in the locality. The key problem may be that the case falls between two main service providers, and as a result is likely to slip through the net of all the statutory services. This may be because the *potential* for poor attainment, violence or bad behaviour are covered minimally or remain unenforced within legal frameworks.

It may be concluded that services are looking to ensure their own performance targets are prioritized and can satisfy inspection processes. Good practice suggests that child wellbeing covers young people aged between 15 and 21, and is addressed equally within children's/youth and adults services. Ideally, an assessment of the young man's needs should take into account how the intersection or overlap between disadvantage based on age, disability and racial difference as well as (possible) poverty, low income and poor housing impacts on his life course. The needs of the whole family may not be within the remit of any one organization, but it may be a good idea to investigate further in case there are hidden issues such as domestic violence or other offending behaviour. The family situation requires clarification in order that assumptions can be avoided, or rumours confirmed, about the lack of support for the young man within the home.

In order to overcome the legal and resource shortfalls illustrated by Practice example 1.1, committed professionals are likely to apply social work laws alongside the Equality Act 2006 and the Race Relations (Amendment) Act 2000. Closer adherence to statutory duties will lead to better targeting of resources and deeper, more rigorous approaches to the development of policy on anti-racist social work practice. It will also allow better open/public reporting of service responses to groups such as Somali young people.

The questions which require consideration by all welfare professionals are strategic as well as routine, but in general daily demands dominate social work responses. In order to undertake challenging duties, however, legal practitioners require global, national and local knowledge derived from personal awareness as well as joint training with related professional groups.

The amalgamation of the equality laws within the Equality Act 2006 suggests a commitment to shared values, as well as improved relations between and across relevant groups. However, the move away from specific laws on 'race', sex and disability may mean that targeted services to, for example, individual women and those with needs based on BME status and disabilities may diminish. This may be a problem for those in need of such services, but in general the change is good for professionals working with increasingly mobile families, facing constant crises which sometimes span two or three generations. The shift from individual assessment of need, for example one social worker with responsibility for a child in a family and another with responsibility for the grandparent, towards holistic responses to the wider family will result in a significant shift in anti-racist practice. Arguably, the focus on the whole unit will benefit family-centred service provision, particularly to BME communities, whose household size is double the British average (Fabian Society, 2006).

Addressing family and intergenerational deprivation is a particular priority within social policy, highlighted by the EHRC in its *Interim Report for Consultation* (Equalities Review, 2007a, p. 11): 'We propose that we see the emerging inequalities in a different way, which recognises chronic and persistent inequalities.' The report goes on to state that vulnerability as a result of class, 'race' and/or gender may lead to disadvantage and, added to misfortune or life crisis (Equalities Review, 2007a), is more likely to result in state intervention. Social workers often intercede at such critical points in the lives of vulnerable people and skilfully resolve immediate as well as far-reaching care problems. It is clear that there is a hierarchy of disadvantage and that some BME individuals and families are likely to receive more state aid than others because poverty, poor housing and related factors curtail opportunities: 'For some groups (most frequently but not exclusively defined by race and religion) disadvantage is effectively being passed from parent to child' (Equalities Review, 2007a, p. 28).

In order to address this, social work organizations need to comply better with anti-racist policies and seek better empirical research evidence and statistical data which supports strategic service planning for families trapped by poor social conditions and diminished life chances. This suggests that those providing services identify barriers and address gaps in order that children and families can break free from the 'penalties' and 'effective cost' of poverty, deprivation and disadvantage (Equalities Review, 2007a, p. 28). The EHRC seeks to monitor equality laws and policy developments in relation to, for example, the educational attainment of children in care.

It may be that social workers, driven by evidence-based practice, will use research findings which track overall trends which link the effects of family or generational deprivation on child wellbeing. Understanding the evidence gathered by national bodies such as the EHRC will help social workers to better frame the needs of disadvantaged children in their locality within a larger (national) framework. Well-informed social workers will support successful progress and provide resources for looked after children equally within schools and care services.

Applying anti-racist laws

The modernization of equality laws is well advanced, but social workers and students may welcome greater understanding of the developments which have taken place over a number of decades. Such legal progress has been critiqued as inadequate over time by social work academics (Dominelli, 2008), but at the time, the Race Relations Act 1976 provided momentous powers to local government and was foundational for anti-racist social work practice in Britain.

Although the legal basis for anti-racist social work practice lies in the 1965, 1968 and 1976 Race Relations Acts, the gathering of all anti-discriminatory laws under the government's equalities umbrella occurred at the same time as professional social work moved further towards incorporating 'race' within the broader, more universal concept of ethical practice (TOPSS, 2002; Hugman, 2005; CSCI, 2006).

Ethical practice per se was not welcomed by commentators who suggested that social workers need to understand the difference between laws which define professional powers and specific duties, for example in relation to mental wellbeing, and laws which provide for general public services, for example in relation to healthcare. It may be argued that anti-racist and equalities laws fall into the latter category.

However, ethical practitioners follow the principle that a law passed in 1976 exists alongside another placed on the statute books today (unless repealed or overridden) and, as a result, provide services which meet both requirements. For example, a mental health professional is able to intervene in, assess and plan the treatment of a service user from a BME background within the provisions of the Mental Health Act 1983, while following core values of anti-racist social work practice set out in the Race Relations Act 1976.

In essence, the expectation is that the relationship between the service user and social worker is morally sound (Sheppard, 2006) because professionals are trusted to responsibly understand and apply personal standards in all their public duties:

> Social workers must adhere to statute and, when lawful, to their employers' procedures ... Occasionally, as with Approved Social Workers performing functions under the 1983 Mental Health Act, powers and duties are designated to individual practitioners. Here they are personally accountable rather than as an employee of a local authority. (Braye and Preston-Shoot, 2002, p. 63)

Inspection bodies such as Ofsted and the Care Quality Commission (previously the Commission for Social Care Inspection) are required to look for evidence of how services are delivered based on principles of good 'race' relations and equality of opportunity.

The Care Quality Commission (CQC) was set up in 2009 and is responsible for the registration, inspection, monitoring, reviewing and quality assurance of residential, nursing, fostering, adoption and domiciliary services. The Commission for Social Care Inspection (CSCI) worked under the provisions of the 2000 Care Standards Act, and the Department of Health National Minimum Standards. The CQC complies with national standards within children and adult services (CSCI, 2006) as well as equality duties:

> CSCI's statutory functions have all been assessed as highly relevant to delivering the objectives of the 2000 Race Relations (Amendment) Act and the 1995 Disability Discrimination Act and are all of equal priority under the requirements of the legislation ... Each of these functions is supported by a number of functions ... using the Equalities Impact Assessment Tool and methodology. (CSCI, 2006, p. 8)

The Race Relations Act 1976 provided a powerful steer to local government, but the provisions were interpreted and implemented selectively. For example, some schools used government funds to employ classroom assistants rather social care staff to undertake outreach work with BME families and communities. Enterprises linked to the Crown and government were excluded.

However, some regional and local authorities used the 1976 Act (and some linked funding) to positively support neighbourhood work such as:

- specialist funding for housing projects targeting BME communities supported by local government, frequently developed by voluntary and independent social care organizations
- specialist assistance for teachers in schools for children with linguistic, religious and cultural needs.

Historically, social work policy and procedure have been based on a range of legislation targeting the public sector, including the Children Act 1989. Section 22(5) specifies that religion, racial origin, culture and linguistic background must be taken into account when a child or young person is being accommodated. But this, and subsequent laws, did not provide for a consideration of how generations of children with particular needs may be disadvantaged as a result of poor care and family circumstances, as well as by religion, culture and ethnicity.

It may be argued that society has not placed sufficient emphasis on preventive welfare measures in statutory child welfare and that a great deal of legislation has come about as a direct result of a series of public enquiries into child deaths. But the Children Act 1989 did define anti-racist duties more clearly than other social work laws, such as the NHS and Community Care Act 1990, and this was subsequently enhanced by the Children Act 2004. Following historical precedent, the Children Act 2004 came into force as a result of the enquiry into the death of Victoria Climbié and the subsequent policy agenda of *Every Child Matters* (Jowitt and O'Loughlin, 2005).

The Laming Report (2003) on Victoria Climbié and the Macpherson Report (1999) on the murder of the BME teenager Stephen Lawrence have both impacted significantly on child protection and 'race' relations respectively in recent years. The former found significant failure in the child protection procedures of a number of local authorities. The latter found that institutional racism contributed greatly to poor police practice (Thompson, 2003).

The Macpherson Report made 70 general and particular recommendations to address institutional racism in the Metropolitan Police force. The CRE's review of legal frameworks resulted in addressing recommendation 11 of the Macpherson Report, which suggested that 'race' laws should be fully implemented by the police. The CRE published follow-up guidance requiring all police forces to define, report and record racist incidents, initiate race relations training and recruit BME police officers (CRE, 2007a; Home Office, 2007). The recommendations of the Macpherson Report were incorporated into the Race Relations (Amendment) Act 2000, leading to greater accountability and a sharper police focus on policing in the London area but the impact on policy and practice more generally has been questioned by the Race Equality Foundation (2008, p. 6) in its review of the work of the EHRC: 'Although mention is made of the Macpherson Inquiry, it is clear to us that the lessons accruing from the inquiry have not been comprehended.'

Policy and practice strive to maintain relevance to legal frameworks, and laws often play a significant part in maintaining focus and upholding standards. The Race Equality Foundation (2008) states that legal tools which counteract racist beliefs may be difficult to implement, but legal sanctions can penalize discriminatory policy and practice. So if a private school bans religious clothing as part of the school uniform policy, they may be challenged under the Race Relations (Amendment) Act 2000 and the Equality Act 2006 on the grounds of discrimination against the relevant religious group.

The Race Relations (Amendment) Act 2000 provides the EHRC with the power to ask public authorities, such as children's services, to produce 'race' equality schemes and policies which explain general and specific duties in relation to school children and staff. This is followed by inspection standards with indicators on how to assess the performance of children in tests and examinations.

A 'race' equality scheme produced by the Office of the Deputy Prime Minister (ODPM, 2006) recommended equality of opportunity and good relations between people from different racial groups and promoted good practice in the following:

■ implementation (outcome-based) plans on race equality impact assessments
■ staff training and guidance
■ race equality within all policy initiatives
■ fairness and equality within pay, learning and development.

The report includes specific actions taken in relation to, for example, computer-based information for staff on when and how impact assessments should take place, an outline of the relevant legislation, and updates on events, issues and research.

The use of census data by other public bodies to address gaps in services may also be inspected (CSCI, 2006; www.local-pi-library.gov.uk). However, such legal powers rely on the thoroughness, competence and ability of staff working for inspection bodies such as the CQC and Ofsted, as well as on the performance management and implementation skills of social workers.

The CRE, replaced by the EHRC, had good community relations at its core. Within this remit, the CRE expressed concern about the impact of contemporary challenges facing Britain, including the impact of increased migration, terrorism and rising extremism, on identity and citizenship: 'Several issues need to be discussed openly: how we live together rather than side by side ... how we encourage new Britons to adopt vital aspects of British life and how we share with new communities' (CRE, 2006, p. 2). Groundwork such as this is likely to be translated into the EHRC aims and objectives as equality is a high-profile area of public concern:

> The Commission's extensive powers and duties allow it to operate both generically and specifically as appropriate. It could, for example, seek to address inequalities in the provision of health care across the board while maintaining a focus on hate crimes that are targeted at race, religion or belief, and sexuality. (CEHR, 2006a, p. 1)

The Race Relations (Amendment) Act 2000 was overseen by the CRE until 2007 and allows for the promotion of good community relations as well as responses to racial hatred and extremist activity. A great deal of background work was carried out at a local level by a network of local race equality councils. The CRE (2006) expressed concern that the future focus on citizenship and cohesive communities may diminish and dilute 30 years of important 'race' relations work. The consultation on this created an interesting debate about the rationale and responsibility for 'race' relations in the public and private sectors both locally and nationally.

In order to address this possible shortfall, the CRE proposed an advisory and mediation body to work alongside the EHRC on issues such as conflict avoidance, resolution and the integration of new migrants within society. The emerging human rights agenda was seen as particularly problematic by the CRE, which pioneered important methods and approaches that empowered communities and neighbourhoods to seek and access, for example, social services.

Thereafter, the EHRC mission statement set out a programme of reform to:

- construct a new framework to challenge persistent patterns of discrimination and inequality
- promote and protect diversity, good relations (both between and within communities) and human rights.

The programme includes a review of inequality and comprehensive anti-discrimination procedures to support the Equality Act 2006 (CEHR, 2006a). In the area of research and education, the CRE recommended the use of a strong evidence base to support anti-racist practice.

The lead for the Equality Act 2006 came from the Department of Trade and Industry (DTI, 2006, p. 18), which was concerned to improve communication and access: 'Cross cutting approach ... equipped to address the reality of many dimensions of an individual's identity and therefore tackle discrimination on multiple grounds through a single access point.' Better communication is an overarching aim for many public services and it may be that the development of the new equalities framework will mean more coherence between related governmental bodies and public sector organizations delivering social work and health.

In response to the government's Equality Bill in 2009, the EHRC supported the idea of public authorities taking account of socioeconomic disadvantage in planning and monitoring services, for example the special health needs of primary age, inner-city school children living in poor housing and on low parental income.

Associated laws on 'race' and racism

A number of additional legal provisions have to be taken into account in the development of anti-racist social work practice, including laws such as the Crime and Disorder Act 1998. Among other things this Act deals with violence against the person, racial hostility and higher maximum criminal penalties where racial motivation is suspected. The Act also adds the offences of racially aggravated violence, harassment and criminal damage to the existing provisions.

The laws which relate to the stirring and provoking of racial hatred include the Criminal Justice and Public Order Act 1994, which outlaws the use and publication of such material, and the Anti-terrorism, Crime and Security Act 2001, which increased the maximum prison term from two to seven years for individuals convicted of incitement to racial hatred.

The Prevention of Incitement to Hatred Act (Northern Ireland) 1970 outlaws criminal activity deemed to stir up hatred against a section of the public on the grounds of religious belief, colour, race or ethnic or national background. However, enforcing equality laws in the context of Northern Ireland is complicated by sectarian differences and the low percentage of BME individuals. Similarly, the Scotland Act 1998 requires adherence to the Human Rights Act 1998, with specific provisions on countering racial hatred to meet the requirements of the Convention Rights (Compliance) (Scotland) Act 2001. The 1997–2010 Labour government required that all emerging laws comply with the Human Rights Act 1998, and that all public authorities follow the European Convention on Human Rights (see Chapter 2). The 2010 Conservative/Liberal Democrat coalition government, however, has changes to human rights legislation as a manifesto aim, and this is likely to herald a knock-on effect on equality and 'race' relations laws.

The problem faced by any national government, however, is that laws on human rights and 'race' stem from a number of international conventions and frameworks. For example, in response to the data evidencing racist public opinion, the European Union in particular continues to provide additional support for equal treatment within a range of directives which may be incorporated into domestic law.

Social activism

Anti-racist social work practice in Britain has been informed by universal conventions and developed as a result of these principles and ideas. Social activism, however, has often been set in motion by problems occurring in other parts of the world, sometimes as a result of the extreme abuse of professional power. This is illustrated by an example of child welfare policy followed in Australia, New Zealand and Canada, which sought to assimilate Maori and First Nations children into European ways of living. It led to the removal of many children into care and resulted in their long-term separation from families, cultures, languages and traditions:

> Many of these abuses have only recently been discussed publicly through the sustained efforts of those affected to tell their stories ... The silences about social work's role are a shameful legacy that practitioners and educators have to address alongside policy makers and the general public in the countries concerned. (Dominelli, 2004, p. 126)

This experience resulted in a major challenge from the indigenous peoples concerned to express concern for past injustices and determine their children's futures:

> In New Zealand, Australia and Canada as in the United States, the rise of indigenous activism paralleled the activism surrounding the civil rights movement … Indigenous strategies for action were pursued vigorously and international links were made through protest action as the mounting of various stands and events. (Tuhiwai-Smith, 2008, p. 113)

It also offered a number of important lessons for international social work beyond the countries involved:

1 That modern welfare policy could actively promote societal ideas which actively oppressed one group in developed welfare-based countries.
2 That child protection officers could confine rather than protect children.
3 The voice of indigenous and colonized peoples could be substantially overlooked and marginalized within service provision.

Britain is also open to accusations of dominance and subjugation, particularly by people from its former colonies. Over a 30-year period after the Second World War, such people left their home countries, settled in Britain and found employment within the public services:

> According to the 1983 ethnic monitoring survey, 6.1% of Birmingham City Council's total workforce was drawn from black communities … the Engineers Department recorded 15.9% … Ten years later the situation has been transformed radically, the figures from the 1993 monitoring exercise showed that the proportion of the city's workforce drawn from black communities had increased to 15.4%. (Solomos and Back, 1995, p. 180)

The BME population grew between 1993 and 2001 to 29.6% in Birmingham (compared to 9.1% in England in 2001). The rise in numbers impacted on social services aimed at younger and older groups throughout these decades, and there is little doubt that demographic changes such as these will continue to exercise policy makers and planners in the future. For example, the proportion of BME children under 16 is predicted to rise along with BME residents aged 65 and over (Simpson, 2007):

> The impact on services depends on how the care of the elderly is balanced within and outside the family … A greater use of institutional support for the elderly would reinforce the impact on care services of greater numbers of elderly. (Simpson, 2007, p. 6)

Over time, newly arrived immigrants became established, settling into positions of relative influence. Personal and professional experiences of welfare resulted in engagement and commentary on social and other public services. Social activism such as this led to an increase in the critical evaluation of public policy. This change in emphasis meant that like-minded white people, also keen to develop quality and social standards, became engaged in the development of ideas on anti-racism. This raised capacity and led to the greater questioning of language, words and meanings.

The English language evolved rapidly in response to the climate of the time and a number of words gained currency in relation to groups disadvantaged by 'race' and/or sex. As Schwarz (1996, p. 81) suggests, the meaning of any word has a 'social history' and its construction is more complex than is immediately apparent. The meanings of words change as they are contested, rejected or accepted by a range of users.

Ideas changed over time and although social workers actively sought engagement with anti-racist practice during this period, they did not always have the knowledge, skills or personal experience of 'race' and racism. During the 1970s, in-depth understanding of 'race' and the effects of racism was limited, and early initiatives in anti-racist practice resulted in behaviour which was sometimes counterproductive. For example, the focus on avoiding offence resulted in zero tolerance of any phrase, however descriptive, such as 'black mark', which depicted the word black in a negative manner (Solomos and Back, 1995).

The overall intention was good, but descriptive words became confused with those which were offensive and discriminatory such as 'nigger', which conversely appeared to be accepted elsewhere, for example within black rap music in later years. The superficial focus on language, therefore, resulted in tacit acceptance of sexist and violent language, while black coffee was banned from social work offices and public sector canteens (Solomos and Back, 1995).

Understanding of the complex and dynamic nature of language in relation to location and context came much later in the 20th century. In the 1970s, many black professionals sought common understanding, and so the word 'black' emerged as a unifying, collective term used to describe BME people united against racism and committed to challenging the behaviour and attitudes of racist individuals and institutions. Sivanandan (1991, p. 34) suggested that the politicized definition of 'black' helped to form the black community in Britain, bound together in the 1960s and 70s by poor living and working conditions, as well as (principally immigration) laws which discriminated against new arrivals to the UK.

Figure 1.1 illustrates the diverse ethnic perspectives and nationalities encompassed by the word 'black'. Such ideas were often used within public sector training to demonstrate unity in simple, hierarchical terms to promote the idea that ethnic minority groups defined by colour would naturally emerge as a force.

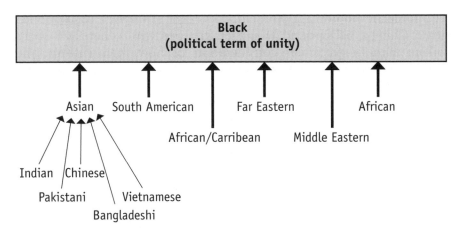

Figure 1.1 Diversity within a unified definition of 'black'

The idea that people originating from such a vast area of the world could be unified is difficult to conceive in contemporary Britain, but during the 1960s and 70s discrimination was overt. Words held a great deal more political power and meanings were dependent on the situation and people involved, so while the idea of 'black' as a political colour provided a solution for some people, it simplified diversity and difference for others (Dominelli, 1997).

Within the unified definition of 'black', segregation rather than cohesion appeared to result in the grouping of large areas of the world, creating a hierarchy of those most and least affected by racism. Cultural and regional subtleties were largely ignored and some groups, for example people from China and Vietnam, appeared less significant than others. Each category could be further divided and subdivided to better reflect geographic, regional and other differences.

Although the simple categorization depicted by Figure 1.1 may look offensive (or even comical) to the 21st-century social worker, at the time it impacted on how law and policy were constructed. This type of classification delayed the development of complex models of social work (Johns and Jordan, 2006), which used evidence on equal rights, poverty, low income and poor housing as well as population profiles and representation. Such thinking also temporarily halted consideration of how relationships could be forged and common understanding developed in a range of ways across cultural, geographical and political divides.

Simple categorization also led to the perpetuation of stereotypes and false homogeneity. In addition, it fixed the characteristics of the individuals and groups who migrated to the UK over many decades, for many reasons and with varied personal histories. The rudimentary nature of this classification meant that the flexibility and openness shown by migrants to new experiences was left largely unexplored, as were collective approaches to unity (Dominelli, 2008). For example, a social worker with a Chinese background would be grouped with other BME social workers without particular consideration of how their cultural and linguistic knowledge could contribute to policy development on anti-racist practice with Chinese communities.

BME immigrants often leave their home countries and everything familiar, including close family, friends, home and environment, for a range of complex reasons. The majority settle in multiethnic areas and relate positively not only with each other but also with white neighbours, who may have recently migrated from countries such as Ireland or Poland. BME settlers arriving in Britain from the 1950s onwards changed and adapted quickly, juggled priorities, used social systems, developed relationships and challenged the status quo (Ely and Denney, 1987).

Since the early 1970s, anti-racist social work practice has benefited from the contribution made by social activists, often of immigrant backgrounds, with a lived experience of racism and a desire to promote individual and group identity. A number of individuals from this period went on to develop theoretical ideas based in disciplines such as sociology (Dominelli, 1988; Brah, 1996; Hall and du Gay, 1996) and social psychology (Augoustinos and Reynolds, 2001), both of which actively contributed to particular ideas around identity formation.

Identity and identification

Issues related to identity and identification in postindustrial society have received particular attention by theorists such as Seidler (2010), who suggests that the rootlessness created by globalization has left some individuals seeking identification with aspects of religion and faith which cross national boundaries:

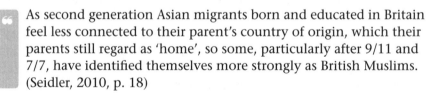

> As second generation Asian migrants born and educated in Britain feel less connected to their parent's country of origin, which their parents still regard as 'home', so some, particularly after 9/11 and 7/7, have identified themselves more strongly as British Muslims. (Seidler, 2010, p. 18)

It appears that the bombings in New York (on 11 September 2001) and London (on 7 July 2005), and other related terrorist activity, had a particular effect on how some people identify themselves, how others identify them, how they connect with others and how they adapt within any given situation. This was illustrated subsequently by many examples of British young men with strong connections to Muslim countries, often with unremarkable pasts, seeking connections through religion and terrorist activity with other young men or groups. The identification of young men such as these, previously based on nationality and citizenship status, changed with the attacks on London, New York and other cities. The bombings heralded a new era of anti-terrorist reaction by governments, which fed Islamaphobia and anti-Muslim sentiment across the western world (Seidler, 2010). The notion of the British terrorist developed quickly and gave some weight to the idea that a core identity could be adapted, enhanced or manipulated to fit any given context, position or individual history. The idea of a transient, transforming identity took hold and did little to support the ideals of multiracial Britain, which espoused social cohesion and cultural/religious difference.

The changing landscape challenged social workers to develop understanding of individual identity in relation to country of origin, ethnicity, cultural/linguistic heritage, as well as political positioning based on ideological or faith-based belonging. Professionals are, however, aware that people change and adapt their identity to fit the context or situation in which they find themselves, although the majority of the population is driven by established universal humanitarian values rather than transitory ideological behaviour.

Social workers arguably have an above average commitment to social justice and come to the task with sound foundations on which the building blocks are added. Figure 1.2 (overleaf) is based on this assumption and provides an opportunity for individuals to examine such ideas in six different interrelated areas of identity. It places the *individual* in the middle and suggests that the most important aspect of their *foundational identity* lies in their ethnic origin and heritage. This is at the core of any individual and is the base on which the other parts are built.

Cultural and linguistic identity has a particular significance because it can offer individuals a chance to show or display aspects of themselves derived from culture (including dress) and language (including accent). It is the day-to-day personality on view. This can be problematic because it can simplify identity and can be used by others to place particular labels on the person and their group, family and community.

The physical context or situation sometimes results in strong identification with a *geographic* place of origin. However, people also become attached to a place of settlement and absorb influences from their surroundings. This may be particularly relevant for social workers and students supporting, for example, children affected by increasingly mobile family commitments.

Political identity builds on cultural and linguistic identity and adds to personal ideology, belief and faith. It can unite an individual to others by virtue of shared characteristics and can be a lifelong commitment to, for example, a cause or campaign. It can also be driven by the need for political statement through action, dress or language. Relationships are often founded on contact and communication with others. These enable greater and deeper understanding of how we are perceived, as well as how others perceive us.

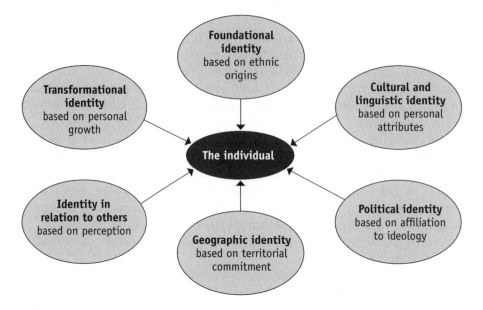

Figure 1.2 Identity and identification with one's own grouping

Finally, in order to substantially identify with one's group, individuals are likely to undergo a process of change and *transformation*. This can lead to a deeper understanding of self in relation to others and feed into the *foundation* of the individual personality.

To further illustrate the relevance of Figure 1.2, it may useful to consider a practice example of a student, Hanna, a young person who has a sound understanding of her family and kinship ties as well as family history.

Hanna: a British social work student identifying with her own grouping

On arriving at university, Hanna feels she has left the immediate influences of her *culture and language* in order to study in another part of the UK. Hanna's knowledge of her personal background and history means that she has a firm basis on which to develop and grow as an individual. Hanna's *foundational identity* means that she is likely to absorb all the experience that this process has to offer.

Hanna has a good idea of her own background, but is aware that she is developing at other levels, for example as a professional. As a first year student, she has a greater understanding of where she stands as a young

practice example 1.2

adult in her own right, and that some of her experiences may result in personal growth in social, economic, *political* and other areas which appear different from her previous life. This is because Hanna is meeting and relating to new people all the time, not only on her own course, but elsewhere in the university and the town.

Hanna likes the place of study and is enjoying the positive (and challenging) aspects of her life as a social work student. She is aware that a learning environment, such as a university, is likely to stretch the values and principles she has brought with her and that the study of professional ethics may result in the questioning of core ideology and belief systems. Like many young people in her position, Hanna is likely to be prepared for the high level of *transformation* which can take place for an individual in this situation.

Although Hanna is a confident young person, she may require a theoretical model which enhances this understanding. Figure 1.2 provides an opportunity for Hanna to examine herself as whole person and to consider what she may bring to, or take from, any given situation, such as a placement in a social work agency. It suggests that personal growth and development is closely linked to the person's situation and location, and that stimulated by a range of influences both close and distant, any individual has some choice in what is taken and what is left behind. Finally, it provides Hanna with an opportunity to assess, evaluate and reflect on her personal history and ethnic background.

Transforming language

The 1970s and 80s were arguably the most interesting time for the development of anti-racist language and terminology. Words were hotly debated among black and white professionals, who, at a time of significant political and social change, were attempting to understand, classify and root ideas and approaches.

The development of ant-racist social work practice has been supported by the particular and transforming nature of the language (Higham, 2006), albeit within an overarching concern about insubstantial progress, for example in the case of indigenous peoples (Tuhiwai Smith, 2008).

Anti-racist social work practitioners have learned lessons from the past and strived to meet equality measures which address ethnicity, gender, age, disability, religion, sectarianism and sexuality. They have also sought an understanding of how such issues intersect in contemporary society, particularly in relation to verbal and written communication. The development of language has a historical, legal and policy basis which bears special consideration for anti-racist social work practice. For example, thinking on black identity has paralleled the development of other related terminology such as cultural heritage and identification, words which have a particular resonance in laws such as the 1989 Children Act. The focus on language needs some consideration and further development mainly because:

- words such as direct and indirect discrimination have legal meaning
- clarification is needed for language which relates to 'race' as a construct
- students and newly qualified social workers look for guidance and understanding
- language is dynamic, but has historical roots.

Words and language relate closely to issues of personal and professional identity for social workers, and terminology continues to generate anxiety and concern, despite the passage of time. Students and practitioners fear offence to individuals through the misuse or misinterpretation of words. In order to minimize this unease, the Glossary in this book introduces commonly used terminology written in a spirit of engagement, rather than prescription and dogma. The words are selected to increase understanding of anti-discrimination and should contribute to the development of attitudes and values, as well as the promotion of anti-racist social work practice. However, many words used in relation to 'race' and racism are disputed, and understanding is dependent on context and location.

Conclusions

Background and history have a particular resonance for those engaged with anti-racist practice and the emphasis in this chapter on these topics provides a useful platform for the rest of the book. The imperative to look back, reflect and learn is a prerequisite to positive action, progress and improvement for social workers driven by ethical and legal standards.

The lessons learned from the past are comprehensive and point to a consideration of motivation and the desire for moral and legal change. In his critique of the British government in constituting the EHRC, Herman Ouseley (2007) suggests that the answer to complex questions often lies in better listening and decision making, based on principles of human justice, equality and diversity. However, Sivanandan (2007, p. 50) warns that constitutional and democratic rights are being eroded in a bid to assimilate, absorb and integrate: 'in search of a flat, colourless, etiolated homogeneity, built on the shifting sands of assimilation and based on shifting British values'.

Developing positive strategies and tactics is a complex task which continues to exercise many activists who wish to promote individual and group identity as well as the relevance of context and time to anti-racist practice. Political ideology remains an important driver for many individuals concerned with the following questions: who are we and how do we identify with others?

> We made Black the colour of our politics and not the colour of our skins. We cannot let ourselves be bogged down in our particularities and miss the wood for the trees. We need an international perspective, even as we take on national and local issues. We need to move in our thinking from the particular to the general and the general to the particular, both at once. And it is then that we can successfully turn individual cases into social issues, social issues into civic causes and civic causes into a national movement. (Sivanandan, 2007, p. 50)

Anti-racist activity has, therefore, an impressive history of mobilizing individuals and groups who have acted collectively to meet political aims based on considered methods and approaches. A great deal of positive change and development has taken place, but a great deal more needs to be done to involve those with alternative and additional views, such as service users, carers and students across the cultural, religious and ethnic divides. The importance of meaning and categorization is also crucial, and words which are analysed and used properly may result in a real change in understanding. Finally, professionals may need to consider how best to proactively promote anti-racist practice in a committed and energetic manner in order to inspire trainees and newly qualified social workers.

Although the developments in language have provided an important milestone for anti-racist practice, such dialogue requires a move towards a common understanding of communication and its impact on shared human existence.

Further examination of how communities live and work together is also worth pursuing. For example, some groups live with ease in parallel communities, sharing common practices based on culture, religion, beliefs, customs and general lifestyles (Cashmore, 1996), while others face a great deal of difficulty. In general, there is substantial evidence to suggest that human contact is often based on common and mutual understanding, rather than difference and conflict.

The points below offer the reader an opportunity to synthesize learning from this chapter on a number of issues and explore approaches which include, rather than exclude, individuals and communities. The relationship between legal and moral duties is also provided as a basis for further discussion, as is the link between holding a belief and acting on it.

implications for practice

Developments in social work often come about as a result of public pressure. In relation to anti-racist practice, professionals and students campaigning for fairness, rights and social justice have also contributed to the large stock of legal and policy frameworks available in the UK. Social workers have developed relevant knowledge and skills and implemented these multifarious statutory provisions while performing complex duties on a daily basis.

Concern about poor practice has highlighted the need for better procedures in all service areas but there is a need for a greater focus on the communication and interpersonal skills used by social workers to support service users who have a complex range of cultural needs. Professionals are key advocates for individuals, children and families and undertake sustained work to redirect individuals towards new opportunities and life chances. Social workers have a responsibility, therefore, to further examine, for example, the factors which result in the passing of poverty and deprivation from BME parents to their children.

Confident and self-assured development of personal and professional identity is a key aim for social workers and students, along with good interpersonal and communication skills. In relation to 'race' and racism, the study of language facilitates this because words can generate positive discussion on common understanding and shared knowledge, as well as complex and contradictory responses.

The oft stated but key message is that anti-racist social work practice is derived from many theoretical positions, and social workers require structured time and space in the workplace to consolidate learning and reflect on emerging concepts and ideas.

main points

- Social work practice has paid insufficient attention to the intricacies of the many complex and interesting questions about the nature, source and act of racism.

- The terms 'racism', 'racial discrimination' and 'racial disadvantage' continue to be used interchangeably. Racial discrimination is the practical criminal result of racism, which is an ideology and/or a belief system.

- The Race Relations (Amendment) Act 2000 and the Equality Act 2006 allow for a clear differentiation between racism as a belief and racism as an act.

- Racial disadvantage comes about as a result of discrimination on the grounds of colour, religious, ethnic, religious and cultural difference.

- Discrimination based on colour activates racist belief and ideology and is unlawful in many countries including the UK which, in the Race Relations Act 1976, defined direct and indirect discrimination.

- Discriminatory abuse of authority, influence and control is forbidden under the Equality Act 2006.

stop and think

- Do white and black people need to 'reclaim history' in the process of understanding and exercising group and individual power?
- Policy and practice superficially question descriptive words such as 'black', while offensive and discriminatory words such as 'nigger' are commonly accepted within, for example, black rap music. What is your position on these differences?
- Do you believe that migrants have developed particular methods and approaches to strategically, practically and morally survive within local neighbourhoods, communities and wider society? If so, think of examples where this has occurred in your own experience.

taking it further

- Higham, P. (2006) *Social Work: Introducing Professional Practice*, Sage, London.
  The focus on practice in this book is extremely valuable, particularly in relation to contemporary thinking on international and national professional definitions of social work and underpinning professional values and principles. In particular, the chapter on values for practice defines key terminology and considers possible obstacles to successful implementation.
- Kundnani, A. (2002) An unholy alliance? Racism, religion and communalism, *Race and Class*, **44**(2): 71–80.
  This considers communal tensions among British Asian communities and how such activity is impacting on the development of cohesive and collective approaches to race and racism. It seeks answers to difficult questions on, for example, how policy and practice can be informed by approaches which empower and 'provide alternatives to the easy and simplistic sense of belonging offered by religious gangs and fanatics' (p. 79).
- Sivanandan, A. (2007) Racism, liberty and the war on terror: the global context, *Race and Class*, **48**(4): 45–50.
  This paper was part of the conference proceedings held at the Institute for Race Relations, which focused on law and civil liberties in relation to refugee/asylum issues facing Islamic communities in Britain. Immigration is related to global capitalism and the author suggested that the 'market state sets the agenda for government policies on immigration and decides who are needed for the economy and who are not' (p. 47). This provided an interesting backdrop to

the other papers, which included Gareth Peirce (2007), This historical context, David Rose (2007), The politicisation of intelligence, and Herman Ouseley (2007), The attack on multi-culturalism. The proceedings ended with a series of responses and a conclusion by Sivanandan (2007, p. 92), which called for solid, unified responses to race and racism: 'We are all in the same boat. So rock it by all means, to get it on an even keel, but don't let's sink it. Let's criticize each other, fight with each others' oppressiveness but only to make our politics more libratory and our unity organic. Criticism, struggle, unity – as the old revolutionaries used to say!'

2 Anti-racist practice in a globalized world

Technology, communication and other changes beyond national boundaries are increasingly challenging the knowledge, skills and values used by practitioners and students. Social workers are increasingly aware that they need to examine the impact of globalization on their everyday concerns as professionals.

This chapter examines the relevant literature and attempts to answer the following question: what are the global forces of significance, and how do they impact on anti-racist social work practice? This chapter will also introduce ideas and principles on globalization which relate to 'race' and racism. The quest for understanding commonly used words will be reiterated here, and the relevant terminology will be defined within the context of social work. Also relevant theories, which link national with global concerns, will be explored through an examination of universal standards. The overall purpose of this chapter is, therefore, to introduce emerging knowledge on 'race' and racism within the context of professional practice in a global context.

Better planning, security and protection have been pushed by successive governments within the UK, both for state as well as individualized provision. The recession added additional pressure leading to, for example, greater emphasis on personal insurance to cover health and social care through illness and retirement. The impact of public sector cuts in 2010, in a number of countries, attracted rapidly transmitted global coverage through newspapers, television and other communication systems. This enabled individuals and societies to see and share experiences with other people in the world.

Global forces are working rapidly to change and enhance society but some groups, held fast by disadvantage and deprivation, remain segregated, divided and semi-isolated in what may be seen as tight/safe communities. Professional understanding of the context and situation of people in such situations is critical, because service users can be resilient and self-determined as well as independent and insular, particularly if they have a history of migration and a broader experience from within, as well as beyond, Britain.

Globalization has resulted in the greater movement of people across borders, and the increase in people from across the world in major UK cities is increasingly being recognized by state and society (*The Guardian*, 24 October 2009). This chapter seeks to capture globalization from a number of perspectives, recognizing that the factors at play are numerous and varied, and that influences may come from both powerful and powerless people in society.

Global ideas and influences

The word 'globalization' is commonly used within the British media in reports on international finance and movement of goods across borders (*Financial Times*, 30 September 2008, www.ft.com), and the relevance of this term to wider societal concerns requires some attention:

> Although increased economic integration has played a critical role in fostering the process of globalisation, most social scientists believe that the popular emphasis on the economic dimensions of globalisation focuses on just one of many aspects. Globalisation also has social, demographic, political and cultural dimensions. (Midgley, 2000, p. 14)

A wider analysis suggests that the economic definition of globalization needs to take better account of the impact of trade and economic integration on, for example, universal labour standards in relation to vulnerable groups such as women and children from BME communities (Midgley, 2000). Held and McGrew (2007) suggest that even liberal countries are driven by global markets and the obsession with national security directly impacts international inequality and world development. The disparity between the rich and the poor is here to stay, therefore professionals concerned with meeting the social and welfare needs of such groups in their locality need to find ways to address the effects of such disadvantage.

Understanding how ideas derived from globalization relate to everyday concerns is challenging. Often concepts make concrete sense only when global events rooted in a distant place or country impact directly on the average person in the street. An example of this is the chaos created by the collapse of a number of banks in the autumn of 2008 in the USA and Iceland among other countries. The crisis initiated a number of national rescue plans, including £400bn made available by the British government to support some British financial institutions (*The Observer*, 5 October 2008). Such injections of public cash resulted in survival for the relevant bodies, but the recession that followed left individual losers, such as investors and homeowners. For example, newspaper reports stated that the drop in house prices was the sharpest in 25 years (*Financial Times*, 30 September 2008, www.ft.com/yourmoney), and the knock-on effect on savings, pensions and household bills, as well as welfare more generally, is yet to determined by the coalition government elected in 2010.

The economic crisis provided a graphic example of how external factors, such as overborrowing by individuals from banks in the USA, along with the recession, directly impacted on the British taxpayer and/or property purchaser as well as welfare provider/user. Those with low incomes were particularly hit by the drop in living standards and the rise in the price of essentials such as food and fuel. This added to problems which social workers helped to resolve.

The international nature of the financial marketplace and its impact on the individual/family was made clearer by the events of 2008, but the relevance of globalization to the discipline and profession remains less obvious. This leaves social workers with the question: why should professionals bother to understand issues beyond personal financial concerns, particularly in relation to anti-racist social work practice? The answer lies in a number of reasons, but the following are particularly interesting to those concerned with social welfare:

- Deeper exploration of international and global perspectives is likely to result in a better understanding of how day-to-day work is influenced by what is happening elsewhere in the world.
- There is a great deal more to learn about the nature, character and process of care developed by social workers in other countries (Powell and Robison, 2007) which could inform anti-racist practice.
- Social workers are increasingly working with, for example, children fleeing poverty and violence (Kohli, 2007) and are looking for appropriate and relevant strategies on anti-racist practice across international borders.
- There is wide recognition that England, Wales, Scotland and Northern Ireland are important players in the global marketplace as they import/export goods and services across the world.
- The four countries of the UK have their own social work standards, legal and policy responsibilities.
- Social work standards for BME populations are different in the four countries of the UK.

Understanding the bigger picture may explain how organizational funding is influenced by larger scale economic events in the world. For example, a number of UK local authorities faced financial difficulties as a result of investing public funds in banks in Iceland. In other words, how the small and the local works, well or otherwise, alongside the big and global:

> All social workers require at least a minimum exposure to ideas about the local-global dialectic, comparative welfare policies and inter-cultural relations ... whilst social work might be considered a local activity, it is not exempt from wider trends regarding labour mobility. (Lyons, 2006, p. 371)

A focused and critical approach to the subject may, therefore, begin with an examination of the terminology used, because words often explain the development of foundational ideas on any subject. So, for example, it could be argued that the language used within globalization is rooted in the movement of people and money across geographic boundaries.

Held and McGrew (2007), Dominelli (2004) and Yeates (2001) have explored the complexity of globalization and suggest that its definition combines the following ideas:

■ the internationalization of the state
■ exploitation of labour and other public resources
■ use of business ideas in welfare provision
■ technical and competence-based approaches to intervention
■ greater control and surveillance within society.

Dominelli (2004) also suggests that globalization has changed the business landscape, and that important decisions are made in places and by people who have little connection with the lives of those they directly influence. This is made increasingly effortless by advances in communication and information technology, which allow people more freedom to talk, share knowledge and engage with the imperfectly regulated wider world. At the same time, individual behaviour is under greater scrutiny in city streets and airports:

> Their interactive dynamics have contradictory outcomes. Enhancing as they do the centralisation of power and decision-making alongside deregulated markets in which corporate elites are free to construct realities that produce highly profitable conditions for investment purposes, they limit the space within which the private individual without resources can exercise choice when his or her expectations for doing so are at their height. (Dominelli, 2004, p. 26)

The meaning of globalization changes in relation to the background, context and perspective of the individuals or groups attempting to engage with it. Fundamental ideas and trends have differed according to the discipline from which they have originated; for example subjects such as social work have emphasized the everyday effects of globalization, while other disciplines have focused on its development on a larger scale:

> So in addition to economic characteristics, to the geographer it implies the compression of time and place incurred in rapid and frequent movements of people and information; while to the cultural anthropologist, it signifies the worldwide spread of McDonald's and Coke and the dominance of the English language. (Lyons, 2006, p. 368)

Within social work, the focus on service user needs has led to the development of theories that, for example, support localized responses and individual and group narratives (Parton, 2002, p. 244):

> Constructive social work is concerned with the narratives of solutions to problems and with change ... Service users are invited to tell their stories using the cultural resources of their communities – local language and interpretation of the problem and the origins of their oppression and exclusion.

Understanding how groups can benefit from cross-cultural communication can enable students and social workers to implement core principles such as empowerment and self-determination in multiracial communities. The aspiration to make sense of the needs of individuals and their families within a global world is a challenge for social workers, particularly if additional factors, such as racism, influence the provision of services. For example, kinship care is used by Lyons (2006) to illustrate the pitfalls of poorly thought through policies on transracial, inter-country adoption in Britain. This analysis suggests that children's services have to train staff to understand processes which allow a successful transfer of family values and behaviours from one country and/or culture to another.

Globalization as a catch-all concept suggests further examination and so in order to broaden understanding, relevant words (often closely related) are introduced in Table 2.1 (Yeates, 2001).

Table 2.1 Understanding globalization

Concept	Meaning	Relevance to social work
Internationalization	This suggests that flexible working practices result in profit accumulation and that the production of goods is increasingly universal, large scale and difficult to grasp at the local and community level	In relation to welfare provision, the idea is widely perceived as a threat to country-based systems and practices which require state control of financial and human resources
Transnationalization	This promotes the idea that national boundaries no longer limit economic, political or welfare activity. Citizens (for example in the EU) can readily cross borders and seek services outside their countries of origin	This approach has improved social work collaboration across borders on public services in relation to, for example, children seeking asylum (Kohli, 2007) and newly arrived migrants with particular religious and cultural needs
Multinationalization	This eases financial movement and production across borders resulting in, for example, expensive fast-food outlets in poor nations	For social work, the concept has resulted in the development of marketplace ideas which are increasingly being imposed by national governments, such as the purchasing of services within and across welfare organizations

Concept	Meaning	Relevance to social work
Universalization	This has resulted in greater global movement of people across countries. Ideas, such as more privatization of health and social care, have also been transferred	This has led to ideas based on, for example, public/private partnerships providing training and development for social workers
Liberalization	This requires the removal of trade regulation between countries	The approach has challenged state-based social work provision provided on a collective basis by society
Triadization	The concentration of power in the three economically advanced regions of the world (Japan/China/India, North America and Western Europe) has often led to authoritarian responses to internal security within, for example, the EU	Global authoritarian responses have resulted in measures such as the approval given by the minister of state for security, counter-terrorism, crime and policing in July 2007 to English and Welsh police chief officers to authorize firearms officers and specially trained units to use tasers when faced with violence or threats of violence
Westernization	This concept is based on the historic idea that countries in the West dominate the exchange of goods, money and culture, leading to cultural uniformity and greater monetary control. Economically powerful countries such as China and India are challenging this position	Colonial ideas and concepts on 'race', culture and ethnicity continue to influence social work thinking
Regionalization	This describes the clustering of countries, such as the EU, into trading areas, with jointly agreed aims and coherent transport links which enable people and commerce to move freely	This allows, for example, the greater possibility of work experience in Europe within social work programmes of study (Lyons, 2006)

Understanding the language used to promote concepts and ideas is a good start, but Yeates (2001) suggests that action needs to follow words, because global change has impacted significantly on social welfare and therefore requires a critique which is beyond the idealistic and rhetorical. For example, professionals, such as probation officers and youth workers, following anti-racist practice principles may have to look for strategies which inform (as well as challenge) counterterrorism measures such as the use of tasers by local police services.

Universalization has also meant that expectations of welfare have changed and individuals are increasingly encouraged to supplement state provision through, for example, personal insurance against poor health and old age. So although Britain holds ideal notions of universal welfare, in reality large numbers of people have to pay supplements for health and social care on a daily basis. In general, however, most people continue to live on below average incomes and only those in good employment or with other financial wealth are likely to pay more for private care.

In the global marketplace, economic advantages are likely to override all other concerns, even those which relate to key areas of public responsibility such as child wellbeing. Yeates (2001, p. 24) suggests that authoritarian responses to internal security concerns are leading to compromises which privilege market forces above ethical and anti-racist considerations: 'This holds that, in response to a perceived threat to their industrial competitiveness, states are likely to engage in behaviour which results in the lowering of their own *ethical* standards.'

Liberalization has also directly impacted on organizational structures and employment practices. For social workers, the General Social Care Council requirements for employer-led continuous professional development, set out in the *Codes of Practice for Social Care Workers and Employers* (GSCC, 2002a), is threatened by the increased privatization of functions such as training, for example on racism and discrimination. As local government hands over such responsibilities to profit-making companies, such as Capita, social workers are spending more of their own time and money on training and development. However, continuous training on 'race' and racism is a prerequisite for a registered, licensed social worker (Social Work Task Force, 2009) and can be requested under *The Code of Ethics for Social Work* (BASW, 2002).

Positive technological advances made through the application of media, television and computers have resulted in the capacity to see and/or relate to other societies, leading to greater awareness of words such as reliance, dependence and need. The increase in global understanding has been brought about by the notion of the shrinking planet and acceptance of international movements such as 'world music' and 'save the planet' (Waters, 1995). Social workers may wish to consider the relevance of cultural and environmental activities such as these in groupwork. For example, young people may benefit from social activities which bring together like-minded black and white groups.

World events, such as the 2012 London Olympics, have the potential to engage human beings in individual, group and countrywide relationships and, as long as there are no other barriers to communication, they are made easier by global systems such as the World Wide Web (Lyons, 2006). The World Wide Web and the internet are, however, beyond state control and can be used by individuals and groups holding anonymized, false or non-existent identities. For those concerned with human rights, communication which is not regulated by society's laws, norms and values can lead to significant problems: 'Humanity cannot be differentiated by race, class or gender in terms of its possibilities and rights' (Waters, 1995, p. 43).

Within social work, the ease of access to computer-based systems has been highlighted by parents and professionals wishing to protect children and young people, particularly those vulnerable to abusive communication with paedophiles and other predators, using the internet. However, computers can be used by service users to develop skills in recognizing and locating potential dangers as well as raising technological confidence.

Communication technology is part of the everyday life experience in practice and education. It is being incorporated into the teaching and assessment of social work students, who are increasingly encouraged to use the internet to inform research and writing. Social care organizations are also promoting email and computerized record-keeping systems within teams and organizations. Mobile telephones are commonly used as a health and safety tool to maintain contact when making a lone or out of office hours visit to a service user.

Although the application of computer-based systems is extensive, social workers are not necessarily skilled in the applications of software in, for example, translating leaflets and publicity into foreign languages. Wider use of information systems requires time as well as interest in the perspective of others. Professionals working with BME communities may consider widening knowledge and skills through the use of the internet, a cheap, flexible alternative to formalized learning.

The ideas and influences introduced here offer a flavour of the concerns facing those who live and work in Britain. The challenges are harder when framed within anti-racist social work because globalization is complex by nature (Midgley, 2000). But even understanding this is a good way into an exploration of ways forward.

The impact of global changes

Demographic changes play an important role in the development of social policy. So the rapid development of globalized systems has eased the movement of money, people, goods and trade across European and other international borders and changed the profile of the British population. For example, London is home to people originating from 160 countries, and 50% of all migrants came to the UK in the last 30 years – one-third arrived in the period after 1996 (CRE, 2007a). This may be because technological advances have made international travel easier and cheaper for economic immigrants seeking to build a new life in the richer countries of the world.

The demographic impact of immigration has meant that the model of welfare advocated by postwar reformists such as Beveridge (Jordan, 1998) is no longer sustainable, but the necessity for responsible care and protection for vulnerable children and adults has grown (Cree and Davis, 2007). Since the 1980s, successive governments have distributed welfare driven by greater efficiency, cost-effectiveness and the rationing of services. In Britain, this has impacted particularly on social work service users (Dominelli, 2004) and at the beginning of the 21st century, only those in extreme need receive state support and aid.

Dominelli (2004, p. 26) suggests that practices which reinforce oppression have to be critiqued in relation to power and control: 'Globalisation is organised as a set of capitalist relations that penetrate every aspect of life to produce winners and losers.'

The increase in the regulation of social workers is seen as particularly problematic, with greater management of contact within and between professional groups, employing organizations and the individuals they serve. The shift away from individual relationships towards bureaucratic management systems is likely to lead to economic and political disadvantage for all public sector service users. Those facing racism and discrimination are likely to face greater barriers because they have below average influence, control and representation within such structures and systems.

The experience of service users disempowered by discrimination within organizational structures depends on how they are perceived, how their needs are promoted and how they are represented. In relation to representation, evidence suggests that social workers are clearly better at advocating for some groups than others (Lyons, 2006). This may be because professionals do not feel skilled or confident in communication which crosses cultures, religions, traditions and customs. Social workers are trained to respond equally to individuals from any group in society, but this means that if there is a mismatch between the social worker and the service user, they are unlikely to accept or acknowledge a skill shortfall. However, accepting a difficulty means that the professional can seek continuous training to fill gaps in their knowledge and understanding. The input must be ongoing because no one individual or family will have the same cultural/ethnic mix, or wish to receive a standard anti-racist response.

Discriminatory attitudes towards particular BME groups, such as Muslims, are reflected widely in society. A survey carried out by the University of Kent of 2,895 individuals on equality, diversity and prejudice in Britain (Abrams and Houston, 2006) found that Muslims suffer a higher level of discrimination based on religion, sex and age, and are more affected by religious prejudice (56%) than Christians (19%). Although Arabs and Muslims are less likely to be accepted as British than any other group, there is little guidance and support for social workers providing services for such groups. There is a continuing assumption that relevant knowledge will be picked up on the job, or that social worker skills and service user needs will somehow be matched (SCIE, 2006). Good practice suggests that local authorities employ a systematic service delivery approach, using relevant socioeconomic data, to target population groups affected by unfair treatment and other disadvantages.

REACH (DCLG, 2007), a report commissioned by the British government on raising the aspirations and attainment of black boys and young black men, provided a fuller analysis of the impact of stereotyping and labelling. This recommended a minister for race to take forward its findings, suggesting that a government lead on issues of 'race' may enable greater clarity on evidence-based anti-racist practice for those, such as social workers, seeking to improve services to BME individuals and communities.

The understanding of losers in society is fundamental to anti-racist social work practice. The formation of appropriate responses, however, also requires an appreciation of economic winners on the global stage, that is, those who have benefited from the abolition of capital controls, ease of movement of finances and the utilization of computerized systems (Dominelli, 2004). High achieving multinational companies fit particularly well into this category because they often function beyond and across national regulatory controls and are seen to epitomize stateless and lawless organizations. The 2008 economic crisis was partly due to the poor regulation of money and people within the financial sector (*Financial Times*, 30 September 2008, www.ft.com).

Deregulated wealth creation/accumulation may not seem immediately relevant to social workers promoting equality and justice in Britain, but the country needs controlled economic consistency in order to provide, develop and build social welfare for established, as well as newly arrived, citizens and residents. Mishra (1999) argues that the only new aspect of globalization in historical terms is the inability of neoliberal, social-democrat governments to meet progressive public policy commitments based on high taxation:

> What economic globalisers fail to acknowledge is that whereas economies can go global, people cannot. While money and capital have been set free to move across the globe, labour remains locked into the nation state, for example by strict control on immigration. By and large people have to live and survive locally. Indeed human communities are defined above all by language and culture and are thus rooted in one place – a geographic location. (Mishra, 1999, p. 116)

For professional social work, the argument for social equality and cohesion within globalized systems is paramount. It is clear that globalization has impacted significantly on the private lives of individuals, as well as that of community and society more generally, and so the imperative to develop personal and professional understanding, particularly in relation to anti-racist practice, grows greater.

Knowledge is power

Information, facts and data are important tools through which knowledge has been historically exchanged and shared, particularly by countries such as Britain which has openly used the British Council and the BBC World Service to introduce and advance western ideas, opinions and beliefs across the world. A number of the principles promoted here, such as professionalization, are enshrined in social work practice.

Another means by which westernization is actively pursued is through the transportation of programmes of study. European and American universities have colleges overseas which provide social work education among other courses. These occur in partnerships with host countries and enable courses to be validated, taught and assessed from abroad. Exchange programmes and the active recruitment of overseas students has resulted in a multimillion dollar expansion in the USA alone, where international education is estimated to be worth $7bn in 1996, making it the fifth most valuable US export (Yeates, 2001).

The UK follows the USA as the country of choice for overseas students. British social work courses are increasingly expanding to incorporate such students within programmes of study, with limited attention to their cultural, linguistic and social needs, and little input on globalization and international social work within the academic and practice curricula. Consideration of the academic and practice teaching skills needed to support overseas students is also limited. Nor has much attention been paid to teaching and assessment methods which address ethnic, religious and linguistic needs.

The internationalization of education is driven by student fees and the expectation that graduates will actively promote Britain's interests in their home countries and transport knowledge of the country and the profession across the globe. Despite their part in the maintenance of global power through knowledge transmission, propaganda institutions like the British Council are widely respected in the world. This may be because many ex-colonies have embedded supremacist ideas maintained by financial and other investments by former colonial powers.

In its report *Making a World of Difference: Cultural Relations in 2010*, the British Council (2007, p. 11) states:

 The people we focus on are professionals aged 18–35 with the potential to become leaders who can influence their country's relationship with the UK. They will continue to be of vital importance to our work. We will ensure that we remain relevant to their needs.

Students are targeted increasingly through the World Wide Web, and the Education UK website (www.educationuk.org) has a database of 450,000 courses and attracts 4 million visitors per year.

In global terms, the educational marketplace is currently dominated by the western world, but countries such as China are also developing their education systems rapidly. The economic advantages have been evidenced and the spoils are likely to be fought over with some enthusiasm in the coming decades (Yeates, 2001). Cultural supremacy is illustrated particularly well by the linguistic dominance of English, the global language of commerce and telecommunications (Lyons, 2006). Critics have suggested over a number of years that English speakers are likely to control large areas of the world, particularly in the southern hemisphere and among groups such as women, where illiteracy remains common and widespread (During, 1995). The economically advanced regions of the world control computers and telecommunication and so their view of the world dominates air space. Those in charge are not only beyond regulation by community or country, but also unlikely to be committed to principles of fairness and justice (Glastonbury and LaMendola, 1992).

Global communication has resulted in the sharing of knowledge on how people live across the world. Despite occasional dips in prosperity, overall living standards are rising steadily within the mainly rich nations. This is being seen, shared and desired elsewhere by those living in economically emerging nations, where disparities between the rich and poor are as significant as differences based on 'race' and/or ethnicity. It may be that one beneficial outcome of globalization is the scrutiny and imitation of universal welfare standards and benefits enjoyed by countries like the UK.

China is an example of an emerging economic superpower which has seen significant change in recent years. Some conclude that the desire for a western lifestyle is a motivating factor for the rapid increase in its wealth, which has seen an unprecedented growth in its share of world trade from 1% in 1979 to 6.4% in 2005, resulting in raising 20% of the Chinese population out of poverty. Of course, this leaves many people with no water and defective sanitation, but along with criticism of poor industrial and human rights practices, attention is also increasingly being drawn to the problems of health and social inequalities by academics such as Professor John Thornton of Tsinghua University, Beijing (*The Times*, 12 February 2007).

Universal standards

Postwar universal human rights charters such as the Universal Charter of Human Rights and the European Charter of Human Rights and the Rights of the Child have been enshrined in national legislation in many countries and are also seen as moral guidance by professional social workers (Banks, 1995).

Although powerful in many respects, it may be argued that global economic factors impact more directly on public policy than do international charters, which have been critiqued to have limited value as instruments addressing material and social wellbeing. At the same time, multinational companies, driven by economic concerns, are setting cultural, social and political values to fit their own needs (Glastonbury and Lamendola, 1992). Waters (1995, p. 70) links globalization to commercial exploitation:

> One of the revelatory discoveries offered by social science in the 20th century is that colonialism and imperialism produce an international division of labour of the social kind. Core or metropolitan societies do capital-intensive, high value adding production while peripheral societies do labour-intensive, low value adding production.

Many companies based in the UK have moved the production of goods to places where workers are paid less. A multinational organization is concerned primarily with profit accumulation rather than social justice, although if it moves to another country, it is likely to increase employment there. However, workers in the home country are immediately disadvantaged, particularly if they are from groups with higher unemployment rates, such as those highlighted in the University of Kent study (Abrams and Houston, 2006). This reported that, in the UK, women and men originating from Pakistan and Bangladesh are twice as likely to have no qualifications and to have the highest unemployment of all BME groups.

Poverty is a significant factor for social workers providing children's services, but it is further compounded if the children are from BME groups (UNICEF, 2007). According to the Fabian Society (2006, p. 136): 'Pakistani and Bangladeshi children are at particularly high risk of growing up in poverty, with a poverty rate of 61%, nearly three times the average.' In order to demonstrate commitment, social workers have to produce clear and specific evidence of how they are targeting groups such as Pakistani and Bangladeshi children (Soydan and Williams, 1998; Fook, 2004). Anti-racist principles suggest that children of all backgrounds deserve services delivered by confident and knowledgeable practitioners, supported by reliable information and well-conducted research based on ethnic, regional and cultural traditions.

Deprivation created by reduced employment prospects tends to result in greater dependence on welfare by individuals and families in crisis. In such a climate, public sector staff have to stretch limited provision to even greater numbers, as well as seek additional resources. They also have to advocate more actively, find alliances and utilize external colleagues and organizations to ensure a service which is equal and fair for all.

When the divide between the rich and poor widens, however, public concern about the provision aimed at claimants, historically considered as the undeserving in society, also increases (Payne, 2005). Social workers based in largely white geographic areas, where the numbers of service users as well as BME staff are small, need additional training which addresses the needs of isolated and excluded service users. They may be well advised to also seek additional fact-based evidence to justify targeted anti-racist services.

A needs-led service which is equal and fair to the wider population, as well as groups such as refugees and asylum seekers, is a challenge facing localities with limited social services funding (Khan and Dominelli, 2000). Within most rich countries, asylum seekers and refugees receive low social service priority, while their total numbers increase every year; for example, the global total in 2003 was 17 million, of which 7 million were children. Over 3,000 of this number applied to the UK from countries such as Somalia, Afghanistan and Iraq, and of these, 3.9% were looked after by social services (Kohli, 2007).

Asylum seekers and refugees suffer from prejudice and discrimination from local and regional media, particularly at ferry ports and airports where established citizens feel threatened and fearful. This suggests that globalization has the effect of destabilizing society and impacting on host communities and newly arrived migrants alike (Kirton, 2000). Situations such as this challenge community cohesion and human rights at a number of levels. In the interests of good communication and fair treatment, social workers have the dual role of safeguarding the interests of local communities, as well as advocating for children and adults traumatized by circumstances beyond their control.

Social workers can learn a great deal from research findings on refugees and asylum seekers in need of safeguarding. For example, evidence on the settlement patterns of newly arrived migrants suggests that a poor reception and/or intimidation are likely to lead to an increased sense of dislocation for those seeking residency (Kohli, 2007).

In a review of major longitudinal studies looking at the resettlement of quota refugees in North America and Australia, Silove and Ekblad (2002) comment on two significant findings. First, it can take up to a decade for people to recover and resettle in host communities. Second, the climate of distrust and hostility towards refugees generally, and asylum seekers in particular, has worsened substantially since the late 1980s (Kohli, 2007).

Asylum seekers and refugees are clear about the impact of poor experiences on establishing roots in a new country. The problems they face include:

■ temporary residency status
■ restrictions on entry to work and education

- poor social support such as language provision
- lack of access to health and social care
- barriers to family reunion
- impact of the alarm and measures combating global terrorism.

Social commentators have critiqued the selective/sporadic/patchy application of human rights conventions in service provision and suggested that welfare-based states, such as Britain, are increasingly turning to public/private partnership arrangements and profit-making welfare organizations (Khan and Dominelli, 2000), even though social workers have a direct responsibility towards migrant groups such as unaccompanied asylum-seeking children (Kohli, 2007).

Consideration and comparison of global standards is a useful way to generate and maintain interest in local services. A country-by-country report on child wellbeing in 21 rich countries (UNICEF, 2007) found the Netherlands to be at the top, and Britain to be at the bottom of a league table in six areas: material wellbeing, health and safety, education, peer and family relationships, behaviours and risks, and young people's own subjective sense of wellbeing. The findings of the UNICEF report (2007) are based on widely recognized measures grouped into 28 indicators of child wellbeing, which include deprivation, achievement and wellbeing at home/school. However, in relation to anti-racist practice, the measures and indicators may be problematic, that is, rooted in westernized notions and generalized to the extent of being meaningless to the everyday concerns of service users living in poverty and/or poor health. The UNICEF report (2007) acknowledges that poverty has to be seen in context because it is based on how individuals compare their lives with those around them and suggests the family at the top of the hierarchy of influences, followed by friends and school. Human relationships are seen as fundamental to sound development and growth over and above money and goods.

Practice example 2.1 describes a young person living in a rich country who may, given referral and assessment, be likely to reach the threshold for statutory intervention from a range of professionals (CWDC, 2007).

practice example 2.1

Joey and subjective wellbeing

Joey is 14 years of age and lives with his mother, of Hong Kong/Chinese origin, who came with her husband to the UK 30 years ago. Joey's mother lacks confidence in using English and relies a great deal on Joey and family friends for interpretation and translation. She has been diagnosed with rheumatoid arthritis and can manage light household chores and so relies on Joey to clean, shop, cook and generally keep order. Joey's father died many years ago and there is very little extended family, but the local Chinese community keeps a close eye on Joey and his mother. Joey's mother has sufficient money and they are both safe and secure. From an outsider's perspective, Joey's subjective sense of wellbeing is generally good, that is, he is healthy, aspirational and has good relations with people.

He works reasonably well at school, but more recently he has become anxious about making the right school examination choices. He does not feel able to share his anxieties with his mother or to alert teachers to the level of work he has to carry at home because this may make public his caring role and perhaps lead to adverse pressure from his peers.

Joey is a teenager who prioritizes his mother's health over and above his own educational needs. His subjective wellbeing is a complex matter and encompasses issues related to identity, age and emotional maturity. Although Joey is living in a relatively small household, he has a developed sense of identity based on kinship, cultural practices and caring behaviours. Research data suggests that compared to other BME families, Joey's circumstances are materially good but he should nevertheless be assessed for statutory intervention (CWDC, 2007).

BME groups have double the number of people in the average British household, the poverty rate among some groups is three times higher (Fabian Society, 2006) and the proportion of BME children under 16 is predicted to rise to 64% by 2026 (Simpson, 2007). This suggests larger, younger, intergenerational households affected by 'chronic and persistent inequalities' (Equalities Review, 2007a, p. 11) passed on from grandparent to parent to child who may still be providing collective, kinship care to nurture and maximize the potential of their children.

The needs of young carers have been highlighted in the guidance on early identification, assessment of needs and intervention in the Common Assessment Framework (CAF) for Children and Young People (CWDC, 2007), which can be seen as an interpretation of universal standards in the British context, albeit in a limited way. This is based on the *Every Child Matters* (DfES, 2004) outcomes, which promote equality principles and economic wellbeing within statutory childcare. The CAF pre-assessment checklist advises the collection of ethnic monitoring data and suggests that confidence, ambition and aspirations are important factors in development and growth. Despite this, the checklist is likely to be used as a referral tool rather than a method which gathers soft and hard information on wellbeing, follow-up analysis and action planning (CWDC, 2007). Table 2.2 illustrates a means by which practitioners can use guidance such as this to enhance anti-racist assessments and develop innovative approaches with BME individuals. For example, the family's practical, cultural, religious and ethical approaches to child welfare as well as their capacity to deal with change may be elicited through the immigration and settlement story of the grandparents and parents.

Table 2.2 Applying universal standards to the assessment of need

Assessment process	Needs
Information	▪ Social and economic factors ▪ Material circumstances ▪ Health, safety and risk ▪ Education ▪ Religion/faith ▪ Linguistic skills ▪ Child-rearing practices used in the family ▪ Influences from overseas/wider family ▪ Caring responsibilities ▪ Sibling/peer relationships ▪ School/leisure experiences
Assessment	▪ Subjective sense of wellbeing, deprivation or disadvantage ▪ Family circumstances and physical environment ▪ Affects of migration, language, culture, religion ▪ Risky behaviours ▪ Norms, customs and traditions passed from grandparents to parent to child ▪ Opportunities available ▪ Shared networks and reliance on kinship ▪ Input from social work and other professionals
Analysis	▪ Self-worth/self-esteem ▪ Capacity/resilience to deal with change such as migration ▪ International connections with family/friends ▪ Family values and behaviours ▪ Management, planning and negotiating skills ▪ Life chances, that is, social capital used to help children succeed in life ▪ Barriers and gaps leading to economic and social failure
Plan and steps for improved outcomes	▪ Integrated kinship-based approaches to child wellbeing ▪ Culturally specific social/public services ▪ Appropriate use of family and kinship, that is, social capital derived from the local community and country of origin

Equality and cohesion

Scrutiny of individual countries often results in praise and chastisement to those highlighted (UNICEF, 2007), but international organizations, such as the UN, are expected to highlight poor standards and make recommendations on how they may be raised across the globe. Critical review and comparison of welfare are generally seen as a positive acceptance of ethical investigation and accountability by individual states. For example, age-related discrimination and racism are universally acknowledged as unacceptable by European countries (Patel and Mertens, 1998).

The European Union (EU) contains 492 million citizens who have 785 representatives from 27 member countries, although the numbers are regularly increasing. However, this representation is selective: the total number of Members of the European Parliament (MEPs) from an ethnic minority background is 15, of which 5 are from the UK. Italy (78 MEPs) and Spain (54 MEPs) have no representation from their significant BME communities. There are just 9 non-white MEPs, 1.1% of the total. At least 5% of the EU population is non-white but statistical data is difficult to find, and some groups are not included, such as the estimated 8 million Roma.

Nations are increasingly being required to address social justice by signing treaties such as the International Convention on the Elimination of All Forms of Racial Discrimination, which has been ratified by 168 countries. A number of provisions of this convention have been incorporated into British law, such as the Race Relations (Amendment) Act 2000. These have also impacted on anti-racist practice through the social work code of ethics (BASW, 2002) and the National Occupational Standards (TOPSS, 2002). Related conventions include the Universal Charter of Human Rights, which has also been enshrined in national legislation and provides moral guidance to professional social work (Banks, 1995).

The arguments set out suggest that knowledge is sometimes used to transfer ideas on, for example, acceptable standards from one part of the world to another. Social work students and practitioners are powerful representatives of the state and will be advantaged as anti-racist practitioners if they understand how knowledge is generated, applied and transmitted (Sewpal, 2003).

The notions of equality and cohesion have particular meanings in the international context in relation to human rights and social justice (Lyons, 2006). The British government is required to report regularly on universal standards and targeted equality issues to a number of bodies, such as the United Nations. In relation to 'race' and racism, relevant national agencies, such the Commission for Racial Equality and latterly the Equality and Human Rights Commission, take the lead in gathering data and responding on a regular basis.

The UK submits periodic reports to the International Convention on the Elimination of All Forms of Racial Discrimination. The Committee on the Elimination of Racial Discrimination (CERD) responds to such reports and expects an action-based response from the UK within a given timescale. For example, CERD commented on the points below in the 15th Report, and the government responded to the points in its 16th Report (CERD, 2003):

■ the provisions of the Race Relations (Amendment) Act 2000
■ the delegation of powers (on incitement to racial hatred) to London's Metropolitan Police

- the increase in the maximum penalty for incitement to racial hatred from two to seven years imprisonment under the Anti-terrorism, Crime and Security Act 2001
- the police complaints system (England and Wales), a police ombudsman (Northern Ireland) and further consultation (Scotland)
- the Community Cohesion Unit at the Home Office
- the National Asylum Support Service
- the inclusion of the prohibition of racial and other discrimination in enforcement machinery of the Constitutions of St Helena, the British Virgin Islands and the Cayman Islands.

The convention therefore requires a regular scrutiny of British law, policy and procedure which targets racial discrimination both on British soil, and also overseas where colonial power still operates.

CERD seeks ongoing commitment on areas of concern such as:

- the increase in racial prejudice against ethnic minorities, asylum seekers and immigrants reflected in the media
- the reported lack of effectiveness of the Press Complaints Commission in dealing with this issue
- the attacks on asylum seekers which have helped sustain support for extremist political opinions
- the disproportionately high numbers of deaths in custody and stop and searches of members of BME communities
- the discrimination faced by Roma/Gypsies/Travellers reflected in higher child mortality, exclusion from schools, shorter life expectancy, poor housing conditions, lack of available camping sites, high unemployment and limited access to health services.

National governments are asked to set up systems to deal with such demands, such as the time-limited consultative Commission on Integration and Cohesion Report (2007), which identified ideas useful for the development of social work policies, such as an integrated community as a place where:

- There is a clearly defined and widely shared sense of the contribution of different individuals and different communities to a future vision for a neighbourhood, region, city or country
- There is a strong sense of an individual's rights and responsibilities when living in a particular place – people know what everyone expects of them, and what they can expect in turn
- People from different backgrounds have similar life opportunities, access to services and treatment
- There is a strong sense of trust in institutions locally to act fairly in arbitrating between different interests and for their role and justifications to be subject to public scrutiny

- There is a strong recognition of the contribution of both those who have newly arrived and those who already have deep attachments to a particular place, with a focus on what they have in common
- There are strong and positive relationships between people from different backgrounds in the workplace, in schools and other institutions within neighbourhoods.

Such bodies seek information from related departments, such as the outgoing Commission for Racial Equality (CRE, 2007b), which provide reports on, for example, birth rates, increased mobility within communities, employment, migration and other areas of global change.

Such reports also provide examples of international practices which directly impact on or challenge a family, community or group. A response from the Commission for Racial Equality (CRE, 2007a) to the Commission for Integration and Cohesion illustrated this by citing the large sums of money crossing borders on a regular basis, in the form of financial remittances (totalling £3.5bn in the UK), sent by immigrant families to dependants in the country of origin. There appears to be little research data on the impact of such financial commitments and caring demands on welfare claimants or social service users. However, there is recognition that individuals and families may be advantaged by such global connections: 'cheap travel brings a sense in which people can feel attachments to other parts of the world, while still enjoying clear and strong "roots" in this country' (Commission on Integration and Cohesion, 2007, p. 15).

A focus on the positive aspects of internationalization is, however, not as newsworthy as the more inflammatory reporting produced by the media on sections of the (mainly Islamic) population. As a result, the threat to community cohesion with Muslim groups has at times become serious and threatening. This is exemplified by the situation following the London bombings in July 2005 (Lyons, 2006) and the monitoring and tracking by anti-terrorist units of individuals such as the Islamic preacher Omar Bakri, leader of the banned Al-Muhajiroun.

Social workers and representative bodies have had little comment to make on the role of the media in inciting racial tension and the resulting policies developed by successive governments leading to ever more restrictions on liberty and human rights.

The CRE, however, did set up an early warning community tension monitoring system through regional hubs and race equality councils. The involvement of a wide section of local ethnic minority communities in this was seen to be critical, particularly as those receiving most attention (such as Muslims) need to develop a position on the use of religious facilities and targeting of young individuals by preachers such as Bakri. Clearly, the diffusion of community frustration and integration of those with extreme views back into the largely law-abiding Muslim community was seen as a priority by the CRE.

The issues highlighted above suggest that the key areas need to be debated more widely within society, particularly as external influences increasingly impact on and divide multiracial Britain. The concern is encapsulated in the question: how can existing communities (at both the extreme and moderate ends) get on with each other as well as with new communities and cultures?

The CRE made its position clear on such questions and stated that, although segregation may exist between some groups, for example Indian and Pakistani, in some cities, it is a divisive and unwelcome force:

> We believe that the research overwhelmingly points to the fact that there is entrenched segregation in many parts of the UK, we argue this because we think that the Index of Isolation is a much more meaningful and important indicator than the Index of Dissimilarity which measures a superficial look at an area rather than exploring what is going on with the communities inside. (CRE, 2007a, pt 49)

The above statement suggests that disenfranchisement is more likely if people are isolated rather than if they are different. The report states that individuals are attracted to neighbourhoods where they feel at ease but that this sometimes leads to separated communities:

> Segregation is not a problem in itself but only becomes an issue if those living in segregated areas are discriminated against in access to labour and housing markets or the development of their human capital is restricted. (CRE, 2007a, pt 53)

The CRE suggests 'safety in numbers' (pt 54) is an important reason why people live together, but this depends on how they feel about the area they live in, and whether they relate well and value commonality as well as difference.

In response to the influx of new groups from Eastern Europe, for example, the CRE commissioned research (CRE, 2007b) on the reception and integration of recently arrived migrants, which recommended good information, appropriate funding and resources, and clear and consistent leadership. This implies that first-hand knowledge results in less discrimination within the framework of a common cultural understanding which challenges myths and misconceptions.

The imperative to set up policy and practice on equality is global as well as local. The British government response is complex as well as contradictory, but it is clear that there is a great deal of work to be done on broader welfare provision, as well as on internal cohesion among communities divided by culture, religion and other ideologies. The social work profession has a powerful, globally recognized ethical position and is therefore able to advocate for those who are isolated and disenfranchised.

Professional identity

The International Federation of Social Workers (IFSW), the European Federation of Social Workers (EFSW) and the International Association of Schools of Social Work (IASSW) have promoted social work as an international discipline and profession. In many countries, social workers enjoy a strong sense of professional identity supported by national associations and regulatory bodies (Dominelli and Thomas Barnard, 2003).

As the impact of limited resources takes hold on the public sector, Parrott (2001) questions the historically understood role and task of social workers in relation to equality and cohesion. It may be that the many positive aspects of the profession should be held onto, but perhaps it is time to consider the inevitable and examine areas which need limited input from social workers: 'community leadership, promoting well being, advancing social exclusion and partnership at strategic level doesn't require social services any more. It's so obvious, let it be' (Parrott, 2001, p. 11).

It is likely that future social workers will primarily carry well-defined statutory responsibilities, albeit shared with other professional groups, which look to provide services conditional on, for example, the nationality and immigration status of the service user. Such practices have been critiqued as discriminatory and exclusionary in the past (Sheppard, 2006). However, it is important to hold on to the contribution social work has made to anti-racist child protection and adult care for example. Perhaps there is a need to maintain the lead provided by social workers to everyday practice in key areas of responsibility such as these, while accepting that responsibility for strategic policy development on 'race' and racism has to be held more widely within the organization.

Professional knowledge, such as on work with children and families facing constant change as a result of mobility (Lyons, 2006), is improving. However, this thinking needs to be better theorized, documented and available to students and social workers. In relation to anti-racist practice, connections can be made with theoretical models developed on, for example, black identity and identification. Cross's five-stage developmental theory of acquisition of black identification (Cross called this 'nigrescence'), as identified below and quoted in Robinson (2002), suggests that individuals who progress through each stage are likely to emerge formed at the end of the process of change and development. Dominelli's (2008) critique suggests that the following stages of development, although rather static, apply particularly to individuals who struggle with, accept or resist racial inferiority:

- *pre-encounter* – identity pro-white and anti-black
- *encounter* – change occurs as a result of a crisis
- *immersion-emersion* – understanding the value of pro-black perspectives

- *internalization* – pride in own racial group
- *internalization-commitment* – expression of new identity.

As providers of services increasingly work together in interprofessional groups, such theories can also be used by social workers struggling with professional inferiority. Examination of how social work identifies itself in relation to other groups may be useful through consideration of the following stages:

- *encounter* – social work's attitude to itself
- *immersion-emersion* – social work's attitude to other professional groups
- *internalization-commitment* – expression of new professional identity.

For example, a newly qualified social worker joining a multiprofessional mental health team is likely to examine their own role, responsibility and status in relation to others in the organization. During the early stages of a career, the social worker will look to the various professional require-ments, such as the National Occupational Standards (TOPSS, 2002), codes of practice (GSCC, 2002a), code of ethics (BASW, 2002), in order to rein-force their worth as a registered, regulated professional. A comparison between the professional codes for social work and other groups, such as nurses, is likely to reinforce the professional standing of social workers and enable them to transform from encountering colleagues superficially to engaging meaningfully with social work tasks. This process may result in a greater identification of their role, responsibility and status as well as enhanced confidence and internalized commitment to core values which promote anti-racist social work practice within interprofessional contexts.

The push towards greater professional confidence and a proactive response to other professions can only be advantaged by a deeper evalua-tion of identity and identification within and across teams and organiza-tions. The minority identity development model offered by Atkinson (Robinson, 2001) is a step-by-step approach for individuals to consider the following:

1 attitudes to oneself
2 attitudes to other members of one's own racial/cultural group
3 attitudes and feelings towards other minorities
4 attitudes towards members of the majority culture.

Dominelli (2008) suggests that a theoretical understanding of identity and identification is particularly relevant to anti-racist social work prac-tice. Robinson (2002, p. 90) believes that:

> An understanding of Cross's model should sensitise social workers to the role that oppression plays in a black individual's develop-ment ... Pre-encounter attitudes have been linked to high levels of anxiety, psychological dysfunction and depression.

Conclusions

The aim of this chapter was to examine the many areas of concern raised by globalization and internationalization. Universal provisions have been linked to areas of national and local interest to illustrate their applicability and relevance. The important work of organizations such as CERD, UNICEF and the CRE, and the UN Committee on the Elimination of Racial Discrimination on promoting anti-racist practice have enabled this chapter to be illustrated by many positive examples of, and recommendations for, good practice.

The words used to describe globalization require consideration in relation to welfare provision and professional practice. The relevance of universal ideas to communities disadvantaged by global factors also deserves some attention, particularly from practitioners delivering services to asylum seekers, refugees and other newly arrived immigrants.

The chapter is also concerned to highlight the challenges facing established migrants and BME groups seeking services based on principles of equality and social cohesion.

Social work is in a relatively strong position and can make a difference to the translation of universal principles into local needs and concerns. The profession is also advantaged by a sound educational, training and professional development base, and social workers can respond individually and professionally by:

- reading widely about Britain's role in international welfare
- learning more about social work practice in other countries of the world
- studying national and international research findings on service users such as refugees and asylum seekers
- developing evidence-based responses using socioeconomic research data found on the World Wide Web
- seeking information and training on culture, religion, customs and traditions
- avoiding assumptions about needs and experiences by seeking individual service user views and perspectives
- offering an anti-racist perspective on extreme measures such as counterterrorism.

implications for practice

Global events affect social work practice on a daily basis. The constraints on public sector funding, brought about by financial mismanagement across the world, is one example of how localized services can be directly hit by large-scale occurrences.

Universal welfare standards have informed work with vulnerable children and adults over a number of years and international research has provided useful data on, for example, indicators of poverty and deprivation in relation to BME children.

Service users with immigrant backgrounds also bring important knowledge and information to any given situation. The process of moving from one country to another results in adaptation and modification which in turn impacts on the transference of important family and kinship traditions and norms across the globe. In order to gain further professional knowledge of the capacity and resilience of such groups, further research is needed on, for example, why some families benefit economically and socially from immigration while others do not.

Social work is an internationally recognized profession and representative bodies, such as the International Federation of Social Workers, are working towards greater knowledge and skill exchange which is likely to enhance professional identity within and across borders. Greater liberalization and regionalization have significant implications for students and newly qualified social workers interested in enhancing their expertise and working in other countries of the world. The value of this experience, however, needs to be better acknowledged and supported by employers and policy makers.

main points

- Despite notions of universal welfare in Britain, individuals are increasingly encouraged to supplement state provision through the provision of personal insurance against poor health and old age.

- Advances in media, television and computers have meant that individuals living in one country can readily see and/or relate to societies across the world.

- Global communication is welcomed by individuals living in developing countries who wish to imitate western welfare standards and benefits.

- There is an expectation that registered social workers, holding qualifications which are recognized and accepted by all members, will be able to work anywhere in the EU.

- The Commission for Racial Equality (CRE) has stated that segregation among Indians and Pakistanis, in some cities, is a divisive and unwelcome force.

- The CRE suggests that they cluster together because they feel safer in greater numbers, but the way people live together depends a great deal on how they feel about the area they live in, and whether they relate well and value common as well as different experiences.

- Do you think that universal conventions should only be there for moral guidance?
- Consider the implications of the UNICEF report (2007) which places the Netherlands at the top and Britain at the bottom of a league table of 21 rich countries in six areas: material wellbeing, health and safety, education, peer and family relationships, behaviours and risks, and young people's own subjective sense of wellbeing.
- In your experience, do you think that there is any truth in the survey carried out by the University of Kent (Abrams and Houston, 2006), which found that Muslims suffer a higher level of discrimination based on religion, sexism and ageism?
- REACH, a report commissioned by the British government (DCLG, 2007) on raising aspirations and attainment of black boys and young black men, recommended a minister for race to take forward its findings. What do you think of this idea?

taking it further

- Abrams, D. and Houston, D.M. (2006) *Equality, Diversity and Prejudice in Britain*, Centre for the Study of Group Processes, University of Kent. A survey of how discrimination based on religion, sexism and ageism impacts on the life chances of black and ethnic minority groups. The study offers useful large-scale data as well as methods and design in relation to research on racism and discrimination.
- Khan, P. and Dominelli, L. (2000) The impact of globalisation on social work in the UK, *European Journal of Social Work*, **3**(2): 95–108. Usefully examines the relationship between globalization and public services, in particular, the relationship between the marketplace and welfare provision in Britain.
- Mishra, R. (1999) *Globalisation and the Welfare State*, Edward Elgar, Cheltenham. Offers the reader background information on the impact of globalization on welfare, employment and political processes and includes a comparative study of Sweden, Germany and Japan. The final chapter on global social policy suggests a reorientation from social rights to social standards.
- UNICEF (2007) *Child Poverty in Perspective: An Overview of Child Well-being in Rich Countries*, Report Card 7, Innocenti Research Centre, UNICEF, Florence. Good example of a study that utilizes large-scale statistics, using interesting (and controversial) research methods. It focuses particularly on disadvantage and how it impacts on children and young people. The report was covered extensively in the British media in 2007, leading to some reflection on the comparison of welfare standards between wealthy countries.

3 Knowledge for social work practice

Introduction

The principles underpinning ethics and values in social work incorporate a range of ideas, including those derived from the regulation of professional practice (Hugman, 2005), as well as from postcolonial thinking on 'race' and racism. A great deal of writing on anti-racist social work practice has charted this work (Dominelli, 2008) and this chapter will build on this by examining the significant influences on anti-racist social work practice, particularly how and where knowledge is produced, who uses and who benefits from it.

Core professional values have been guided and influenced by international conventions, agreed as overarching rules by a disparate range of countries across the world. The 1948 Universal Declaration of Human Rights was founded on underlying principles such as human dignity and civil and social rights. These principles were all-embracing and therefore too big to use in daily life. They are particularly difficult for poor people, living in less developed areas of the world, who reasonably argue that ethical living is a luxury more easily afforded by rich people in countries like the UK. The British welfare system is relatively well resourced in global terms and thus offers those working within it the opportunity to meet the particular and specific needs of individuals and groups.

State-led welfare has enabled British social workers to respond to core and universal principles beyond their immediate remits. For example, professional perspectives have contributed to theory building on 'race' and racism which has improved and informed anti-racist practice. BME activists and writers working in subjects such as social work, sociology and social policy have also influenced practice knowledge. Among other things, they have reflected on, and challenged, preconceived notions being applied to images of BME individuals and communities (Owusu-Bempah, 2000; Chand, 2005). Social workers, faced with ever more complex service demands, have looked to advocates of anti-racist practice for guidance on methods and models which respond ethically, efficiently and effectively to daily challenges and dilemmas.

The development of knowledge which looks critically at practice has meant that social workers and students have taken time to reflect on the influences of personal experience on professional practice (Fook, 2000). Professionals recognize that racism challenges existing values and requires release from certainty and expectation handed down by previous generations (Baldwin, 2004).

Background knowledge

Attempts to formulate universal human rights and social justice are long-standing and well recorded in contemporary literature (Banks, 2004; Hugman, 2005). For example, the Stoics believed in human rationality rather than chaos. Greek philosophers espoused philosophical thought through observation and deduction and ensured that their principles were enshrined in guidance on medical practice (Hugman, 2005). The Romans, although oppressive and violent in the extreme to those they colonized/enslaved, espoused core, essential principles of natural justice. Citizens of Rome could appeal to principles of natural justice against unjust laws and seek to defend their rights and freedoms.

Ethical knowledge has developed over time and is reflected in the regulatory codes and registration requirements (GSCC, 2002a) for a number of professional groups. The British Association of Social Workers (BASW, 2002) code of ethics has incorporated a range of universal ideas to meet contemporary organizational needs, so Section 4.4.1.j appears to direct employers and managers towards fair and equal treatment: 'To treat workers fairly and in accordance with the principles of natural justice.' While common threads have been built on by societies over generations, ethical knowledge as a layered, multifaceted entity requires some introduction, particularly to students and inexperienced staff keen to understand the links between personal ideology and professional commitment.

Influences from far and wide can be found in the fabric of the modern welfare state and, more particularly, in the regulation of professional practice. For example, ancient rules such as those set out in the Hippocratic Oath sought to guide early medical practice through the following principles (Hugman, 2005):

- coordinated instruction and registration
- training which benefits patients
- prohibition of abortion and euthanasia
- condemnation of the abuse of power of a doctor over a patient
- confidentiality between doctor and patient.

For social work practitioners, the principles set out here provide the basis for formalizing contact with service users on, for example, setting boundaries around relationships, communication and record keeping. They are also a foundation for professional codes which address professional integrity, quality and standards, appropriate qualifications, individual registration and continuous professional development.

Payne (2005) charts a range of ideas from overseas, including those from China and Japan, which inform contemporary social, family and community care. The significance of religions such as Buddhism is widely accepted, but Payne cautions against ideas driven by religious and philosophical thought deeply embedded in history. He suggests that Buddhist teachings have not necessarily adapted well to contemporary society and that, compared to other formalized faiths, Christianity has responded better to the idea of the welfare society:

> Buddhism ... encourages adherents to accept the status quo fatalistically and discourages the idea of responsibility for those outside a personal circle, it seems to set its face against more general welfare and this has led some to the view that the ideology of Christianity was crucial to the development of social work. (Payne, 2005, p. 18)

This suggests that religion has to adapt and transform essential ideas to encompass modern welfare principles, such as civic duty, in order to respond to the concerns and demands of those beyond, as well as within, its immediate following.

The influence of faith and religion on society is long and enduring. In the formalization of social work values, the imperative to understand and respond to spiritual as well as practical needs has resulted in faith and religion receiving greater attention. Religious thinking has not, however, been visible in the literature on anti-racist social work practice.

Class is another area which requires further attention, particularly in relation to BME groups. In the 19th century, the class system maintained aristocratic supporters of the British monarchy, many of whom used their power, wealth and influence to found the civil service and related professions. Forsythe (1995) suggests that the charitable origins of social work were firmly based on class divisions. A great deal of philanthropy was aimed at pacifying the poor and keeping them in their proper place. Notions of superiority filtered down to every layer of society, and those who were substantially different and in need of civilization were actively excluded: 'The class-based context of society, therefore, made for a model of social care administration by superior stewards who sought obedience and individualistic morality from their appreciative recipients' (Forsythe, 1995, p. 4).

Contemporary welfare ethics are based on universal ideas shared and agreed by the countries involved in the Second World War (1938–45), motivated by an unprecedented post-conflict desire for international stability, safety and wellbeing.

The development of modern-day global conventions took a number of years, beginning in 1938 with what can only be described as a shameful examination of human rights at the Evian Conference. This was set up in response to the atrocities of the Third Reich against its own citizens, and in particular followers of the Jewish faith.

The results of the Evian Conference were inconclusive, based on a lack of recognition or commitment by the 32 countries present to challenge the policies of the then German government. This inertia contributed to the subsequent massacre of 10 million oppressed individuals, many of whom were disabled, gay, lesbian, Gypsy and of Jewish and Polish origins (Forbes and Mead, 1992). There is evidence that, in a bid to create an Arian master race, the German SS employed a large number of doctors to research the creation of a cognitive and physical elite by applying ideas based on eugenics. This resulted in the gas chambers being used in the first instance to exterminate children and adults with disabilities.

The relevance of historical knowledge to modern anti-racist social work practice is illustrated by the links between fascism and racism within sociological literature:

> it is quite clear that the history of contemporary racism has been influenced in one way or another by the experience of fascism and the anti-semitic political mobilisations which were a key feature of fascist movements ... the usage of the very term racism is in fact closely related to the rise of Nazism and the racial theories they advocated and put into practice. (Solomas and Back, 1996, p. 50)

Postwar responses included the setting up of the United Nations (UN) in 1945 and the subsequent adoption and proclamation, by the General Assembly of the United Nations Organisation on 10 December 1948, of the UN Universal Declaration of Human Rights. This was later seen as traditional and middle of the road because it did not provide sufficient clarity on what follows on from fundamental rights in relation to 'race', religion and sex (Thompson and Melia, 1988). For example, Article 3 simply states that 'every person has the right to life, liberty and security of person'.

Critics of the declaration also suggested that the underrepresentation of developing nations in the drafting process meant that insufficient attention was paid to the constraints faced by individuals living in poor and extremist societies. It was, therefore, unworkable in countries based on religious, for example Catholic and Islamic, doctrine.

The 30 articles were written by Eleanor Roosevelt, chairperson of the drafting committee, and founded on key principles which were subsequently enshrined in British law, including the Human Rights Act 1998, the Equality Act 2006 and a range of social work legislation such as the Children Act 1989. The basic tenets of the Universal Declaration of

Human Rights, defined below, were derived from age-old universal rules, but with added civic, economic and social rights, embedded in political notions of cross-national collaboration, mutual aid and unity:

- *Human dignity* – developed from the basic tenets of every world religion, that is, the right to be treated as an individual.
- *Civil and political rights* – interpreted by many as a negative position because at that time governments were encouraged not to interfere in basic rights such as freedoms of speech, the press, religion and assembly.
- *Economic and social rights* – encompassed the responsibility of nation states to provide shelter, healthcare, education, employment and security in old age.
- *Solidarity* – allowed an important commitment to individual duty and international cooperation in relation to the environment, peace, development, self-determination and justice across national borders.

The next major declaration appeared in 1950 with the European Convention for the Protection of Human Rights and Fundamental Rights and Freedoms. Article 14 states:

> The enjoyment of the rights and freedoms set forth in this Convention shall be secured without discrimination on any ground such as sex, race, colour, language, religion, political or other opinion, national or social origin, association with a national minority, property, birth or other status.

Forbes and Mead (1992) suggest that while the convention appeared to provide wide protection from a whole range of discriminatory acts, it was designed to have crucial limitations:

- it secures only the rights laid down in the convention itself
- it does not grant an independent right to the freedom from discrimination.

The relevance of this for employment rights is particularly important. The convention itself does not guarantee protection against occupational discrimination or unequal pay within the countries who signed. A great deal of policy and practice on this emerged subsequently through challenges to poor employment practices, resulting in case law. This may be why the BASW code of ethics includes fair treatment in its guidance, and why the right to follow religious practices is adhered to by many employers. The latter came about over many years as individuals successfully won rulings to pray and dress according to their faith and belief. As a result, discrete spaces for cross-denominational worship in the workplace are more commonly available.

In relation to the individual rights and needs of the wider population, Blakemore and Boneham (1994) suggest that European countries have responded differently, rather than cohesively. So, for example, Islamic headdress is outlawed in schools in some European countries, such as France, whereas it is commonly seen in British schools. This is because accepting difference in its many forms requires a great deal of societal commitment as well as national confidence. The desire to support one disadvantaged group over another is also dependent on national priorities, which may, at any given time, privilege some groups, such as BME children, over others, such as recent migrants and asylum seekers.

The harmonization of the EU has increased the sense of a common European identity, promoted by the power of the merged economies through common passports, currency and ease of travel. Skin colour is not a barrier to freedom of movement, and heterogeneity continues to be widely celebrated by Europeans of all ethnic backgrounds. This may suggest equality for all EU citizens, but, in reality, racism permeates the countries within which they reside.

Until the late 1990s, British citizens made use of the European Court of Human Rights in Strasbourg, which dealt with human rights breaches in a long distance, time-consuming and expensive manner. The British Human Rights Act was enacted in 1998 and finally allowed cases to be processed within the domestic judicial system (Johns, 2005). This was an important milestone for social work service users who had previously found the laws and courts based in Europe difficult to access.

Social work practitioners have found the Human Rights Act 1998 extremely influential in court cases, particularly in relation to the rights of the child and family (Wilson et al., 2008). This and related provisions, such as the UN Convention on the Rights of the Child and the Adoption and Children Act 2002, have to be balanced in cases of permanency and guardianship, for example, where account has to be taken of objections to adoption based on cultural and religious beliefs.

Universal conventions have provided an important backdrop to national legislation, but targeted guidance, such as the International Convention on the Elimination of All Forms of Racial Discrimination, has also allowed cross-checking and benchmarking of ethical principles across national borders. Such instruments have been used to landmark important historical events and support related commemorative activity. For example, the UN holds an International Day for the Elimination of Racial Discrimination on 21 March every year to mark the Sharpeville Massacre, a milestone in the political mobilization of black South Africa. Interestingly, the UN website provides one example of an activity on human rights in Fiji to promote this day, while all other activities appeared to be held at Geneva. It may be that greater interest by individual countries in the central message has been lost with the passing of time.

In Britain, the extensive knowledge built by organizations such as the UN on human rights has been utilized by successive governments to bring individuals and communities together to examine universal principles for use in welfare provision. From the mid-1960s onwards, the Commission for Racial Equality (CRE) produced information and data which promoted universal, European and domestic conventions, directives, laws and policies. It supported individuals through employment tribunals and court proceedings and provided examples evidencing the prejudice and unfair treatment faced by particular groups in society, such as the Irish and Traveller communities. The CRE generated legal knowledge, improved laws and developed policy, along with the Equal Opportunities Commission, on the employment rights, pay and working conditions not only of black people, ethnic minorities and women, but also of the wider population.

Over many decades, social work embraced the demands made by organizations such the CRE. Critics, however, suggested that the professional response was overly influenced by a commitment to personalized relationships with service users, founded on the core ethical code of 'respect and service' (Clark, 2000, p. 69) and the Kantian principle of moral duty and reasoned thought. This may be because personalized practice is limited by the knowledge applied by professionals within such relationships. For example, if a social worker or a student intervenes and provides a service simply based on stated need, they may not necessarily address deeper rooted issues of identity, or complications raised by racist or discriminatory behaviour by or towards the service user and/or the professional.

Experience suggests that the knowledge used in social work by those who deliver and those who receive services has too often been at odds. This may be because the professional position has been either too broad/universal or too narrow/particular. Payne (2005, p. 6) suggests that a great deal more knowledge needs to be accrued and recorded on a range of perspectives, including those which incorporate the lived experience of BME individuals, women and other 'ordinary people'. Deeper understanding is more likely to lead to competent practice which can encompass bigger, alternative ideas within local, specialized demands. Some of this knowledge is already available, framed within the mobilization and empowerment of BME individuals and groups during the 1980s and 90s. Such activity was highlighted and actively supported by theorists such as Solomos and Back (1995, p. xi), concerned to share research-based knowledge which evidenced the multifaceted nature of the subject: 'A rounded analysis of the politics of race ... to deal with the complex intertwining of national, local and everyday processes of racialisation.'

Such writers were concerned that political, community and other thinking had to be closely related to the development and implementation of global instruments such as the UN Convention on the Rights of the Child. Professionals concerned with developing anti-racist practice had to link universal standards and local procedures in order to make sense of civic duties, obligations and responsibilities as well as individual rights.

Human rights are founded on collective principles, that is, that groups sign up and agree to abide by the rules set out. Ethical collaboration across the world is a good idea as long it is properly followed through. The grand gesture usefully brings countries together and commits them to the overarching idea, but little is done to challenge those who ignore or abstain. Unless nation states cooperate, endorse and comply, the losers are likely to be the most vulnerable in society. For example, the Convention on the Rights of the Child has the signatures of every country in the world bar two – Somalia, which had no government, and the USA (UNICEF, 2007). The USA abstained because the convention contradicted the existing law and practice in several states which authorize the execution of young people aged 16–18. In 2004, of all US prisoners, 38.6% and 15.2% respectively were of black or Hispanic backgrounds (US Department of Justice, 2010). These figures suggest that a percentage of prisoners must be both under 18 and non-white, although statistics on this age group were difficult to find on official websites.

Markers in social work knowledge

Social work has a significant theoretical backdrop on which to base its future development. Some of this has contributed to professional pride and some has provided a source of learning. Much of it requires examination in relation to contemporary thinking on anti-racist practice.

A great deal of formalized charitable work began in the UK during the Victorian era (Healy, 2005). One of the founding organizations was the Charity Organisation Society (COS), set up in 1869 to coordinate means-tested services. It was based on the notion of the deserving and undeserving poor and the philanthropic idea that the criteria for supporting the underclass, regardless of 'race', gender, sexuality and disability, was best decided by the moralistic rich. Supremacist ideas focused on the civilizing influences of class, Darwinian principles of physical/mental fitness, and religious ideas of moral regeneration:

> Full restorative private charitable intervention would only be offered to those who satisfied the investigator's criteria of thrift, abstinence, industry and so forth. The rest would be allotted to the Poor Law for minimal intervention based on less eligibility ... As far as race was concerned it was generally believed that the Anglo Saxon race was superior to all others and that whites were superior to blacks in intellect, ethical behaviour, mental capacity and physique. (Forsythe, 1995, p. 1)

The COS and other similar charitable organizations were significant in the development of contemporary social work practice. Jones (2000) proposes that British social work is founded on an ideology which privileges moral characteristics above socioeconomic circumstances.

Eileen Younghusband (1967) also suggested that social work practice has developed to encompass democratic, humanistic ideas based on individual and group relationships and is therefore at the heart of any friction, conflict or controversy which occurs within and between families, individuals and communities:

> No profession is more deeply involved in problems of the rights and responsibilities of the individual and those of society nor so close to practical problems of implementing the great democratic ideals of liberty, equality and justice in all complexities of individual people's lives. (Younghusband, 1967, p. 5)

Younghusband further suggested that ethical practitioners need to know the difference between instrumental, for example immediate and concrete, and ultimate rights, for example global. This is because the pressure to produce practical outcomes, such as better housing or income for one young care leaver, often overrides broader principles, such as universal welfare benefits for young people up to the age of 21: 'a value – any value – is essentially a standard, a yardstick by which to measure a criterion by which to decide amongst alternative possible lines of actions' (Younghusband, 1967, p. 5).

Practitioners and students faced with the daily challenges of needs-led services use individual and universal principles to set standards in relation to thorny questions such as: what is *just* good enough, or *just* satisfactory in social work practice? They struggle to define good practice, but are aware that their interventions have to be explained, justified and accountable. So, if an elderly Asian woman requests female-only bathing facilities in a mixed-sex hospital ward, health and social workers struggle to uphold ethical practice with limited resources. Responses are based on personal judgements, and so a key question for professionals is not just about the service provided, but: is the service *just okay*, or is it *better than okay* for the individual involved? This question relates to the universal principles on which anti-racist practice is based. If the elderly Asian woman is offered a one-off arrangement for a female-only bathing facility, would this be the end of the matter? Or should all female patients expect to have this service available? Should women-only services be available to BME people or to everyone? In other words, should a private bathroom be at the behest of a practitioner or should the hospital change its structure to meet the right to dignity, respect and choice? It is likely that the majority of professionals take their responsibility towards patients keenly, but, depending perhaps on the profession involved, some may be less inclined to advocate and create policies more generally.

Younghusband (1967, p. 9) concluded that people offer rights (such as

choice) based on value assumptions, and that professionals are as suscep-
tible to discriminatory behaviour as any other individual: 'like everyone
else, social workers are steeped in the prejudices and moral assumptions
about desirable behaviour of their own particular sub-culture'.

Social workers have responsibilities as ethical practitioners, but they
also have rights to personal values, which include the right to be different, have an individual voice, be oneself and feel safe. They have a right
to explore and debate personal attitudes and values derived from family
and background, within a safe working environment and a protected,
well-supervised space.

Younghusband advocated that the British Association of Social Workers
produce ethical guidelines to support social workers facing personal and
professional ethical dilemmas in order that they 'learn better how to change
negative community attitudes; to work for the increase in tolerance and
understanding; to help other people to examine their own values; and to
promote certain values held by the profession' (Younghusband, 1967, p. 9).
In a radical move, she suggested that social work values should be imposed
onto wider society and maybe other professions.

In response to such concerns, BASW produced *The Code of Ethics for
Social Work*, which provided broad guidance based on humanitarian and
democratic principles promoted by Charlotte Towle in 1965. The code
was first published in 1975 (and amended in 1985, 1986 and 1988) and
stated that:

> social work is a professional activity. Implicit in its practice are
> ethical principles which prescribe the professional responsibility
> of the social worker. Basic to the profession of social work is the
> recognition of the value and dignity of every human being, irre-
> spective of origin, race, status, sex, sexual orientation, age, disabil-
> ity, belief or contribution to society. The profession accepts a
> responsibility to encourage and facilitate the self-realisation of
> each individual person with due regard for the interest of others.
> (Watson, 1985, p. 1)

The updated code of ethics is available on the BASW website (www.basw.
co.uk) and now incorporates a range of guidance for social workers,
managers and researchers. References to anti-racist practice are minimal,
although Section 4.1.6 (BASW, 2002) focuses on cultural awareness in
relation to the following:

- impact of own ethnic and cultural identity on others
- practitioner knowledge of service user identities and affiliations
- differences in values and beliefs
- provision for qualified interpreters.

A later section deals with workplace responsibilities and suggests that professionals: 'Challenge and seek to address any actions of colleagues which are racist, sexist or otherwise demonstrate prejudice' (BASW, 2002, p. 11).

Banks (1995) suggests that it is important to distinguish between different rights, particularly those which are based on a negative premise and those which are positive in nature. She also separates those which are legal from those which are moral, and those which are absolute from those which are conditional, and offers the following definitions:

- *Negative rights* (or liberties) – relate to the freedom to do something without interference, for example free speech
- *Positive rights* – state a claim against someone else to do something, for example medical treatment
- *Legal rights* – valid claims by virtue of the legal code or customary practice, for example the right to vote
- *Moral rights* – valid claims bestowed by a moral code, for example the right to be treated with honesty
- *Absolute rights* – apply unconditionally to everybody, for example the right to respect
- *Conditional rights* – qualified in relation to certain conditions, for example the right to liberty which can be withheld on certain grounds.

Arguably, such rights are applicable to social work within any context but Banks proposes that the BASW code of ethics is essentially driven by either absolute, for example the right to trial, or conditional rights, for example the right to freedom of speech. She puts forward a list of rights which can be adapted for anti-racist practice:

- to be treated as an end, that is, respected as a human being first
- to self-determination, that is, empowered and enabled
- to be treated as a unique individual, that is, offered a voice
- to a professionally competent service, that is, properly trained staff.

Although these rights are either supported by law or by a moral position, they pose an important question for anti-racist practice with groups who are not seen as primary service users, such as newly arrived immigrants, refugees and asylum seekers:

> Many of the people seeking social work help, or required to have contact with social workers, may have been already denied full citizenship rights, and/or may find it difficult to exercise their rights due to poverty, lack of confidence or lack of competence ... Except in areas of social work which are subject to the law, such as child protection, mental health or probation work there have not been clear rules or guidelines about who should be offered social work help and what the nature of the help should be. (Banks, 1995, p. 101)

There is a great deal of debate within social work about the quality and quantity of intervention, particularly with individuals and groups who do not meet legal and policy criteria for services. Arguably, a great deal of knowledge on welfare provision has been derived from existing practice based on local and regional concerns, as well as responses to crisis situations relating to low income or poor housing, for example. Such immediate knowledge and experience often lead to the development of practice wisdom more likely to maintain and sustain that which is closest and most relevant to the locality and neighbourhood. So, a safeguarding team in adult services in a largely white, rural area is unlikely to see a newly arrived 18-year-old refugee living and working in a local takeaway as a priority, unless they are assessed as vulnerable under relevant law and policies.

Social work is justifiably proud of the superior position it holds in examining and implementing professional principles (Clark, 2000). However, in relation to anti-racist practice, it needs a consistent, coherent and substantial commitment which informs attitudes, behaviour and good conduct. The BASW code of ethics and the professional codes of conduct and practice are ideal professional instruments where such principles can be developed.

Building professional knowledge

Social workers hold a great deal of practice wisdom and need to discuss existing and developing ideas constantly with other people. Dominelli (2004) offers the following ways to make and share ideas:

- mutuality through joint and shared work
- interdependence and reliance on others
- solidarity
- the possibility of reciprocity and exchange of knowledge and skills
- understanding of our own and others' entitlement to societal resources.

Social workers are compelled by altruism and common humanity as a professional group and are aware that knowledge is better if widely shared, easily available and accessible in form and presentation.

Schön (1991, p. 24) suggests the following hierarchy of applied knowledge and states that 'basic science yields applied science. Applied science yields diagnostic and problem solving techniques which are applied in turn to the actual delivery of services.' This theoretical perspective can be interpreted as Figure 3.1. This implies that knowledge is derived from the superior empirical science base, and that a high percentage of social work theories may have emerged from academic thought, rather than professional experience. The hierarchical privileging of theoretical (basic and applied) science does not account for the important influence that social work practice has had on the core ideas and principles on which foundational knowledge is based.

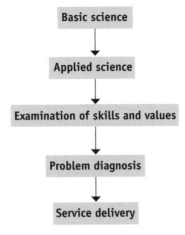

Figure 3.1 Schön's hierarchy of knowledge

Source: Adapted from Schön, 1991

Social work knowledge may be derived from alternative perspectives which are informed by evidence and reflective and competent practice respectively. Evidence-based practice is based on empirical research and reflective practice theorizes practice wisdom and experience. In relation to anti-racist practice, a combination of the above ideas can be developed into the model in Figure 3.2.

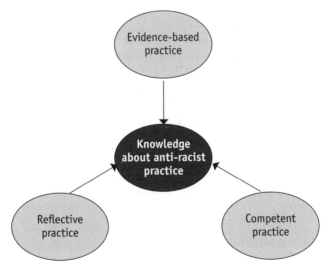

Figure 3.2 Sources of knowledge for anti-racist practice

Evidence-based, reflective and competent practice can also be examined and related to the following five social work methods advocated by Healy (2005):

- Problem solving
- Systems perspectives
- Strengths perspectives
- Anti-oppressive social work
- Postcolonial approaches.

These five approaches can be developed to promote policy and procedure on anti-racist practice, as illustrated in Table 3.1.

A great deal of work on anti-racist practice requires a fundamental understanding of personal strengths and weaknesses and how these impact on professional life. It is, therefore, highly unlikely that the models above are without complication. Nor is the path to learning and development on 'race' and racism measurable in purely scientific terms, because so much of human behaviour is based on value judgements, loaded with morality and affected by anxiety and fear (Rapley, 2001).

Anti-racist practice is challenging for those championing the issue. Many people feel isolated within their teams and organizations, while others feel unable to deal with the feelings generated by the subject. 'Race' and racism often lead to self-questioning as well as the examination of individual upbringing or family experience. In order to promote ethical practice, employing bodies have a responsibility to ensure that individuals and teams are supported in the development of competence in working environments which are healthy, safe and open to learning.

Social workers can demonstrate a sustained obligation to core social work values by reflecting on methods used by them to engage services users on a daily basis. The learning gained from this process is likely to enhance expert knowledge of the safeguarding needs of, for example, a BME boy living with his mother in a domestic violence situation. It is through processes such as these that professionals can develop effective strategies to assist self-determination and empowerment: 'In this way expert professional social workers are able to create critical knowledge which potentially challenges and resists current forms of domination' (Fook, 2000, p. 118).

The commitment of social work to reflective practice suggests that egalitarian adult learning principles inherent within the process of thinking, learning and doing continue to be highly valued. An important component of this is the individual's ability to evaluate, feel, act and review (Baldwin, 2004). As the following quote shows, the cycle of adult learning presupposes that evaluation is central to positive growth and development and that it has to occur both at a personal and professional level:

Table 3.1 Knowledge on anti-racist social work practice

	Problem solving	Systems	Anti-racist practice		Postcolonial
			Strengths	Anti-oppressive	
Evidence-based practice	Critical use of research and data which are scientifically neutral	Anti-racist approaches which are checked, quality assured, monitored and reviewed	Understanding derived from everyday evidence. Development of models which work well	An understanding of wider oppression and its relation to local practice	Practice based on an understanding of relationship between global and local evidence
Reflective practice	Decision making based on lifelong learning and continuous professional development	An understanding of how professionals, teams and organizations systemically fail service users	Examining and learning from own prejudice and bias. Using learning to inform good practice	Breaking down component parts of all work to critically examine and learn	Positive, evaluation, recognition and learning from history which is shared within and across teams and organizations
Competent practice	Impartial and objective organizational decision-making processes	Full implementation of the race relations laws in all areas. Individual and institutional awareness of barriers to provision	An understanding and application of self in relation to 'race' and racism	Checks that bias and prejudice are avoided for all service user groups. Good practice impacts on all services	Policy and procedure which reflects learning and development from past injustices and is owned by organizations

> Learning is often about letting go of fond and long-held beliefs. This was a painful experience, for example, for many social workers engaging in anti-racist training, as they learnt about their long-held but unconscious prejudices. Learning is personal and potentially threatening. It is particularly anxiety provoking when it happens publicly, for instance, with students or social workers.
> (Baldwin, 2004, p. 43)

It may be that one lesson from the past is to use reflection more positively in relation to the development of anti-racist social work practice. For example, students taught the history of welfare and social work may deconstruct it, that is, pull it apart and examine it in detail, and relate it directly to injustice and inequality in contemporary Britain. A way forward may be to examine history, question philosophical and postcolonial thought, and assess the ways it fits in with current and urgent concerns.

Another area of examination may be the link between theories of 'race' and racism and how they show up in the structures and systems of the social work or social care organization. How are anti-racist laws interpreted? Where does the knowledge, policy and guidance lie? Who is taking the lead in managing performance in this area? Who is responsible for overall implementation?

Students and novice social workers sustain their commitment to the profession because they believe that it has an ethical and moral basis. They may also be motivated by individual ideology. The reasons why an individual is attracted to, and remains committed to, the profession are extremely important for personal growth and continuous development. The profession still considers itself a liberal, needs-led provider of public services, but this commitment is challenged by daily dilemmas. Social workers get pulled and pushed in different directions, driven and motivated by overwhelming material demands, while striving to maintain ideological priorities.

Policy makers, leaders and managers pay limited attention to this area and so ignore the real link between motivation, recruitment and retention. There is, therefore, a particular need for more research on how professional dilemmas impact on personal values and moral positions.

Building interprofessional knowledge

British social workers are increasingly functioning within the context of integrated and interprofessional (children and vulnerable adult) services and are more likely to be influenced by the cross-fertilization of ideas, both within and across the profession and discipline. Healy (2005) suggests that social work may learn from other professions by sharing ideas and methods which cross institutional contexts and geographic locations.

The increasingly interprofessional response to service needs has steered social work towards sharing two areas of ethical practice recognized by related agencies providing social welfare, such as health and education, that is, anti-oppressive practice and anti-discriminatory practice (Dalrymple and Burke, 1995; Thompson, 2006). Closely linked to anti-racist practice, the former is concerned with structural and institutional transformation, and the latter steers change and development through the application of law. Both perspectives offer politicized ways of conceptualizing difference and diversity.

Other ideas advocated within interprofessional working are based on ethnicity and ethnic difference, associated with the characteristics of unity, harmony and cohesion. The overarching approach here is that BME individuals and communities are ethnically different from the general population and so require structures which enable unification and conformity (Thompson, 2006). This suggests that large groups can somehow be brought together in a unified mass, and that the transformation of character and morality is more important than material circumstance or basic human need (Jones, 2000).

Interprofessional methods have to meet individual needs based on ethical practice. This leads to research and theory building. For example, social workers based in a multiracial school may be working with teachers, education welfare officers, school nurses and administration and ancillary staff. In general, each group will understand the needs of their organization and the service it provides. Some individuals will be bound by their own codes of practice and professional values, while others will use principles based on personal/family experience. This situation will persist because welfare workers are trained to meet operational demands, and unless the whole group agrees to discuss the basis on which the individuals engage with each other, it is likely that the models and approaches used will remain undeveloped. Evidence-based practice, however, requires individuals and groups to work together and collaborate as a team on a daily basis. This is difficult to attain particularly in areas such as anti-racist practice.

In order to raise capacity, practitioners may need to look to other parts of the world for the development of interprofessional approaches which, for example, utilize service user potential and strengths. The family group conference (Healy, 2005) is a model that strives to maximize the capacity of the wider as well as the immediate family to plan and provide care for their own children and young people. The family is required to attend a series of meetings where issues are discussed and decisions made. The meetings are normally facilitated by a professional who may be a social worker, teacher or youth worker. The views of those present, most particularly those of the child or young person, are incorporated, agreed and recorded.

The collective planning model originated from New Zealand as a result of concerns about the overrepresentation of Maori children in the welfare system (Morris, 2002). The approach has been used in Britain for a number of years, but there are issues about the viability of transporting models which are particular to the cultural and ethnic needs of one group, region and country. Presumably, family group conferences work well in New Zealand because the model is culturally applicable, understandable and useful to the relevant family and kinship units. The client-centred approach assumes that family care is widely understood and common across the globe, even if practice is variable.

However, within a British context, innovations such as this bring particular problems. The model is based on the premise that the family group in question has positive qualities as well as a strong desire, common purpose, strength and commitment to caring for and safeguarding a child or young person. It also requires that the range of professionals involved with the collective responsibility for assessment, intervention and provision are all equally dedicated to an ongoing relationship based on goodwill, effective communication, understanding and commitment to the process. There is an assumption that the family and practitioners have a good working knowledge of how family group conferences work, as well as interprofessional policy and procedure. Finally, there may be an unchecked belief that those involved in the process respect each other's positions, and are able to act in an anti-racist and anti-discriminatory manner.

Although family group conferences are constrained by problems such as those mentioned above, they do have a significant advantage in involving professionals from related disciplines who bring important knowledge and perspective to any given situation. Most professions are concerned with the development of expert knowledge, and approaches which make sense in the family and community context. Some practitioners, such as teachers, are advantaged because they have sustained, long-term relationships with children and a great deal of knowledge of the locality and neighbourhood which crosses cultural and religious divides. Methods such as these require adaptation to national and local contexts if they are to offer valuable alternatives to collaborative working and allow greater choice for service users with multiple needs.

Interprofessional working has been widely promoted in recent years, but Doel and Shardlow (2005, p. 52) suggest that the push to develop policy and practice may lead to 'trivialising' rather than maximizing social work knowledge. In building relationships with allied professionals, social workers may wish to examine how they are seen by others. One of many images of social workers is that they feed and maintain service user dependency (Healy, 2005) and stifle rather than enable change, confidence and self-esteem. Social workers who are committed to empowerment, self-determination and the sharing of power may find this hard to accept but ethical principles need be regularly checked for certainty.

In working interprofessionally, it is useful to relate the global to the local as it refocuses universal principles and translates them into legal and policy responsibility:

> Equality before the law is a crucial aspect of the rule of law. Equality in the abstract is not enough to ensure social justice ... Equality is realised by explicit endeavour rather than being presumed. (Dominelli, 2004, p. 237)

Building personal knowledge

Substantial and open consideration of individual worth and value is informed by other international perspectives. Frankenberg (1993, p. 140) believes that the liberal movement in the USA is in danger of 'entrapment' and suggests that the following statement needs to be acknowledged and acted upon: 'First, that race makes a difference in people's lives; and second that racism is a significant factor in shaping contemporary US society.'

Although the national context and history of issues of 'race' varies between the USA and Britain, BME individuals are defined by the colour of their skin in both countries, and racism remains widespread in both countries. Racist ideas are derived from the past and it may be that social work now needs to fully and actively engage in envisioning the future. This may require rethinking on how personal knowledge is used to inform, excite and motivate future generations.

In-depth examination of the impact of personal knowledge on role, task, status and identity will always increase the professional confidence of those engaged in social work. However, the workplace is likely to be driven by employer demands for skills on, for example, report writing rather than consideration of how the wording in reports may prejudice and bias understanding.

Ideas which focus on building capacity are, however, receiving particular attention in social work, and include the creation of a knowledge base which unifies professionals who work with BME communities (Singh, 2006). Approaches such as these are better informed and increasingly build ethical confidence in developing, collating and promoting evidence-based anti-racist practice (Dominelli, 2004).

The move away from negative approaches, such as reprimand and blame (Healy, 2005), towards understanding how social workers think and work (Owusu-Bempah, 2000) is more likely to critically focus on the relationship between personal ideology and professional practice.

Social workers are asked to apply law, policy and procedure on a daily basis, but legal interventions are often seen to relate to service user rights, rather than processes which may be applied to practitioners. However, laws relate to all members of society and understanding needs to begin with the person. Social work students, growing and developing as professionals, may need to examine the impact of rules and regulations on their own personal beliefs, attitudes and behaviour. Exercise 3.1 provides an opportunity for students and practitioners to examine the dilemmas inherent in using laws which may contradict personal/religious principles.

Exercise 3.1

Using law in practice

Aim: To relate the provisions of the Race Relations (Amendment) Act 2000 and the Human Rights Act 1998 to interprofessional policy and practice.

Task: Consider the following dilemma and formulate a response, individually or in small groups.

You are a social worker in an interprofessional voluntary sector organization working with young adults in residential care. The team manager has brought this dilemma to you in a bid to formulate an agency response on religion within anti-racist policies.

A new team member is a Jehovah's Witness and has strong beliefs and objections, for example to blood transfusions, which are likely to impinge on their practice. Article 9 of the Human Rights Act states that individuals have:

> the right to freedom of thought, conscience and religion; this right includes freedom to change his religion or belief and freedom, either alone or in community with others and in public or private, to manifest his religion or belief, in worship, teaching, practice and observance.

Individuals have a right to follow religious beliefs in the workplace but this entitlement is conditional upon the context and situation. The organizational policy has to state the restrictions and/or parameters around religious behaviours, along with a clear legal basis and rationale for the decisions made. The overarching aim of the policy should be to protect rights and freedoms.

Consider the conditions you would develop in the organizational policy within wider legal responsibilities.

Individuals carry layer upon layer of knowledge built up throughout life, and how this knowledge is used within the process and application of learning is an area of particular concern to anti-racist practice. For example, practitioners may learn skills framed as mental maps to implement procedures in social work practice and develop concepts which impact directly on attitudes and behaviour (Carpenter, 2005). Greater insight into the way we think and act is likely to lead to a better understanding of life as it unfolds and the capacity to face challenge and confrontation.

Anti-racist social work practice requires professionals to have an advanced understanding of the aspects of their personal background, family ties, local and regional identity, friends and colleagues which impact on others, regardless of ethnic or cultural background. Exercises 3.2, 3.3 and 3.4 offer an opportunity for a step-by-step approach to the understanding and development of identity. Exercise 3.2 is about self-perception, Exercise 3.3 is about the multidimensional nature of individual identity, and Exercise 3.4 offers readers the opportunity to see themselves as others see them. Professionals such as social workers require a high level of insight into how their own background and experience influence their interactions with those around them. This understanding is incremental, that is, built over time, in order that the person involved can meaningfully incorporate the range of information made available to them. The process of personal and professional development is often shared with others and so these exercises can be undertaken individually and then shared in pairs and groups. The order in which they are taken may vary and contents may be adapted to fit the situation and context.

Exercise 3.2

Personal knowledge of self

Aim: To understand the perception you have of yourself, your identity and your self-image.

Task: Begin with two people, then form a group of four, and then feedback to the larger group.

1 Turn to your partner and consider your *personal* identity and self-image in relation to your family, upbringing, geography, region, education, culture and religion.
2 With your partner and the couple next to you, list the ways in which your personal identity impacts on your professional persona. Bring back ideas you are prepared to share with the group.

People may identify themselves in a number of ways, as well as carry a number of labels and stereotypes assigned to them by others. This additional labelling is particularly likely if a person is young and male, evidenced by the many young men targeted simply on the basis of skin colour, such as Jean Charles de Menezes. He was an innocent Brazilian electrician shot seven times by police marksmen who mistakenly identified him as a terror suspect in the aftermath of the London bombings in 2005.

Multiple identities are carried by, and assigned to, many women from BME backgrounds, particularly those visible by religious clothing. So, not only are individuals striving to identify themselves, but they are also struggling with categories placed on them by others. Despite this, a government report defines Britain more positively as super-diverse and transnational: 'Research suggests that trans-nationalism does not hinder integration, it helps it – as trans-national identity may give people the confidence to express their attachment and engage with wider society' (Commission on Integration and Cohesion, 2007, p. 34).

Exercise 3.3

Understanding the multidimensional nature of identity

The figure below can be copied and used with a small group of students and/or practitioners. Facilitators may wish to assure participants of confidentiality and other ethical rules to ensure a safe learning environment where disclosure can occur. Facilitators need to be aware of the potential for anxiety or nervousness created by this exercise.

Aim: To identify the characteristics students may ascribe to themselves in order to understand how they perceive themselves.

Task: The individual places him/herself in the middle and then ticks the means by which individual identity is defined. The figure may differ according to who fills in the circles, as those from BME backgrounds are likely to have a strong sense of self in relation to dress, religion, age and sexuality.

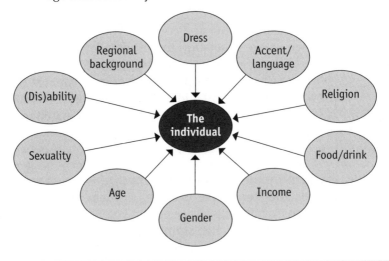

The above illustration can be used to enable individuals to express and declare knowledge they wish to share with others by following Exercise 3.4.

Exercise 3.4

Defining our own identity and relating to others

Rules of confidentiality must be discussed and agreed in order to ensure a safe learning environment where the differences referred to can be discussed.

Aim: To allow practitioners to acknowledge, recognize and see themselves from the perspectives of others. It will enable understanding of identity beyond that based on race, culture and ethnicity. These words have been deliberately excluded from the above illustration, as every individual has a racial, cultural and ethnic background regardless of their skin colour.

Task: The exercise is best undertaken in pairs in the first instance and should be fairly light-hearted, but allow time for discussion afterwards.

In pairs, each person draws a simple image of her/himself with coloured pens in the middle on a large piece of paper. The drawing needs to be circled and a spider diagram created, similar to the above, using words which best describe the characteristics each person would ascribe to her/himself. Each person draws two spider diagrams, one for her/himself and one for how she/he sees the other person in the pair, using words which she/he believes best suits her/him. When the two drawings are complete, the pair compare the spider diagrams for her/himself with that for the other person. Allow time for discussion in pairs.

When ready, seek agreement from the others to share only relevant and appropriate information with the wider group, drawing generalized conclusions about identity, awareness of others, and stereotypes.

Those undertaking the exercise may look for excluded words used to self-identify such as 'social worker' and 'professional'. Regardless of where they work, social workers are sometimes seen as child snatchers and because of this are not always open about their title. It may be, however, that some participants will identify themselves thus in an environment which is safe and inclusive but others may shy away from using their title if they fear questioning, scorn or contempt.

An area rarely declared in social work circles is religion and spirituality. Although many care organizations are founded on liberal Christian principles, little is known about how this influences contemporary social work practice. Many social work students, professionals and academics, however, wear badges (literal or in the spoken/written word) which identify their political, ideological allegiances and campaigning commitments, but few dare to display Christian symbols. A person wearing a turban is treated with appropriate, often superficial, respect but a polite, middle-class intake of breath greets a person wearing a crucifix which demonstrates a religious rather than a fashion commitment.

Faith and religion require a great deal more attention and yet social work is dominated by its Christian heritage (Forsythe, 1995; Healy, 2005). The profession conservatively sticks to existing structures and systems, which exclude those who wear turbans or are in any way different from positions of power and influence.

Anti-racist advocates have always promoted the idea that critical scrutiny and understanding of self will result in improved service delivery for all service users, not just those from BME backgrounds. More ambitiously, well-founded anti-racist practice is likely to support ethically confident, evidence-led practitioners who may further embed their professional identity, build on sound interprofessional relationships and contribute to wider social policy.

The notion of social work identity, however, needs ongoing attention because social workers continue to suffer from poor confidence and low self-esteem, and are constantly alarmed by the professional stereotypes and labels assigned to them by others. Negative attention from the media adds to professional self-doubt and leads to concern about the use of power and judgement inherent in their roles as managers, supervisors and educators. Unless curbed and constrained, this sense of anxiety may be passed on to students and the cycle of poor professional confidence perpetuated.

In relation to anti-racist practice, personal knowledge incorporates an understanding of self based on identity and identification. The discussion so far has been largely concerned with BME individuals who have been perceived as having a problem with 'racial' identity and identification (Maxime, 1996). Developing anti-racist practice, however, requires greater attention to white identity in social work literature. Insufficient focus may be because the description of self has tended to focus on categories such as 'race', gender and class, which tend to generate a them and us scenario and result in overly simplistic group stereotypes (Fook, 2002).

Frankenberg (1993, p. 197) is concerned that identity is defined relative to white cultural norms:

> Whites are the non-defined definers of other people or to put it another way, whiteness comes to be an unmarked or neutral category, whereas other cultures are specifically marked 'cultural'. Similarly discussions of race difference and cultural diversity at times revealed a view in which people of colour actually embodied difference and whites stood for sameness.

Being white is indefinable but positive. Being black is definable but negative. Clear perception of white culture and identity leads to the understanding that, although difficult to define and lacking character and shape, the concept is a point of reference for all white people when appraising and evaluating others. This leads to the marginalization of BME people, thereby making them superfluous.

Sorting people into groups may be the thin end of the discriminatory or racist wedge, but does it help to make sense of the world and promote understanding? Is it a means by which an in-group looks after its own by excluding all others? Oakes and Haslam (2001) contend that the real problem does not lie with categorization but with the act of racism itself.

However, personal and professional identity is increasingly fragmented and fractured. There are many layers representing difference and change (Hall, 1996) which we are constantly working to understand and make whole. Breakwell (quoted in Maxime, 1996, p. 101) suggests that notions of identity, self-concept, character and personality are often confused: 'used interchangeably and, on examination of the literature, refer to the same process and phenomena'. Welfare professionals desire a place in the social and political sphere, but often find this goal hard to achieve.

Hall (1996) deconstructs identification and sees it as a combination of common origins and shared characteristics. These may include moral experience, based on early influences derived from a range of sources, including the media and friendship. Practitioners working with children will know that children are more inclined to see things they have in common with others, than things which are different. As young people grow and develop, differences become more visible to them. Thereafter, their personal and professional ideology is framed more through difference than commonality:

> Identities are about the process of becoming rather than being: not who we are but where we come from, so much as what we might become, how we have been represented and how that bears on how we might represent ourselves. (Hall, 1996, p. 4)

Identity is dependent on the meanings people attach to the concept and can therefore be either a choice or labelling by others. So self-identification, based on cultural, social and political influences, has been perceived as a positive way forward. For example, a young person with a mother born in Jamaica and a father born in England may see themselves as mixed heritage or British, depending on their self-perception and motivation.

Individual identity develops through history, language and culture. Like social workers, young people should choose difference rather than be constructed by difference. Only then can they build a positive self-image: 'Black self-concept – the appreciation that black identity or black self-concept – is an active developmental process which is exposed to various influences within and without and can be selective and/or adaptive' (Maxime, 1996, p. 101). Arguably, white people conceive their own image more positively than BME people in Britain because society supports and enhances whiteness on a daily basis. The influences which impact on BME groups have to be similarly powerful in order that black individuals benefit from the same feedback as their white counterparts.

Exercises 3.5, 3.6 and 3.7 are inspired by important work undertaken by Rooney Martin and other community work trainers in Sheffield in the 1980s and, used individually or in a groups, are designed to encourage thinking on the wider influences.

The focus in Exercise 3.5 relates to whiteness rather than on being black or an ethnic minority and partly challenges the idea that BME people are defined by their skin colour and white people are not. However, the changing nature of society means that everyone is better placed to examine identity and identification, so Exercise 3.6 provides an opportunity for BME individuals to examine the nature of being black in British society. Finally, Exercise 3.7 enables another growing section of the population, people of mixed 'race', heritage and parentage, to consider the links between these areas and other aspects of identity.

Participants may not have considered personal identity from this perspective and may find the discussion interesting, particularly if it includes consideration of words and terminology (see Glossary at back of book).

Exercise 3.5

Being white

Aims: ■ To examine personal experiences and knowledge of being white in British society
■ To understand ethnicity and culture in relation to self
■ To consider commonalities and differences.

Tools: Use a large sheet of paper on a flipchart stand and felt tip pens to write statements and comments. This demonstrates that the exchange is open, honest and valid.

Task: Consider each statement, add comments and discuss influences, meaning and feelings.

Statement	Comment/feelings/reactions
Being white and young	
Being white and middle class	
Being white and a majority	
Being white and educated	
Being white and Welsh/Scottish/Irish and English	
Being white and a professional	
Being white and rich/poor	
Being white and a student	
Being white and provincial/city based	

The terms used are deliberately provocative and can be added to and changed. The material produced will be rich and multi-faceted but may generate powerful emotions. Those undertaking the exercise may wish to allow substantial time for briefing and debriefing at the beginning and end. The large paper can be used immediately to discuss the comments, but also kept and stored to compare when the exercise is repeated later at the mid-point or final stages of the placement.

Being black

Aims: ■ To examine personal experiences and knowledge of being black in British society
■ To understand ethnicity and culture in relation to self
■ To consider commonalities and differences.

Tools: Use a large sheet of paper on a flipchart stand and felt tip pens to write statements and comments. This demonstrates that the exchange is open, honest and valid.

Task: Consider each statement, add comments and discuss influences, meaning and feelings.

Statement	Comment/feelings/reactions
Being black and young	
Being black and middle class	
Being black and a minority	
Being black and educated	
Being black and Welsh/Scottish/Irish and English	
Being black and a professional	
Being black and rich/poor	
Being black and a student	
Being black and provincial/city based	

The terms used are deliberately provocative and can be added to and changed. The material produced will be rich and multifaceted but may generate powerful emotions. Those undertaking the exercise may wish to allow substantial time for briefing and debriefing at the beginning and end. The large paper can be used immediately to discuss the comments, but also kept and stored to compare when the exercise is repeated later at the mid-point or final stages of the placement.

Being mixed 'race', heritage or parentage

Aims: ■ To examine personal experiences and knowledge of being mixed 'race' in British society
■ To understand ethnicity and culture in relation to self
■ To consider commonalities and differences.

Tools: Use a large sheet of paper on a flipchart stand and felt tip pens to write statements and comments. This demonstrates that the exchange is open, honest and valid.

Task: Consider each statement, add comments and discuss influences, meaning and feelings.

Statement	Comment/feelings/reactions
Being mixed 'race' and young	
Being mixed 'race' and middle class	
Being mixed 'race' and a minority	
Being mixed 'race' and educated	
Being mixed 'race' and Welsh/Scottish/ Irish and English	
Being mixed 'race' and a professional	
Being mixed 'race' and rich/poor	
Being mixed 'race' and a student	
Being mixed 'race' and provincial/city based	

The terms used are deliberately provocative and can be added to and changed. The material produced will be rich and multi-faceted but may generate powerful emotions. Those undertaking the exercise may wish to allow substantial time for briefing and debriefing at the beginning and end. The large paper can be used immediately to discuss the comments, but also kept and stored to compare when the exercise is repeated later at the mid-point or final stages of the placement.

The exercises in this chapter provide an opportunity to build understanding of personal and professional identity. It may be that the exploration offered in this chapter will result in recognition of the emotional ties individuals have to that which is common, mutual and unifying rather than that which is different, alien and rare (Hall, 1996).

Conclusions

Anti-racist practice requires social workers to understand themselves, gain confidence and apply knowledge derived from historical as well as contemporary sources. They are likely to do this better if they work closely with related professionals and service user groups. This is critical because it may prevent practitioners from, intentionally or unintentionally, privileging one individual, group or community over another. No matter how principled the profession is in its rhetoric, ideals have to be real and open to challenge.

The commitment to core values suggests that the profession wishes to inform and develop the role and function of key practitioners. Those involved in managing competence are particularly aware of such processes and committed to gathering evidence on core values. Social work is at an important point in its development as a profession (Social Work Task Force, 2009) and can confidently argue for ethical knowledge which better informs operational needs. Equal recognition of practice and theoretical knowledge must be agreed if issues such as anti-racist practice are be prioritized.

Practitioners and teams face many barriers to critical practice, sound decision making and the professional use of judgement. Social workers are increasingly challenged in their statutory duties and have been criticized for overly following rules and procedures (Dominelli, 2004) which counter core principles and values. Despite this, anti-racist practitioners positively inform organizational thinking over time, however narrow and constrained. They look closely at emerging standards, see if legal/policy duties are being met, suggest incremental knowledge-led changes which improve their roles and responsibilities, and contribute to universal ideas and principles.

This chapter seeks to connect universal, professional and personal knowledge to the development of personal capacity and identity. The links between the founding ideology and contemporary anti-racist social work practice need to be considered positively and ways forward examined in detail in order to maintain ongoing commitment.

implications for practice

The generation and transfer of knowledge is an important aspect of professional social work and developments in this area will be increasingly supported by national institutions, such as the proposed College of Social Work (Social Work Task Force, 2009).

The day-to-day knowledge used by practitioners is derived from a range of sources and built over time. Social workers carry details, facts and particulars which are held together like pieces of a jigsaw puzzle, but the amount, relevance and quality of the information held in each piece is dependent on the person and the context.

Understanding the processes used by individuals to acquire, improve and develop knowledge is an important goal for social workers seeking to enhance their own and others' learning. However, professionals need time to examine the quality and quantity of information held and used by them and whether it is constrained or limited by operational demands. To illustrate this further, if total practice knowledge held is in four main areas (that is, like four pieces of a jigsaw puzzle), what does each piece represent? Do the pieces fit together? Which piece dominates and is privileged in relation to the role and task at hand? Which pieces are being used more than others at any given time?

Practice know-how is used on an everyday basis to support service users but it is likely that knowledge on anti-racist practice will be vaguer and less defined. Because information on anti-racist practice is likely to be confined to a small section of one piece, the challenge for social workers is to pay greater attention to the bigger jigsaw puzzle and embed anti-racist practice within all four pieces.

main points

- The common threads of the welfare state and the regulation of professional practice are found in ancient rules set out in, for example, the Hippocratic Oath (Hugman, 2005), which sought to guide and support medical intervention.

- The 1948 Universal Declaration of Human Rights was founded on human dignity, civil and political rights, economic and social rights, and solidarity. But critics have suggested that the underrepresentation of developing countries in the drafting process makes it unworkable for some.

- Change requires an advanced commitment to core values. Fook (2000, p. 118) implies that professional confidence may be a prerequisite to the successful development of such a commitment: 'In this way expert professional social workers are able to create critical knowledge which potentially challenges and resists current forms of domination.'

- Baldwin (2004, p. 43) suggests that 'learning is often about letting go of fond and long-held beliefs' and the process is often difficult, threatening and complex.

stop and think

- Belief systems have impacted substantially on contemporary social work practice. Do you think such ideas have also contributed to the image and position of BME individuals and groups?
- Do you support the view that British social work is founded on an ideology which privileges 'character and morality rather than material circumstance' (Jones, 2000, p. 120)?

- Social workers are steeped in prejudices and moral assumptions about desirable behaviour (Younghusband, 1967). What do you think?
- Is there any basis in the view that the historical stereotype of the undeserving and vulnerable service user is stretched further by the image of the, often black, foreigner landing on British soil and abusing the welfare state?

taking it further

- Clark, C.L. (2000) *Social Work Ethics: Politics, Principles and Practice*, Palgrave – now Palgrave Macmillan, Basingstoke.
  Clark provides an interesting political analysis of practice-based ethics by suggesting that social work has developed a professional response based on personal relationships, that is, on the ethic of 'respect and service' framed within the Kantian theory of moral duty and reasoned thought. Principle-based practice is limited, however, by the complex nature of human interaction and intervention which relies on the value of an individual and may result in behaviour which is racist or discriminatory.
- Payne, M. (2005) *The Origins of Social Work: Continuity and Change*, Palgrave Macmillan, Basingstoke.
  Historical developments are often seen as progressive, but too little has been recorded of knowledge based on the lived experience of BME individuals, women and 'ordinary people'. Equality is a crucial aspect of the rule of law, but it may be conceptually abstract and inadequate in ensuring social justice.
- Schön, D.A. (1991) *Reflective Practitioner: How Professionals Think in Action*, Ashgate, Aldershot.
  Schön offers an interesting analysis of how professionals think and examines a hierarchy of applied knowledge: 'basic science yields applied science. Applied science yields diagnostic and problem solving techniques which are applied in turn to the actual delivery of services' (p. 24). Part 1 provides an invaluable contribution to the debate on the application of professional knowledge through approaches such as reflection in action.

4 Reshaping organizations and professional practice

Introduction

The aim of this chapter is to examine how new thinking in anti-racist social work can inform organizations, as well as guide the work of individual practitioners. This will be considered in relation to wider developments in the acquisition and application of knowledge and skills in policy, practice and research on 'race' and racism. The objective is for a better understanding of legal duties, targeted training/development and effective communication, within and across organizations, in order that social workers can be properly equipped and supported to undertake their responsibilities as service providers, team members and employees.

Social work has a reputation for overreliance on practice wisdom to inform complex human interactions within teams, organizations and service user interventions. Although learning derived from everyday work experiences has its value, it has to be supplemented with educational and training opportunities, in order that practitioners can confidently embed anti-racist and anti-discriminatory principles in everyday processes (DH, 2008).

Well-trained social workers respond more effectively to, for example, BME children with particular needs, but in general, developing anti-racist knowledge and skills is likely to benefit all service user groups (Dominelli, 2008). Critics, such as the Equalities and Human Rights Commission (EHRC), suggest that managers and leaders need to incorporate equality and human rights routinely within business-based decision making (*The Guardian*, 25 November, 2009).

In order to support this, the chapter includes models and exercises which promote individual and group understanding of organizational context, professional role and responsibility. This chapter is relevant to all staff, including managers, social workers, students and practice teachers/educators.

In the social work literature, anti-racist professional practice has been conceived and promoted in two broad areas. The first has focused on improving services for groups, such as vulnerable children (Gilligan and Akhtar, 2006) and adults (Blakemore and Boneham, 1994). The second has provided broader guidance on anti-racism (Dominelli, 1997) and ethics and values (Hugman, 2005). Such works have examined a number of areas, such as the application of universal principles to improving services, and offered guidance on approaches such as communication and other interpersonal skills.

While the work is important, the complex link between theoretical principles and operational concerns requires continuing attention by leaders and managers, particularly those who are inclined to follow the human instinct to meet minimum standards (*The Guardian*, 25 November, 2009). In an evaluation of the dilemmas inherent in balancing practical demands with ideology, that is, working with world views on a day-to-day basis, Clark (2000) suggests that it may not be possible to square the two at this point in time. This may be partly because the ideas shared by people in the past are not always applicable to the 21st century. A great deal of historical social work literature is based on values which may be dated and therefore no longer viable for contemporary practice. Social workers are continually seeking answers to complex ethical questions in relation to, for example, methods of intervention. Many have looked to learning gained from direct work with individual service users, families and groups. This material has been evaluated in social work literature but theory building has been constructed from individualized experiences rather than systemized, longitudinal research. For example, there is a need for social work approaches, informed by evidence, which address poverty and deprivation (Williams and Soydan, 2005).

However, empirical research is being conducted and published on competent practice with groups such as unaccompanied asylum-seeking children (Kohli, 2007), which seeks to promote appropriate and relevant methods of working based on universal values and principles. Theory building such as this requires replication in other areas, such as political science, and by other powerful groups, such as white feminists.

Feminist thought and activity has influenced social work practice for many decades and throughout this time has been critiqued for lacking insight into the needs of BME women (Dominelli, 2008). White feminist literature has frequently patronized and labelled BME women by placing them in the position of victim and/or as newly arrived immigrants (Fekete, 2006).

There has been limited research on how BME women perceive and contribute to their own image and even less on the impact of ethnicity, culture, religion, spirituality and faith on family and childcare. Fekete (2006) suggests that alternative anti-racist perspectives such as these continue to threaten some elements of the feminist movement who view anti-racism as liberal 'protection and privilege' (Fekete, 2006, p. 12). The assimilation of extreme patriarchal cultures within the less patriarchal/sexist cultures of the West is deemed by Fekete (2006, p. 13) to be 'culturocide'. Thinking such as this suggests that white feminists need to look to historical lessons learned from colonialism and imperialism, and to actively contribute to the development of BME feminist perspectives within professional practice.

Anti-racist practice in organizations

The British government's drive to modernize social work is key to contemporary developments in all areas of welfare provision (Johns and Jordon, 2006). The process of modernization has been supported by bodies such as the Commission for Racial Equality, who accepted the need to develop new thinking on welfare aligned with principles of good business and acceptable standards. The focus on individual choice and responsibility, rather than collective understanding and responsiveness, is also increasingly being supported by the social work care councils through National Occupational Standards. It is, therefore, unlikely that the General Social Care Council (GSCC) for England and Wales will challenge social work provision which balances business and welfare objectives while it still exists. The government announcement in 2010 that social workers will in future be regulated by the Health Professions Council is a further challenge to the independent professional voice promoting public sector values.

The increase in the use of marketplace models within children and adult services has, however, been cited as one reason for the move away from community and neighbourhood responses which have traditionally been seen as more able to encompass ideas based on empowering individuals and groups (Dominelli, 2008).

Within this scenario, social work is dealing with significant structural change, in the way it provides services to children and adults, and also in the way it demonstrates its core values and principles. As a profession, it is being assimilated and absorbed into statutory, voluntary, independent and private organizations. Payne (2009, p. 59) argues that the majority of social care organizations now carry 'hybrid' duties, and have to manage a mix of funding and staffing from a range of sectors.

Evidence suggests that BME service users continue to be seen in negative ways, wherever the service is situated, because provision is limited by the understanding of, and commitment to, the needs of BME individuals and families (Forbat, 2004). This shortfall can, however, be addressed by policy makers through greater links to the government's wider modernization and equalities agenda. Organizations can pay particular and specific attention to anti-racist social work skills and ensure that practitioners are better educated and trained in assessment, intervention, review and monitoring in relation to identity, culture and religion/spirituality. Social work providers need to make a business case as well as an ethical argument for greater investment which may include a rationale for immediate as well as wider benefits. The need for greater efficiency is supported by government departments that are increasingly providing guidance on how to make 'quick gains' as well as achieve 'longer term goals' (DH, 2008, p. 26). For example, the effective use of scarce resources within the personalizing of services can be used to argue for better communication and contact with and between BME individuals and families (Payne, 2009).

In developing policy and practice, the inclusion of local knowledge on culture, ethnicity and identity issues must be stressed (Owusu-Bempah, 2000). The modernization of child welfare builds on s. 22(5) of the Children Act 1989 which forcefully guided child and family-centred practice. It may be argued, however, that the Children Act 1989 promoted as well as constrained subsequent practice with children with specific religious, cultural and linguistic needs. Social workers following the spirit of the Act struggled with the practicalities as well as principles set out within it. For example, placement policies promoted child/family matching, but there was limited research evidence on the key constituents of a successful looked after placement and the assessment skills required to assess the cultural and ethnicity needs of a BME child. Poorly trained, but ideologically driven social workers followed such policies uncritically, aware that questioning may set them aside from professional perspectives and challenge liberal thinking. As a result, half-hearted attempts to meet the requirements of the Children Act 1989, and subsequent childcare laws, continue to this day.

The scarcity of family placements, along with limited resources, restricts choice and self-determination for BME individuals, even within the recent move to personalize social care (Payne, 2009). This is illustrated by past practice. For many years, a number of London boroughs, unable to meet childcare, adoption and fostering needs themselves, bought services from organizations based in (possibly cheaper) areas of the country. This sometimes resulted in children from BME origins being placed in largely white, rural settings supported by workers with limited access to necessary local provision (such as food).

Meeting the needs of BME children and other service users has, however, become easier in recent years. The 2001 census provided important data on Britain's multiracial population – 9% categorized themselves as an ethnic minority or of mixed 'race' background (ONS, 2001). This suggests that the profile of the country has changed in unprecedented ways. For example, London alone hosts residents who speak 300 different languages, originating from 160 countries (CRE, 2007a), and Birmingham is home to 29.6% BME people. The majority of BME people in the 2001 census are likely to be British by birth, history and commitment, and for those providing children's services, this suggests greater potential for matching children and families for fostering and adoption. However, diversity in the general population does not always lead to this, that is, social workers are not necessarily better able to place children with families with similar cultural and religious backgrounds. Although the majority of UK residents share similar experiences, family and kinship care is likely to be individual and different across BME as well as other groups.

Faced with demographic changes within local populations, organizational investment in skills that enable professionals to better identify, assess and review needs is needed more than ever. Minimal or inconsistent adherence to law and policy is not ethically viable in multiracial Britain and agencies need to ensure that their equality duties are met within strategic planning and inspection processes (DH, 2008). Social workers require training which allows them to seek a deeper understanding of how individuals value their own culture, ethnicity and religion in relation to family and kinship care. Demographic data shows that children and young people in contemporary Britain are likely to place emphasis on different aspects of their identity than prior generations (ONS, 2001).

Anti-racist practice requires confident decision making by strategically motivated social workers, who see 'race' and ethnicity among a number of important factors. Practitioners who follow such ideas will understand that, given the options available and all other factors being equal, children from BME backgrounds are likely to make the same lifestyle choices as any other child. For example, within fostering and adoption, some BME children may prefer to opt for a life with white carers because they are richer (Owusu-Bempah, 2000). Others may be more influenced by pressure from peers on where they want to live, rather than professional arguments on matching based on culture and/or religion. Social workers should care for and attend to the needs of children making sensible choices, even if they opt for personal care or relationships which challenge long-held professional values set out in childcare law and policy.

Reflecting on such ideas and using evidence-based approaches are likely to lead anti-racist practitioners and organizations further towards competent, realistic, child-centred assessments which match ethnic, cultural and linguistic requirements regardless of colour. Even within resource constraints, social work agencies can make a business case for interventions which promote a better fit between the individual child, the community within which they reside and wider family/kinship ties.

An organization is defined by the methods by which it operates and the way it is seen by its target audience. Examples of learning from the past suggest that approaches and communication can be improved by simple changes aimed at specific groups. During the 1970s, social service reception areas displayed posters asking those with limited English to ask for interpretation and translation. These signs were written in English and so service users with poor literacy and/or confidence were unable to read them and/or ask for assistance. This was compounded by the look and staffing of the reception area. On entry into the building, service users often faced receptionists with limited training or knowledge of languages other than English.

This situation has improved in recent years and most organizations now ensure that public information is available in a range of languages and caters for people with linguistic as well as learning differences. Reception staff are better trained and valued, as the gateway to the organization, and can routinely call on related services and workers such as translators, interpreters and advocates. Contemporary examples of good practice such as this have been mirrored in settings where good business is the overriding factor. So, for example, local branches of major banks regularly translate posters to attract targeted, and financially successful, customers from Poland.

Training and education enable the development of organizational policy and practice, particularly on core values such as the Kantian ideas of intrinsic worth, desire and choice (Banks, 1995). However, teams and organizations have the challenging responsibility of transforming these ideas into the daily routines of the job in hand through the sound performance management of individual staff and students.

Senior practitioners and social work managers have to ensure that anti-racist laws are implemented in a realistic, ethical manner which fits well with the team and organizational culture. Good management and leadership are likely to be supported by context-specific reflection, evaluation and debate, which takes account of structural constraints and the motivation to tick boxes.

A positive way to learn from and develop best practice is by scoping (*The Guardian*, 25 November 2009), auditing and evaluating anti-racist initiatives and projects. Past experience has shown that, for example, organizational approaches on the wording of social work assessments and probation reports on young people have resulted in greater management scrutiny of assumptions and discriminatory language used in formal record keeping. However, the Equality and Human Rights Commission recognizes that institutional language remains a contested area of practice and suggests that linguistic change is most effective if it is led by staff and service users rather than organizational directives (*Times Higher Education*, 6–12 August 2009).

Developments such as the above indicate that practice wisdom is a powerful force in service delivery which meets many legal, policy and practice goals. Kadushin (1968) proposes that change is easier to swallow if it is built on existing know-how, collective thought, habit and custom. Demands which require a rapid and unfamiliar response may entrench attitudes and are less likely to change patterns of behaviour, particularly in sensitive areas such as 'race' and racism:

> Change creates anxiety. It requires giving up the familiar. It requires a period of discomfort during which one is uneasy about continuing to use old patterns of behaviour but does not feel fully comfortable with new behaviours. The threat of change is greater for the adult student because it requires dissolution of patterns of thinking and believing. Change requires disloyalty to previous identification. (Kadushin, 1968, p. 2)

In-service training for social workers has included core values and principles for many decades and so the assumption is that such practice wisdom has a sound ethical basis. However, a working knowledge of 'race' and ethnicity within performance management cannot be assumed, because most guidance on ethical competence for example, provided by the government and regulatory bodies such as the General Social Care Council, is generic in nature and agencies interpret and prioritize anti-racist practice to meet local and regional policy needs.

Continuous professional development is now part of the registration requirements for qualified social workers, as is the training and supervision provided for newly qualified social workers. Students follow degree-level education where practice is closely supervised. In addition, all students and operational staff have to follow the professional codes of practice and code of ethics (BASW, 2002).

Public services work in partnership with universities to provide qualifying and post-qualifying training for social workers. The joint assessment of qualifying social work students takes place over a three-year span within portfolios of evidence which demonstrate suitability and fitness for professional practice. The direct links between education and practice are vital to the recruitment and retention of future staff and so all employers (large and small) are required to provide continuous professional training for new and established staff (GSCC, 2005).

Modern, business-minded organizations need to ensure that training on ethically sound, evidence-based practice is routinely included in their programmes, to support the professional application of law, policy and procedure (DH, 2008). Evidence suggests that social work is increasingly being delivered by a range of public, private and independent sector organizations employing staff from disparate professional backgrounds. Even within such modified, hybrid workplaces (Payne, 2009), there are ample opportunities for the integration of anti-racist social work practice based on the following principles:

- Regular reporting of legal and policy duties
- Public commitment to equality duties and measures
- Strategic planning which incorporates service and staff needs
- Innovative responses to structural and institutional constraints
- Guidance and training on anti-racist practice at all levels
- Good communication across and within organizations.

Managing anti-racist practice

One of the key areas of responsibility for managerial staff is to provide a clear and rational steer to students and colleagues on what constitutes anti-racist practice within a context which is increasingly focused on operational, reporting and inspection demands predicated on business-based management and accountability models. Most managers are skilled at implementing and demonstrating a daily commitment to best practice and high standards to a range of service user groups. They allocate resources according to operational demands and guide staff who may be lethargic and resistant to change.

Within this demanding scenario, senior practitioners are aware that commitment to anti-racist practice is an additional performance demand in a busy workplace and that it requires redirected and/or additional resources. In order to pursue it further, managers have to be committed to the ideas and skilled in justifying equality measures to funders and politicians using service-driven, principle-based arguments.

A skilled manager will aim to support the development of anti-racist knowledge and commitment to the same level as that accorded to other procedural and operational demands. They may do this by pinpointing areas where practice can be embedded in standards, for example on managing risk with BME mental health service users (DH, 2008).

Good practice requires a consistent and relevant focus on anti-racist knowledge and skills within management processes such as supervision of students and newly qualified social workers. This can be undertaken through case-related discussion of the diverse needs of service users and/or through examination of individual values. Managers will find the setting of anti-racist standards in supervision a useful way to measure individual service delivery expertise over a set period, such as the newly qualified social workers year or a student practice placement. A positive approach such as this will impact on social work interventions and organizational behaviour. It will also highlight the challenges faced by practitioners and improve management support for staff working with BME communities.

Greater attention within performance management is likely to lead to an understanding of the fit between anti-racist practice and procedural guidance, such as *No Secrets* (DH, 2000), which asks for an effective response to the abuse of vulnerable adults based on good interagency and interprofessional collaboration within and across organizations. *No Secrets* implies that competent and well-defined communication is at the heart of a successful organization, and that responsibility for this needs to be defined at all levels.

The organizational structure suggested in *No Secrets* is an interesting example of how connections can made between sectors, that is, children and adult services, key organizational roles, and the practice implications of policy on 'race' and racism.

The Laming Report on the case of Victoria Climbié highlighted poor cultural understanding and inadequate lines of communication between and across organizations as key causes of the death of a black child (Gilligan and Furness, 2006). On this occasion, poor protection resulted in the loss of a child, but the development of policies on safeguarding adults suggests that an older service user from a BME background is equally vulnerable to such mediocre and deficient practice. Lessons learned from child protection may be applied across all ages, sectors and organizations.

Inter- and cross-agency collaboration has received a great deal of attention by government, and partnership working is well understood within health and social care. The Laming Report (2003) recommended better sharing and transfer of information, but despite this, systematic approaches continue to elude many organizations.

Figure 4.1 originally appeared in *No Secrets* (DH, 2000) and is a simple and adaptable approach which can be used by organizations aiming to review and improve two-way communication (suggested by the arrows) both within and between teams and professionals.

Strong communication between operational staff, supervisors and managers

Good communication between senior managers and public authorities

Poor communication between chief officers, executives and councillors/cabinet members

Figure 4.1 A model illustrating different communication dynamics

There is an urgent need to develop and apply models which aid good communication, such as the example in Figure 4.2.

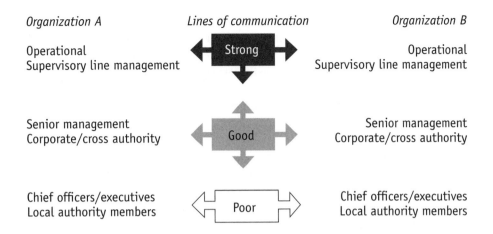

Organization A	Lines of communication	Organization B
Operational Supervisory line management	**Strong**	Operational Supervisory line management
Senior management Corporate/cross authority	Good	Senior management Corporate/cross authority
Chief officers/executives Local authority members	Poor	Chief officers/executives Local authority members

Figure 4.2 A model illustrating good communication

Poor communication at more senior levels may be because a great deal of training has focused on operational policy and procedure on anti-racist practice. Procedural frameworks are seen to empower and support practitioners in their daily interventions with service users and to contribute to the broader discussion of role and responsibility of, for example, the registered professional rather than the chief executive or local councillor.

Phillips et al. (2006) suggest that good communication is central to collaborative working and needs to be promoted at all levels to maximize social work interests as well as anti-racist practice (Bhatti-Sinclair, 1999). Professionals who are interactive are likely to value contact with colleagues, be able to advocate, for the profession and service users, be skilful in negotiation and understand the importance of easy-to-digest, accessible information. Interprofessional relationships are particularly good if the parties involved trust each other's knowledge and expertise (Phillips et al., 2006).

Models that map communication such as Figures 4.1 and 4.2 can be reproduced by any organization to show how and where contact is taking place with related agencies as well as how communication is flowing within and between its own teams. Ideally, the model of communication should illustrate the importance of communication at all levels of the organization.

Consideration of approaches which enable and promote critical reflection and evaluation of the status quo is likely to lead to a better understanding of how structures and systems help or hinder the development of good practice externally and internally. Such examination should result in a positive assessment of strengths and weaknesses and highlight opportunities and challenges. Figure 4.2 provides an opportunity to examine, transform and improve communication at all levels of the organization in all operational and strategic areas.

Understanding the possibilities and constraints provided by structures is one way to enable change and development. Approaches to development require information on what is already available, who is taking responsibility, and where responsibility should lie in order to provide management information on effectiveness, influence and gaps in services. Understanding how teams communicate and function may enable managers to allocate specific anti-racist responsibilities to committed, energetic members of staff.

The *No Secrets* (DH, 2000) management system provides a structure which incorporates large sections of the organization, including publicly accountable local government councillors or cabinet members who may have little contact with frontline staff but are powerful individuals in relation to anti-racist practice. This is because they are elected and often hold important knowledge of the locality and community, rarely utilized in the provision of social care services. So the development of anti-racist practice may include consultation with elected members on, for example, the social needs of elders from the Somalian communities.

Social work organizations have duties at a number of levels including operational, supervisory and managerial and these are overseen by employers, chief officers and elected members. Although the organization as a whole has responsibility for anti-racist practice, responsibility has to be allocated for a number of tasks such as management, health and safety, accountability, information, planning and so on. In order to address anti-racist practice in a systematic manner, these responsibilities have to be allocated and reviewed at a number of levels within the organization. Table 4.1 provides a chart which lists some of the areas covered by public sector organizations and can be used, changed or developed to incorporate equality impact and other demands. For example, operational staff are likely to have some input into strategic planning as well as other areas such as health and safety. This has to be made clear and related directly to anti-racist practice. Relevant responsibilities can then be allocated to them as well as other employees, managers and members.

Table 4.1 Responsibility for anti-racist practice within the organization

Policy and practice	Operational (including students)	Supervisory	Managerial	Corporate/ cross authority	Chief executive	Elected members
Strategic planning and reporting						
Health and safety						

Policy and practice	Operational (including students)	Supervisory	Managerial	Corporate/ cross authority	Chief executive	Elected members
Resources						
Workload management						
Information systems, data collection and storage						
Supervision and accountability						
Safeguarding/ protecting service users						
Continuous professional development						
Quality and standards						
Education and training						

In order to develop this idea further, Table 4.2 (overleaf) illustrates how one section from Table 4.1 on strategic planning and reporting can be used to incorporate ideas on anti-racist practice in employment.

Understanding social work policy is critical to providing appropriate services, and each of the above categories should be considered in relation to the following:

- the service delivery responsibilities of key professionals and organizations
- service user rights based on statute, policy and procedure
- equality duties and service impact in relation to particular groups such as children or adults
- discriminatory practices on the grounds of race, religion or belief, gender, disability, sexuality and age of consent and age discrimination.

Policy and procedures are often, however, clearer to those delivering and supervising service provision than to those managing and overseeing the organization. The duty of corporate/executive-level staff to eliminate institutional racism cited in the Laming Report needs to be better understood, mainly because a number of other child protection inquiries evidence poor practice by middle and senior management.

Table 4.2 Examples of organizational development on anti-racist practice

Policy and practice	Operational	Supervisory	Managerial	Corporate/cross authority/sectors	Chief executive	Elected members
Strategic planning and reporting	▪ Staff contracts and procedures ▪ Induction standards ▪ Access to computerized and paper documents ▪ Information/ training on how to access anti-racist law	▪ Regular and systematic inclusion on agenda ▪ Introduction of policy, procedure ▪ Critique of systems ▪ Assessment of individual commitment	▪ Examination of structural racism and discrimination ▪ Management of team performance ▪ Strategic reporting on training and development needs ▪ Advocacy on behalf of service users ▪ Systems and procedures for whistle-blowing	▪ Assessment of different professional approaches ▪ Learning from others ▪ Joint working on innovatory approaches ▪ Collaboration on and comparison of standards between areas/ sectors	▪ Development of policy and guidance on 'race' and racism ▪ Overarching planning and reporting responsibility clearly set out and reported ▪ Targeting of specific service user groups such as black children with special educational needs	▪ Training in anti-racist practice ▪ Knowledge of geographic area and ethnic minority population ▪ Committee responsibility for anti-racist practice ▪ Biannual reporting based on national targets

Putting procedures, such as whistle-blowing, into place is made more difficult by the process of law making in the UK. Johns and Jordon (2006) suggest that the legislative framework is principally designed to support individuals through the courts, which means that those who have faced racism have to first pinpoint and then have the courage and tenacity to pursue their case:

> The futility of tackling discrimination by simply forbidding it, as formal equality seeks to do, is clear. But the core weakness is theoretical. Because it focuses on the individual, it fails to recognise structural forces at work and this prevents a serious challenge to discrimination. (Johns and Jordon, 2006, p. 1277)

The case for equal opportunities in the workplace has been well made by those who make, write about and implement legal provisions, but how policies can be better promoted in the workplace is a question which continues to tax individuals, teams and organizations. It is clear, however, that the problem lies in implementation rather than in the letter of the law (Williams and Soydan, 2005).

In-service training has been seen as a means by which organizations demonstrate their commitment to greater knowledge and understanding. Although valuable, standards have been inconsistent and managers have been content to provide a light touch approach to anti-racist practice. A good example of this is training on diversity and difference – a model which provides a safe, apolitical analysis of how groups relate to one another. For senior and middle management, beleaguered by an increase in business approaches to welfare and scrutiny of professional standards, this has provided an easy response to (often) hard-hitting legislative requirements. In essence, approaches such as diversity and difference lack an analysis of structural and institutional power and are seen as ineffective, liberal responses to promoting a level playing field. They also focus on personal and attitudinal change, rather than legal and policy requirements. Another significant problem lies in the isolation from, and lack of alignment with, other public sector responses such as those promoting anti-discrimination, human rights, social inclusion and cohesion.

Approaches which offer comfort zone responses to anti-racist practice create considerable problems for national bodies such as the EHRC, responsible for the Race Relations Act 2000, which requires concrete evidence from public sector managers on how 'race' equality is implemented (Forbat, 2004) in the following form (Equalities Review, 2007b):

- a definition of equality
- a case for equality
- a public bodies framework for measurement
- better use of data
- identified and targeted action on persistent inequalities
- better accountability for those delivering services.

An equalities review should specify public functions which affect people differently, based on ethnicity, and offer three-yearly monitoring and review of plans. The reviews must include information on staff from BME backgrounds in relation to performance appraisals, training provided and grievance/disciplinary actions. All employees, students and service users can seek information on the race equality schemes and plans from the relevant organization, that is, a trade union, local councils for racial equality, or the EHRC. In addition, the review must set out the roles of inspection bodies, as well as those of political, managerial and community leaders. Although the EHRC has a wider function than the CRE, the aims and objectives suggest a robust and systemized approach to transparency, community action and exposure of those neglecting their duties to the Equality Act 2006.

Managing equality requires skills which enable and empower staff – a partnership based on agreed principles such as joint work targets, open communication and shared tasks. The focus is on developing individual strengths beyond case management and wider institutional and structural constraints. Following such principles, good management practice is likely to incorporate the following approaches and skills:

■ Problem solving which focuses on improvement in performance
■ Identifying problems and responding appropriately
■ Reflecting and promoting evidence-based practice
■ Interpersonal skills which include active listening and responding
■ Providing feedback which is detailed and useful
■ Being explicit, understandable and accurate
■ Building confidence by setting and meeting specific goals
■ Avoiding uniform responses to complex issues and concerns
■ Relating well to individual levels and abilities
■ Using methods and approaches which model good practice.

Senior practitioners who follow such principles are likely to avoid paying attention selectively, or attributing certain group characteristics to individuals. They will also challenge group assumptions, labelling and stereotyping, and critically examine the notion of value-free management. Individuals keen to work in anti-racist ways are also likely to adhere to a few simple rules:

■ Recognize and challenge team or group bias in an appropriate way
■ Theorize anti-racist practice in an informed and confident manner
■ Validate experiences of discrimination and/or oppression
■ Develop good interpersonal and communication skills within, for example, report writing
■ Clarify professional behaviour and boundaries within teams and organizations.

In particular, the implementation of anti-racist law and policy in an organizational workforce development agenda needs to include the support of well-trained staff interested in developing anti-racist practice, as well as the recruitment and retention of social workers from BME communities. Examples from methods used to support student learning, such as shadowing, mentoring and coaching from team members, may be utilized to support confidence building and the acquisition of relevant applied knowledge. Equality laws have provided the basis on which to promote good employment practice but they have to be used with sound judgement:

> Essentially, the idea is to eliminate unfair discrimination, and, in employment at least, reduce discrimination to justifiable grounds. This can be defined as a person's merit: ability plus effort in the interests of recruiting the best person for the job. (Johns and Jordon, 2006, p. 1276)

In general, it is important to avoid the replication of old ideas and to look beyond and adapt traditional methods and approaches to management (Coulshed and Mullender, 2001). Many organizations have emphasized diversity and difference in corporate training. However, judging individual performance is a complex interpersonal process and those involved in assessing professional competence may find the following list provides useful indicators or pointers to blocks or barriers to understanding:

- Selective use of words and actions
- Tendency to generalize, stereotype and label
- Focus on certain characteristics in relation to certain groups
- Collective assumptions and perspectives (individual or team) based on working rather than theoretical knowledge
- Viewing individual needs as a set of problems
- Devaluing the process of reflection and evaluation
- Limited understanding of evidence-based anti-racist practice
- Insufficient understanding of individual and group bias
- Poor interactive and interpersonal skills
- Low confidence and defensiveness
- Partial understanding of collective, collaborative and team working
- Lack of fluency in communicating ideas and validating experiences
- Limited understanding of self in relation to others
- Weak empathetic skills
- Capacity to learn and develop reduced by past experience.

In order that it is a positive and worthwhile experience for all concerned, performance management requires a complex analysis of how role and task are perceived by those managing and those being managed. The list above may be taken, changed and adapted to meet individual need within performance management or supervision processes, and the points can be related to 'race' and racism and focused on staff and service users from BME groups.

Managers faced with a social worker, student or related professional who demonstrates one or any of the above characteristics and finds points made within feedback or challenge difficult to grasp must consider blocks in communication and how these may be addressed by the individual, the team and/or the organization.

Another important factor in managing performance is the recognition of differential power and imbalance in status and role. Senior and/or experienced staff are advantaged by greater and deeper knowledge of structure and institution, but discussion of how and where power is located rarely takes place. This may be because the need for precision and transparency is difficult when many public sector organizations are functioning within rigid hierarchical structures and systems.

Finally, the role of a public sector manager in relation to anti-racist practice includes many skills, but knowledge and understanding of the following are particularly important:

- The impact of national requirements on the anti-racist practice of staff and students
- Management responsibility for organizational goals in relation to equality measures
- Systems which allow individuals to challenge institutional racism and discrimination
- Management and supervision styles which enable and support professional development
- Approaches which value individuals in the wider organization
- Modelling which demonstrates core values and principles
- Insight into their own attitudes and how it may impact on management practice.

Regulating anti-racist social work practice

The increase in regulation and registration of the social care workforce has resulted in an important focus on managing ethical performance, set out in the GSCC *Codes of Practice for Social Care Workers and Employees* (GSCC, 2002a). Employers are further guided on management responses to operational and strategic leadership in business, workforce and change management, marketing, selection and recruitment and employee training and development.

The greatest challenge to managers lies in the complexities of measuring the attitudes, values and behaviour of staff and students. Although the National Occupational Standards recommend an integrated focus on equal opportunities, equality and diversity, there is little on how to guide and support professionals to meet the specific and detailed demands of anti-racist practice.

Practitioners seeking specific guidance on methods can look to staff responsible for equality issues and/or line managers who are likely to offer existing instruments which track continuous professional development. Methods such as this, however, may be well developed in some settings, but are not necessarily evaluated or critiqued substantially in the social work literature for transfer or replicability in anti-racist practice. However, existing knowledge on performance management in one sphere can be linked to that in another related area. For example, the EHRC offers guidance on the tracking and collection of data on racist crime which can be used by social work managers to monitor bullying and harassment.

Regulating competent anti-racist practice is a key responsibility for any public sector employer, and so the imperative to assess social workers' and students' understanding of this topic within management and supervision systems is growing. The development of processes which introduce and track individual knowledge, skills and values in the career life cycle is particularly important if anti-racist practice is to be understood and owned within any organization.

Staff and student learning has to include a critical evaluation of dilemmas, arising from practice contexts and local case examples, as well as an understanding of wider social and racial disadvantage. A process such as this is more likely to result in meaningful and informed professional, as well as organizational change which promotes as well as owns core social work values:

> A potential contradiction is whether social work aims to foster lifestyles and behaviours that are the responsibility of service users themselves (empowerment and emancipation) or aims to support collective identities which do not allow for diversity (adjustment). (Higham, 2006, p. 187)

Organizations and managers committed to anti-racist practice will ensure that critical reflection occurs routinely in one-to-one supervision as well as beyond, within and across teams and organizations. However, the assessment of anti-racist practice requires a complex set of skills, as well as organization-specific knowledge. The task has to be undertaken, therefore, by those who can confidently share internal as well as external wisdom and practice experience.

In order to pursue a systematic approach, those responsible for performance management may consider adapting the following questions when supervising social workers and students (Equalities Review, 2007b):

- How is equality defined by the team and organization?
- Does the organization have an anti-racist framework for evaluating service delivery?
- Does the organization include targeted action on persistent inequalities in its strategic planning?

- If data is collected on BME groups, do employees have easy access to it?
- How do individuals and teams account for delivering services to targeted groups?
- Do all staff have easy access to equality documents?
- How are individuals tested on knowledge of anti-discrimination?
- Are new members of staff asked to make a case for anti-racist practice by managers?

Questions such as these will provide a way into discussions on personal drive and commitment, as well as knowledge of how anti-racist practice is seen by the wider organization. Pursuing anti-racist practice requires not only a fundamental understanding of key operational issues but also of what constitutes a good, positive and safe working environment where people are able to explore issues and concerns openly and respectfully.

Equality in the workplace

Tew (2006, p. 34) suggests that commitment to empowering practice is complicated by structural disadvantage and that this is because there is a

> tendency for empowerment to be defined for relatively powerless people by those with vested political or professional interests ... *power to* may be seen to fit with a dominant Western masculine vision of individual competition and achievement, it may have less resonance with those who lack privileged access to social and economic resources.

Overarching organizational principles and goals may lie within law and policy, but sources and levels of power are often with individuals who have substantial understanding of the culture and makeup of the organization. Often, values are shaped by groups and individuals in whispered intangible ways which may be difficult to understand and challenge. Anti-racist practice can be developed if managers and teams examine and define the nature of such interactions and openly share this knowledge with the wider organization through verbal and written communication.

There is a widely held assumption that social workers follow professional imperatives relating to good communication and interpersonal skills such as good time keeping, understanding the importance of greetings and goodbyes, offering people time, maintaining good eye contact and demonstrating humility. Those actively committed to anti-racist practice are likely to ask service users and staff how these rules of engagement can enhance and sustain communication.

Along with good interpersonal skills, service users value minimum change and consistency and greater attention to mid- and long-term planning from their social workers. For service users from BME backgrounds, this is particularly important because staff who maintain contact are likely to gain skills and expert knowledge as well as deeper bonding with the individuals, families and communities. Sustained commitment may also lead to empowering practice and greater service user involvement in decision-making processes. This, in turn, will enhance trust in service providers and offer greater opportunities for comment as well as the sometimes unwelcome but necessary challenges to poor practice (*The Guardian*, 25 November 2009).

Tew (2006) suggests that power is better used cooperatively within a framework of openness and problem resolution linked to personal and professional goals. The case scenarios in Exercise 4.1 provide an opportunity to examine immediate reactions and responses within one-to-one supervision or team meetings followed by detailed exploration and discussion. Each sketch may be developed or changed and made relevant to the context or setting as necessary.

The social work desire to feed dependency (Healy, 2005) needs to be watched, so it is wise to be aware of the need to protect, collude, control, nurture and overempathize in each example. Facilitation, thoughtful consideration and enabling are positive approaches which are likely to lead to fruitful results.

In order to be useful, learning must be a shared among participants rather than a test for one individual. It is important to examine the power inherent in the relationships of those involved prior to using the case examples, as openness is a key principle of a safe learning environment.

Exercise 4.1

Equality scenarios

Aims: The main aim of this exercise is to allow individuals or groups to explore the issues raised and share experiences, ideas and imaginative thinking.

Task: Discuss either a selection of cases or the whole set (as time allows) and examine feelings, responses and strategies at an individual and institutional level. The case examples may be considered in total or chosen to emphasize a particular aspect which may be of concern. Time should be taken to think through relevant issues, and in all cases, consideration should be given to the issue of 'race' and racism.

This is not a knowledge test, although the exercise requires a clear understanding of how anti-racist practice may be reflected in daily work. Please be aware that responses may be multifaceted, complex and even contradictory at times:

1 A service user has refused to accept a visit from a BME social worker and asked that their case be transferred to you, a

white social worker. In order to protect the BME social worker, the manager has agreed to this request. Consider your responses as a colleague and examine the feelings, emotions and organizational issues.

2 You are a BME social worker and a recently recruited BME social worker complains that they have been the subject of a negative comment about their ethnicity from another BME colleague who is also your friend. Consider your course of action and plan how you may respond to this at a professional as well as personal level.

3 A member of the operational staff has asked for guidance on regional accents from you, the team manager. The colleague has suggested that you should check with other agencies and clients on whether or not they can understand what a newly appointed colleague says, as they come from a different area of the country. Discuss the issues and consider the relevance of professional codes of practice.

4 An overseas student has been on placement for three months in your placement agency and the university has informed the line manager that the student has recently declared previous convictions which occurred in their home country and did not appear on the records of the Criminal Records Bureau. The agency is generally happy with the student's work but needs to address this issue and the team is asked to comment. What is your view as a member of the team?

5 A colleague has shared their strong religious beliefs with the team and with you as a friend. They have recently revealed to the line manager that their faith does not allow acknowledgement or acceptance of gay and lesbian relationships. This issue has been openly debated within the agency, but what is your view on this?

The information provided in the case scenarios is limited by design, based on the premise that social work decisions are often made on partial information which may lack detail and/or is received indirectly. Readers, however, may elaborate and expand the ideas in order to add depth and realism.

Anti-racist practitioners are likely to find these scenarios difficult, as they raise complex issues about conflicting emotions concerning the balance between service user and staff needs (scenario 1), divided loyalties and operational priorities (scenario 2), prejudice based on regional difference (scenario 3), honesty and openness (scenario 4) and homophobia based on religious belief (scenario 5). Exploration of anti-racist practice is likely to result in the examination of how individuals develop discriminatory attitudes and behaviour. Consideration may also be given to guidance provided by supervisors, managers and assessors on matters which involve interpersonal relationships and communication skills. Wider discussion may also examine the impact of such practices on service delivery and the development of policy to improve good team and organizational practice.

If used in one-to-one, peer or group supervision, the scenarios are likely to raise a great deal of debate on attitudinal and behavioural responses. Readers are encouraged to look for assumptions, stereotypes and conclusions which may *not* be supported by sound evidence.

Challenging attitudes and behaviour

Addressing poor practice is more difficult when knowledge on the issue is limited, so it is useful to encourage the gathering of literature, evidence, data and other information in any organizational context. Sharing of this corroborates, substantiates and promotes good practice, which in turn leads to the development of policy and procedure. The following guidelines may be useful for students, supervisors and practitioners wishing to use and develop tools and materials such as Exercise 4.1 with colleagues and students:

- Read widely to raise your awareness of the issues of racism, discrimination and oppression within a broad context
- Seek information and training on anti-discriminatory law and policy
- Develop proficiency in reflective practice and self-evaluation
- Understand the principles of receiving and giving useful and constructive feedback
- Gain information on strategies used to challenge discrimination
- Enhance your own natural ability to learn from experiences (negative and positive)
- Consider in detail the effects of labelling and stereotyping
- Make effective use of supervision to develop your knowledge, skills and values
- Work positively within hierarchical structures and systems.

Challenging racist or discriminatory views and attitudes is a complex, sometimes necessary task, but individuals are more likely to use positive and constructive feedback if the basic rules of courtesy and respect are followed. If attitudes and actions are challenged at the appropriate time and place, and as soon as possible, the recipient may appreciate the relevance and necessity more fully, particularly if the guidance below is followed:

- Base the feedback on hard facts and detailed and specific information
- Ensure the feedback is evaluative and focuses on the issue and not the person

- Offer opportunities for the supervisee to engage, respond, reflect and build on feedback
- Be sensitive to tone and body language.

It is important that the challenge is proactive and appropriate in order to avoid overreaction and feelings of hurt and disappointment. A good experience is likely to lead to personal and professional self-examination and greater insight into self and others.

Challenging is always difficult particularly for individuals who find themselves faced with teams with discriminatory attitudes and behaviour, even though this may not be entirely intentional, for example jokes based on racial stereotypes. Exercise 4.2 provides an interesting scenario for you to examine.

Exercise 4.2

Challenging strategies

Aims and objectives: To examine approaches and strategies that support sensitive yet effective challenging to consider how the use of facts, tone and body language can enhance feedback to develop listening and reflective skills.

Scenario: You are a manager supervising a recently appointed overseas social work assistant from Iraq in a local authority children and families team. The probationary period is nearing its end and you have to provide a report on the colleague's competence in order that they can receive a permanent contract in the organization. However, you are concerned about a number of issues including:

- the colleague does not appear to be settled in the team and has been demonstrating signs of frustration since arrival
- another member of the team has heard the colleague say that they dislike children and wish to work for an international charity as a researcher
- unprofessional behaviour has been reported because they have not followed signing in/out and sickness procedures and taken longer than agreed lunch breaks.

You have arranged a special supervision session to discuss the above issues with your colleague.

Task: A role play of a supervision session, lasting approximately 15 minutes, can be undertaken in pairs. One person can act as the manager and another can act as the social work assistant. Where applicable, the two people can be observed by a larger group who can contribute to the subsequent discussion.

Before proceeding to role play, both people may wish to spend a few minutes considering the agenda for the supervision, strategies which challenge assumptions and a plan of action. They may also wish to think about feelings and how to avoid generalized anger, blame and frustration.

Both the manager and the social work assistant must base their responses on the key constituents of positive feedback, that is, that it is specific/descriptive, addresses the problem, is tough on the issues but not the person, focuses on future learning rather than past mistakes, seeks a solution, and leads to positive change.

The practice example can be seen from three linked perspectives: anti-racist, managerial and organizational. Anti-racist practitioners may see this case as a poor cultural match between the organization/team and the worker rather than a problem of racial and ethnic difference. The three problem areas may be indicators but may not combine, and a good manager will look for explanations, with a view to resolving each issue separately. They will not assume that the social work assistant is failing the probationary period at this stage and will compare their performance to the agency's probationary requirements and ethical standards.

The manager will ensure that the colleague's nationality and/or immigration status are openly discussed, but will be aware that the colleague may be stereotyped and labelled in relation to 'race' by the team and/or organization. The manager will ensure that the colleague has been provided with ample opportunity to report complaints and grievances.

If, however, the three areas of concern are linked and demonstrate serious incompetence, the manager will have to agree a plan of action to ensure that the colleague is offered the requisite opportunities to change or enhance their performance. If necessary, the manager will have to take steps to make a fail recommendation on the probationary report. Although the manager must follow ethical principles, they will ultimately make management decisions which promote anti-racist standards and protect and safeguard service users.

Managing research in practice

Research evidence supports understanding of racism and provides a foundation for new forms of anti-racist practice. Any empirical study undertaken in practice is likely to aim for results which are outcome based, service related, participative and inclusive. Smaller studies set their sights on local concerns and larger, better funded projects target national and international issues. Those which relate to anti-oppressive practice tend to ensure that the gathering of data is related to personal, institutional and structural power because consideration of, and confidence in, empowering approaches are likely to spark new ways of thinking and doing social work:

> In particular, the phenomenological perspective acknowledges the centrality of power relationships between different actors in the construction of what is accepted as 'truth'. Such an epistemology is highly compatible with a professional preoccupation concerning the unequal access of people to economic, social and political life on the basis *inter alia* of their ethnicity, gender, disability or income level. (Laird, 2003, p. 253)

Social work research is likely to impact on professional behaviour as well as inform service user perspectives. Researchers should therefore be encouraged to develop appropriate methodological research processes which incorporate ethical considerations. The desire to change organizational structures/systems as well as learn more about themselves as professionals is an additional motivation for those committed to evidence-based practice.

Students utilize research findings routinely when reviewing literature for course assignments and dissertations particularly if the title/subject relates to anti-racist practice. There is also some emphasis on evidencing theories on ethics, values, human rights and social justice within social work practice-related assessments. Research and analysis skills developed at the qualifying level can be substantial and should continue to inform subsequent professional practice. Ideally, social workers should be thinking as researchers, sharing findings, seeking further training and contributing to research studies as they progress through their careers.

Understanding methods, approaches and findings is extremely useful but the development of anti-racist practice requires additional skills in synthesizing and extracting ideas which inform interventions with, for example, older people (Phillips et al., 2006).

The focus on research in relation to 'race' and racism is likely to lead to greater scrutiny and incorporation of anti-racist perspectives in processes and findings. It may also result in greater contributions from interested frontline practitioners and students to methods and approaches used in local research studies. Figure 4.3 illustrates the circular process that should feed the anti-racist vision and aims of any organization or team. The cycle suggests that ideas should be continuously honed, developed and used to inform evidence-based practice.

Students and practitioners are concerned with equality and social justice, as well as the gathering of evidence which reflects anti-racist practice policy, practice and procedure. In order to contribute positively to research initiatives, many look for clear rules and codes which can be agreed by participating researchers and those steering and/or managing the overall aims.

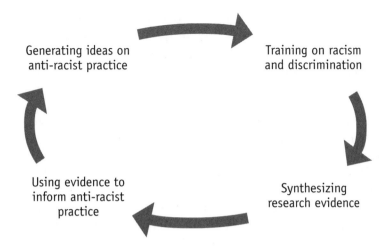

Figure 4.3 Linking ideas, training and research evidence

Consideration of anti-discriminatory and anti-racist practice has to be incorporated within research processes and should inform communication and interpersonal skills. In order to pursue this, researchers may need to consider the following questions and share thinking with others participating in the design, testing, data collection, analysis and dissemination of the findings:

- *Research design and management:* What will be the composition of the team responsible for the aims, objectives and process of the research? Will the provisions of the Equality Act 2006 be applied to the research design, application and published results?
- *Research team and steering groups:* Will they receive training on anti-racist research or consultative support?
- *Research instruments and tools:* Will all participants be treated in a fair and just manner, and how will anti-racist perspectives be included?
- *Ethics proposals:* How will 'race' and racism be addressed, studied and reported? Will the study reflect the population profile of BME groups in the geographic area and how will their needs be included?
- *The contribution of researchers from BME backgrounds:* How will individuals be involved, valued and participate positively in the development of methods and approaches?
- *Human rights principles:* How will researchers respond to ethical concerns such as respecting the right of participants to take responsibility for themselves? What are the contingency plans if discriminatory attitudes and behaviour are shown towards the researcher and/or other participants?
- *The wellbeing of all research participants:* Preventing harm and/or adverse effects to research participants includes the consideration of ethnicity, culture, religion and faith – how will this occur?

- *Informed consent:* How will this be gained from participants with particular linguistic, cultural or learning needs? What are the additional staff and financial resources required to meet these needs?
- *Privacy and confidentiality:* How will this be tested against different cultural and religious ideas and traditions, for example within pilot studies?
- *Openness and honesty:* Will researchers have the opportunity to explore the difference between openness and honesty in order to avoid misunderstandings and misinformation which may later be translated into research findings and thereafter quoted as 'truths' (Laird, 2003)?
- *Linguistic and cultural difference:* Will consideration of this include well-considered responses based on appropriate advice to avoid, for example, the use of poorly selected, trained and supported interpreters?
- *Attitudes and values:* Will the research design incorporate additional support, briefing and debriefing for key staff?
- *Research findings:* Will the overall aims of the research include consideration of how the results, conclusions and recommendations will be shared and disseminated in a linguistically accessible and culturally open manner with participants and other key players?

Research undertaken within any setting is likely to emerge from a range of organizational and individual experiences which confirm or contribute to the status quo and/or existing cultural norms. Fook (2003, p. 362) cautions against the idea of value-free research and stresses that cultural imperialism has often restricted or limited research horizons: 'differences must be defined in terms of their variation from some accepted norm. In this way the norm is preserved, as it is seen as a benchmark by which other perspectives are defined.'

Examining and setting out key principles in research design is the first step to implementing anti-discriminatory and anti-racist practice. It is also important to question the value of knowledge gained by researchers located within social/class/educational structures and with professional and personal identities, motives and agendas likely to impact on the questions asked, methods used and conclusions drawn.

In addition, the power base on which research is conducted requires further consideration as subjects are often powerless and have little or no control over the methods and findings. Social work values have to be integrated in empirical research design and approved by ethical committees run by organizations and courses of study. These can be built on and developed to incorporate anti-racist practice.

The notion of a bias-free and uninvolved researcher requires some thought in relation to 'race' and racism because the research process is likely to generate and uncover a great deal of feeling. This has been evidenced in studies which examine issues such as domestic violence, where the research design incorporated a number of prerequisites, such as the development of a trusting relationship between the researcher and the researched over a prolonged time period, in-depth knowledge of the relevant issues and utmost confidentiality (Bhatti-Sinclair, 1994).

Impartiality is an additional problem as research subjects sharing personal and traumatic experiences are likely to seek affirmation, empathy, encouragement and acknowledgement from the interviewer. As a result, researchers may be drawn into sharing, confirming and soothing the interviewee's pain in an unplanned and unexpected manner. It is therefore imperative to examine methods and materials early in the process and pilot, review and adapt them to enable this aspect to be managed sensitively, particularly if research is conducted in the workplace and/or with service users.

The value of research in practice is worthy of consideration as it is an important tool to enhance and promote anti-racist policy and procedure in the following areas:

- Definition of the status, role and task of those with responsibility for research and evidence-based practice within the organization
- Outcomes of research in relation to targeted policies and procedures, for example on child wellbeing
- Management of student and staff research
- Monitoring and quality assurance systems on research outputs
- Development of research methods and approaches which improve and enhance student and staff confidence
- Understanding of broader societal concerns in research design, such as same-sex marriages and the effects of migration on children and families
- The application of international and national ethical frameworks and national social work/social care codes of ethics and practice, for example on the rights of the child, within research processes
- Effectiveness and efficiency of research resources in relation to the BME population
- The impact of the research on anti-racist policy and practice.

Conclusion

The wider as well as particular developments in policy, practice and research on 'race' and racism were considered in this chapter in order to inform new ways of working and communicating within and across organizations. The emerging approaches to 'race' and ethnicity in relation to the management of staff, services and students have also been explored. Positive models and approaches which enhance personal and professional relationships between the key players both within and across organizations are critical to social work policy and practice, and the ideas introduced here may be taken further by readers in order to relate them better to context and setting.

There is a particular argument made to promote the critical application of anti-racism within research in practice. Empirical evidence provides a sound basis for the acquisition and application of knowledge and skills, both in service provision and in relation to staff and students who are open to critical and reflective methods and approaches. Tools and instrument which enhance, support and change performance and develop effective communication can only be purposeful and useful additions to the existing responses to anti-racist and anti-discriminatory practice.

implications for practice

Contribution to organizational changes requires the acquisition and embedding of new ideas and letting go of old ideas built over many social work generations. People are inclined to enhance, complement and re-create what they know, often regardless of whether the ideas are good or bad. Transformation requires weeding and filtering of existing as well as new knowledge, but pruning is painful and often resisted. However, efficiency changes are familiar to public sector workers, and airing, sifting and refining ways of doing social work can be used productively to move people and organizations in the right direction.

Practice research provides value-added evidence to support transformation in areas such as 'race' and racism, particularly if findings and recommendations show ways to improve service provision, contact and communication with BME service users. In order to successfully inform change and development, however, research results have to be made readily and easily available. Students and social workers are both contributors and users of research but they rarely challenge researchers on the need for better accessible evidence. BME professionals are particularly well placed to contribute to research processes in relation to, for example, how ideas around 'race' and racism are conceived, who undertakes research and whether the findings are applicable to anti-racist practice.

main points

- In order to develop anti-racist practice, social work professionals must use the principles set down in legal and policy frameworks, such as the Race Relations (Amendment) Act 2000 and the Equality Act 2006, in developing overarching policy and everyday procedures.

- Children's social workers need to use empirical research findings to develop competent practice with specific service user groups such as unaccompanied asylum-seeking children (Kohli, 2007).

- Effective and well-defined communication is at the heart of a good organization and responsibility needs to be defined at all levels.

- Wisdom derived from everyday practice may be valued by professionals but it does not always lead to the development of social work theories.

- Understanding the possibilities and constraints provided by organizational structures is one way to enable change and development. What do you think?
- As a student, do you feel that being well informed on anti-racist practice is likely to give you greater confidence and fluency as well as increase your credibility as a social worker?
- Is anti-racist practice a step too far in a busy workplace?
- Do you agree with Fook's (2003) suggestion that cultural imperialism has restricted and limited research horizons and therefore value-free research is not possible?

taking it further

- Gilligan, P. and Furness, S. (2006) The role of religion and spirituality in social work practice: views and experiences of social workers and students, *British Journal of Social Work*, 36: 617–37. Provides an interesting evaluation of 127 students and social workers' views on religion and spirituality, and a useful legal and policy backdrop to the relevant issues. It also identifies beliefs, views on curriculum content and offers guidance of demonstrable knowledge in student assessment, comparing British and American attitudes to intervention. It is a good example of a research project which elicits individual views on a sensitive but relevant subject.
- Johns, N. and Jordon, B. (2006) Social work, merit and ethnic diversity, *British Journal of Social Work*, 36: 1271–88. The aim of this paper is to consider the issue of merit and diversity within the wider policy focus on community cohesion. The authors suggest that 'policy structures used to pursue diversity, or at least to remove any barriers to diversification, are inherently flawed' (p. 1271). There is some analysis of the historical developments which have led to this approach and an important connection between morality and utility. The authors suggest that individual merit needs to be linked to ability, identity and effort within a group or organization and that structural diversity is the desired goal.
- Kohli, R.K. (2007) *Social Work with Unaccompanied Asylum Seeking Children*, Palgrave Macmillan, Basingstoke. Empirical research on competent practice with unaccompanied asylum-seeking children, which aims to promote appropriate and relevant methods of working based on universal values and principles. The author sets out the demographic arguments, reviews relevant literature and evaluates the findings of a study examining the contributions made by social workers to the lives of unaccompanied children and young people.

- Williams, C. and Soydan, H. (2005) When and how does ethnicity matter? A cross-national study of social work responses to ethnicity in child protection cases, *British Journal of Social Work*, 35: 901–20. The authors assert that there is limited evidence on effective social work responses to ethnicity despite professional claims to the contrary. Using a vignette measurement tool in Denmark, Germany, Sweden and the USA, the study has data on assessment and intervention methods used by social workers to address specific needs on culture, race and ethnicity. The conclusions suggest that while the UK has law and policy on the issue, many European and other countries rely on universal principles applied through individual discretion, which often result in western ethnocentric services to vulnerable children.

5 Service users, 'race' and racism

Introduction

This chapter introduces relevant literature, law and policy. It also focuses on the advantages, threats and influences of service user participation in social work, and links this to the development of anti-racist practice as it applies to organizations, practitioners and service user groups. The chapter evaluates these areas, considers service user experiences and examines the barriers to service provision.

There are many reasons why service user perspectives need to be considered in relation to anti-racist practice. It is widely acknowledged that understanding service user points of view is compelling for social workers for a number of professional, as well as moral reasons (Forbat, 2004; Cree and Davies, 2007). There is also a great deal of scope for contrasting service users' experiences with those of BME groups, both service users and more generally, particularly within processes designed to consult and include marginalized groups in society. Comparison is likely to indicate that BME communities and service user groups share a number of features as public sector stakeholders. There is particular value in exploring the experiences of the two groups in relation to the following:

- the lived experience of all service users
- the development of a range of service user perspectives
- the contribution service users have made to their own services.

The backdrop to the ideas on the involvement and empowerment of service users in welfare provision is significant, and examination of a wider literature may contribute to the discussion on how lessons from the past can inform future work. For decades, service user activists argued for the importance of a direct input from service users into organizational policies and procedures, and highlighted barriers, such as professional control, which obstructed these developments (Leach, 1996). As the years passed, wider messages from BME groups improved the way in which BME and other service users were involved in the planning and delivery of public services. Critics (SCIE, 2004a) subsequently argued that service user consultation has focused on existing provision, rather than on more comprehensive developments in organizational structures and systems. For example, social work providers have sought service user comment on selected areas, such as performance and inspection targets, rather than across all levels of service delivery.

Humphreys (2005) argues that the knowledge used in social work and social care is derived from three essential sources: practice intelligence, applied research and the lived experience of service users. These areas are, however, valued differently within professional social work. For example, work-related policy, organizational procedures and protocols have informed research and evidence-based practice more than service user views.

The privileging of professional knowledge over learning from service user experiences has meant that the testing of methods and approaches has not been thorough or wide-ranging. A number of reasons have been cited for the poor development in this area including:

- social workers continue to lack clarity about their roles
- social workers are confused about how to develop sincere and authentic relationships with service users and BME communities
- organizations are threatened by external scrutiny and perceived interference in internal processes.

Added to this, resources have remained static or diminished, while the responsibilities of the average social work team have expanded. So organizations have not necessarily prioritized service user involvement, like anti-racist practice, or integrated service user perspectives into comprehensive, systematic approaches.

This suggests that social workers need to be clear about their practical, emotional and ethical responsibilities when engaging, in the short, medium or long term, with individuals and groups. Clarity about their responsibilities is likely to lead to a better reception, result in greater professional/organizational confidence and better use of time and effort.

Service user groups interpret the slow response as an ongoing retention of control and a lack of commitment by professionals. They feel undervalued by a system set up to meet their personal needs and less able to contribute to its development. Despite this, some pressure groups continue to campaign for better legislation and improved standards in relation to, for example, students and newly qualified social workers.

The push for services informed by service user perspectives has led to documents such as *Putting People First: A Shared Vision and Commitment to the Transformation of Adult Social Care* (DH, 2007). These documents recognize the expert knowledge brought to the task by families, carers and personal advocates, as well as the value of collective responses and campaigning networks. In the process of acknowledging service user strengths in policy documents, the government has also added ideas based on individual needs such as consumerism, choice and the control of personal resources. Such notions are encapsulated in the modernizing social care agenda of *Putting People First*, with greater self-assessment and person-centred planning through, for example, telecare, that is, the use of information technology to engage with service users at a distance from direct services (DH, 2007).

It appears that in the process of acknowledging service user input, policy makers and professionals have refined the approaches and modified the language to describe the key stakeholders. Words from other spheres, such as commerce, have been imported and used to avoid the stigma and embarrassment attached to the label 'service user'. However, the relocation of such terms to social welfare has created additional problems. For example, the word 'consumer' suggests choice and control in relation to goods and commodities, but social work service users do not necessarily have the same power as other purchasers.

In any case, the idea that service users are consumers in a commercial sense is not only untrue, but works against the principles of equal access and empowering practice. This perspective is akin to the 'colour blind' approach (see Glossary), promoted to suggest a level playing field where black and white people are treated equally within a society where racial prejudice is common and widespread. There is no doubt, however, that people who access social/welfare services feel degraded by labels such as 'service users' (Cree and Davis, 2007). There are a number of reasons for this. One may be that many groups, including BME communities, feel grouped together as a homogeneous mass in a manner which strips them of their individual, cultural or any other modes of identity: 'many people who use services have not wished to be defined in this way ... they come from all classes and cultures, they are young, old, female and male, with disabilities and without' (Cree and Davis, 2007, p. 3).

The difficulty of defining and identifying people was acknowledged in Chapter 1, but for the purposes of this chapter, the term 'service user' is used to describe individuals and groups seeking and receiving publicly funded interventions. Also the words 'participation', 'involvement' and 'consultation' describe processes used to include service user perspectives in the design, development and delivery of services. Although participation may be used interchangeably with involvement, the difference between the two words requires further consideration. Involvement through consultative processes usually means asking for token comments on existing/well-developed policy and practice, while positive inclusion and genuine participation is likely to result in involvement at all levels, with the requisite sharing of power, knowledge and resources.

Background

Service users have been seen as a problem within welfare for a long time (SCIE, 2004a). For example, needy families were defined as inadequate by the Poor Law Amendment Act 1834. This Act moved away from the provision of poor relief in the community and provided workhouses where men and women were segregated in sometimes harsh and tyrannical conditions.

Between the 1920s and 1950s, the Eugenics Society actively promoted the idea of better breeding for families unable to manage parenthood, along with ideas of supremacy based on racial differences. Similarly, other groups such as the mentally ill or older people were seen as deficient or desperate, and the value placed on disadvantaged and discriminated against groups by society at the time was reflected in the public services provided (Payne, 2005). A great deal of such thinking is buried in the past, but it may be argued that some of these ideas persist, promoted by writers such as Herrnstein and Murray (1994), who stress primacy based on intelligence, illustrated by differing patterns in marriage, child birth and dependence on welfare.

Morris (2002) argues that the early beginnings of social work contributed to the slow development of service user involvement, which took hold during the latter half of the 20th century. The twin notions of consultation and participation were supported by the Seebohm Report in 1968 and promoted by the community development (Leaper, 1968) and social change agenda (Calouste Gulbenkian Foundation, 1968).

A great deal of empowerment work happened with BME communities as a result of this attention, and the process of development produced some important lessons for other groups. However, the intention behind this activity was later viewed with some scepticism – principally because community and 'race' relations were seen by the then government as a means by which newly arrived and dysfunctional BME immigrants could be assimilated into mainstream society (Anthias and Yuval-Davis, 1995).

The Race Relations Act 1976 was a significant milestone for anti-racist practice, mainly because it created the Commission for Racial Equality and local race equality councils to encourage contact with, and representation from, BME groups. However, a great deal of this work did not maximize collective strength or address the tensions created by the poor services and employment prospects faced by inner-city communities. The effects of systematic deprivation eventually led to the 1981 race riots, subsequently investigated by the Scarman enquiry into civil unrest (Thompson, 2006). Among other findings, the Scarman Report (1982) suggested that poor communication and community interaction was a significant issue for those living in such neighbourhoods. It concluded that, although racism was personally significant, it was also a matter of real concern to society and the country (Thompson, 2006). The report strongly recommended community consultation as an important way forward.

Anti-racist practice was also politically difficult during this period. BME communities appreciated the findings of the Scarman Report, but felt that pubic sector responses to the report and similar initiatives lacked integrity and authenticity. Public bodies sought comment and feedback, but required it in a particular form from groups and neighbourhoods who were ill-equipped to deal with the complexities of civil unrest. In order to improve communication and the exchange of ideas, public sector organizations looked for community representatives with an overarching finger on the pulse. In reality, many of these people were removed from the everyday concerns of their own and/or any other community, and were able only to represent their personal and family views. Such individuals were unable to have a broader understanding or analysis of community and neighbourhood, and could not contribute impartially and fully to the development of anti-racist policy and practice. Because of this, active participation took a great deal of time to bed down.

However, when community representation started to make a difference, the individuals involved got drawn into the system and became further removed from the key concerns of the people they represented:

> People who become active in local politics are not necessarily in touch with the feelings and aspirations of those they professed to represent ... Their very positions, not to mention their class positions, tended to isolate them from their client group, since they necessarily had to operate more and more like (and with) local government officials. (Anthias and Yuval-Davis, 1995, p. 176)

However, the basis for change within 'race' relations was of its time and, therefore, politically charged by the ideological nature of the subject, which meant that developments were often fragmented and divisive (Solomos and Back, 1995). The early experience in 'race' relations provides important lessons on how best to achieve service user representation within pre-existing organizational structures and systems. Although contemporary social policy has examined some of these complexities, BME groups and service users continue to remain marginal in institutional decision-making systems.

Contemporary law and policy

The NHS and Community Care (NHSCC) Act 1990 placed a legal duty on public authorities to consult service users. This was supported in 1998 by the government White Paper, *Modernising Local Government*, which placed emphasis on consultation with the individual, rather than with a family, group or other system of social cohesion (Lawrence et al., 2003). The underlying principles of quality, scale and economy led to significant changes within the public sector which included a greater involvement of those receiving services (Davies, 2005). However, with a few notable exceptions, social work practitioners did not seriously embark on the integration of service users' contributions (Humphreys, 2005) until the drive to consult and involve took hold within the modernization agenda: 'Involving service users and carers in the education and training of social workers is higher on the policy and practice agenda than ever before' (SCIE, 2004b, p. 3). This is despite decades of collective action from stakeholder groups promoting personalized services, such as direct payments, based on principles of choice and self-determination (Braye and Preston Shoot, 1995). Critics suggested that, if the change agenda was to be truly beneficial and useful, all the stakeholders had to address the power inherent within the existing organizational structures and systems (Pinkerton, 2002).

The NHSCC Act 1990 set in place the idea of public bodies competitively purchasing services from a range of private, voluntary and independent sector organizations. This resulted in a change of ethos and philosophy in relation to public sector financing, beginning the move towards direct payments and the personalization of services. Commercial ideas flourished on what was historically deemed by some to be the sacred ground of public service envisaged by the Beveridge Report (Payne, 2005). However, the use of business ideas was evaluated as partial and narrow, as it took little account of care organizations with limited interest in the generation of funds and profit making. For example, a residential home for children, primarily funded by the public sector, is unlikely to focus on profit making. The children will be looked after by staff such as care managers and may exercise limited control of the services available to them.

Aware of this, local government followed the NHS by developing internal markets, that is, contracts within organizations for purchasing and providing services, and public/private partnership arrangements, for example joint contractual arrangements used to finance new hospital and school buildings. The tighter focus on budgeting changed the philosophical roots of public sector organizations and the relationship between service providers and service users:

> Quasi-markets are 'markets' because they replace state provision with more competitive, independent services. They are 'quasi' because they differ from conventional markets in a number of important respects. On the supply side, as with conventional markets, there is competition between service suppliers. On the demand side, consumer purchasing power is not expressed in terms of cash but in the form of a budget confined to the purchase of a specific service. (Hoyes and Means, 1993, p. 288)

Efficiency and effectiveness were cited as the rationale for the quasi-markets, but this created a number of difficulties in relation to value for money, choice and equality not only for service users, but also for the terms and conditions of the mostly low-paid public sector employees:

> Equally, a central focus on costs may reduce choice for the individual consumer since expensive but preferred care options may be dismissed or ignored by the care manager, although it could equally be argued that such an approach ensures the maximum number of clients can be helped for any given amount of resources. (Hoyes and Means, 1993, p. 293)

Ellis and Whittington (1998) suggest that the range of staff engaged in delivering services includes receptionists, telephonists, drivers, building maintenance staff, managers, clerical staff, caterers and volunteers, along with social workers, care assistants, community nurses, occupational therapists, physiotherapists, chiropodists and general practitioners. There is an expectation that such staff will have the necessary skills and knowledge to perform assorted, complex functions in a manner which is both efficient, effective and incorporates service user views.

The modernization agenda also provided an articulation of the social care role and responsibility within a mixed economy of care (Means et al., 2003). For some BME communities, this policy resulted in specific targeted residential and day services staffed by workers with a knowledge of identity, culture and religion.

However, critics suggested that the marketplace ideas not only limited access, but also prolonged existing problems for BME service users. A great deal of debate also occurred during this period concerning the relationship between carers and those being cared for, particularly within the disability and feminist movements. However, despite concerns about the quality of care provided to BME individuals, the issue received minimal attention (Ahmad and Atkin, 1996):

> The complexity of the difficulties facing users, carers and service providers is addressed in a recent review of the relationship between African and Caribbean communities and mental health services by the Sainsbury Centre for Mental Health (2002) ... which reports that prejudice, cultural ignorance and fear of violence influence assessment and leads to treatment that relies heavily on medication and restriction. (Means et al., 2003, p. 172)

The changes in the public sector were also significant for social care workers attracted to the profession because of its service values. Many anti-racist practitioners, in particular, wondered about the validity and reliability of the methods used to involve and empower service users. The modernization agenda defined professional responsibility, but the need for better guidance and training on involving service users was still needed (Thompson, 2006). BME social workers also sought recognition of the voluntary contribution made to BME-based services and neighbourhood projects.

In essence the modernization of social services neither addressed diminishing resources, nor dealt with the move away from core professional values such as empowerment, choice and self-determination. For antiracist practitioners, the reforms offered confusion rather than certainty, promoting service user involvement on one hand, and undermining core values and principles on the other. The long-term fallout from this was seen to limit innovation, originality and improvement for all stakeholders including individuals, families and organizations (Lloyd, 2002). Subsequent development of the personalization agenda addressed the need for service user-led interventions, planning, budgeting and self-directed care supported by partnership-based professional input (Payne, 2009).

The change in the nature of the service user–professional relationship within the personalization agenda raises interesting questions for participation more generally. Engaging properly with service delivery processes lifts the expectations of those invited to have a say. It further implies that social workers have equal status with service users. Arguably, the former group comprises individuals who have high professional, institutional and economic position, while the latter group consists of those at extreme disadvantage and holding minimum resources. This suggests that a partnership is compromised by the power inherent in knowledge, skills and values available to those involved. Power relations between social workers and service users are fundamentally different, although the desire to share power is established and is, therefore, worth examining further.

Service user power

The poor application of prejudiced ideas and stereotypes can play a significant role in power relations. Prejudice is a judgement formed prior to any given experience, and can be harmful if acted upon negatively (Cashmore, 1996). If prejudice is combined with power, it adds additional strength to any unfair act, as suggested by the equation power + prejudice = discrimination. For social workers, this assumes that professional power has to be used in conjunction with personal prejudice to discriminate against a person or group. This idea presupposes that discrimination can only occur if it is acted on by the individual, group or organization.

The source of a great deal of social work power is the authority handed down from employers to employees holding well-defined professional positions within which they dispense their legal and moral responsibilities. Social workers also have personal attributes such as 'race', gender, class, age, sexuality and (dis)ability (Brown and Bourne, 1996). Professionals are seen to have advantages such as these, along with educational attainment, well-paid jobs and work-related status.

Service users rarely possess the professional advantage bestowed by structures and institutions but they may benefit from their 'race', class, age and sex and, in relative terms, by education, employment and income. They may also have the power to initiate individual and/or group prejudice towards others, in the same way as professionals.

Differences in power have been cited as critical to the development of 'user-led change' (SCIE, 2004a) for all groups. But lessons from anti-racist practice suggest that participation based on the lived experience per se does not always lead to social and political change (Solomos and Back, 1995).

Professions need to empower service users in order that they can offer a balanced critique of the administrative, operational and decision-making processes. For example, greater attention needs to be paid to good planning and preparation for meaningful involvement. Discussion of the effective use of resources such as funds which meet both service user and professional needs more equitably has to take place at all levels in any organization.

Service users need to examine behaviours which are defensive and resistant, as well as those which are overconcerned with personal histories, and focus instead on understanding where power is located and how it can be influenced: 'User/carer interests are often described as personal rather than strategic ... illustrating mismatch between the client's experiential perspective and language and the managerial provider perspective and language' (SCIE, 2004a, p. 15). This suggests a systemized approach to collaboration, and a shared consideration of the purpose, standard and quality of engagement, possibly through joint training and development. Strategies such as this are likely to allow deeper, collective examination of the service user–social worker relationship based on efficient and effective practice.

Consistent and ongoing communication is also likely to lead to greater understanding of stresses and demands. Social workers may relate to service users at a number of levels within a working day, and therefore undertake multiple and varying tasks. Service users may carry a range of the responsibilities while living with a high level of personal, health and other needs. Both sides see a snapshot of responsibilities held by the other at any given time. For example, a service user contributing to staff recruitment is likely to see a social work manager on an interview panel in isolation from their other service duties. A social worker is unlikely to see the service user representative undertaking a part-time job, as well as carrying out caring/family obligations.

In relation to developing anti-racist practice, responsible staff may need to consider the additional institutional hurdles faced by BME service users wishing to be involved in selecting or managing staff. The motivation behind the invitation also needs examining because too often the views of BME service users are sought on BME-related rather than generic tasks. This is based on the assumption that BME service users have expert knowledge only on BME issues rather than wider expertise on recruitment, selection and related processes.

Social workers and managers seeking to involve BME individuals in, for example, the appointment of staff may consider sensitively checking their assumptions about racism, such as all BME individuals are anti-racist, as well as about the breadth and depth of their knowledge of the relevant recruitment processes. Responsible staff should also ensure that service users are properly briefed on their role and responsibility, as well as invited to take part in planning, preparation and information sharing in a user-friendly and accessible manner.

The value of service user involvement to organizational practice is demonstrated by well-planned and coordinated arrangements. If service users feel their contributions are appreciated, they are more likely to provide feedback which is developmentally useful and non-threatening to professional and organizational responsibilities.

Service users may have a great deal of individual knowledge as consumers, but they may not have a deep understanding of how organizations function internally or manage the daily grind of allocating and rationing resources. The duty to act in a realistic and principled manner which avoids waste is a responsibility well understood by welfare professionals, but may be less clear to service users (Beckett and Maynard, 2005).

Service users may be unaware that they are unlikely to have significant influence on any organizational processes beyond the immediate task, because most organizations function in hierarchical ways to meet their duties, and are unlikely to easily give away their influence and power. However, organizations committed to empowering practice are likely to examine the institutional power held by their own staff, as well as to appreciate the type and quality of influence held by service users within and beyond any given situation. Locating the sources of influence may shift the balance of power and ease the path to change and policy development.

Those in senior and middle management positions are seen to hold considerable power over those seeking services, particularly in relation to organizational information. Sharing resources is a critical prerequisite for service user involvement and must be valued and prioritized if seeking and utilizing service user feedback is the desired aim. Gaining service user input suggests that it is used systematically to improve services; however, a great deal more thought needs to be given to the effective use of the information collected:

> In public services, consumerism is seen as essentially a cultural stance involving an organisation's willingness to be open to receiving and acting on customer views, then this may in any event be a misreading of much private sector practice, where frequently it is only the largest and latest customer who holds significant power. (Willcocks and Harrow, 1992, p. 114)

Service user participation and feedback has to be valued and supported within the organization regardless of individual status. Managerial responses have to demonstrate equal and fair treatment to those with the least authority, the smallest influence and the greatest disadvantage. This is problematic for many BME communities with limited understanding of organizational systems and cultures. The knock-on effects of poor awareness and confidence may result in greater dependence on family and community systems for social welfare. Within such a context, BME individuals may be disadvantaged by a low status in society, as well as poor access to social services. Organizations interested in responding strategically to such groups may need to use socioeconomic data from the locality or region to analyse the relationship between family and kinship to social need.

Service user participation is a priority for the locality and region, but also for the strategic aims of national organizations and their governing bodies. The issues raised, however, have been the same. A project that evaluated representation on the General Social Care Council found that service users brought an individual perspective and were not always formally or directly accountable to social care user groups or other individuals (SCIE, 2003a). The value of their perspective to the organizations involved was, by default, limited by personal experience and history. Organizations seeking service user involvement at a higher strategic level may need to seek representation from larger groups with relevant experience in order that they can be seen as representing powerful groups, as well as individuals with personal histories (SCIE, 2003a).

People can be disempowered in many and varied ways. For example, evidence suggests (SCIE, 2004a) that although organizations are committed in theory to the participation of service users, practical responsibility for attendance at meetings and events is often left to the individual. The person representing a service user group or BME organization may be an older person, a woman or a disabled person. Whatever the issue, they are likely to be left to manage the practicalities of access and other physical constraints. There is little research in social work on the participation of older service users who may also be women and/or from BME backgrounds. Ageism is a cause for real concern within British society (Thompson, 2006), and many citizens and campaigning groups regularly promote age-related welfare rights. As a result, such services have received some policy attention from the government, illustrated by the announcement by the then Minister for Care Services Liam Byrne that 'social care is at the heart of what the government is trying to do over the next four to five years' (*Community Care*, 2005, p. 14). Some local authorities have addressed this within the development of adult services by seeking data on service take-up by older citizens and BME people in particular. An increase in the overall pool of older service users is likely to lead to greater intervention demands, as well as more participation and feedback.

Developing anti-racist practice on service user involvement

Despite policy drivers and local government responses, there is continuing concern that although anti-racist practice has been built on black perspectives, there is a need to include particular input from BME as well as other service users (Singh, 2006). The problem is that BME service users may be abstaining from developmental work, as well as the wider service user movement, because they feel their influence is undervalued and they wish to remain segregated within their own communities (Singh, 2006):

> Black and minority ethnic groups may have difficulty in subordinating their objectives to the narrow [service] agenda and may be unwilling to act as collaborators ... it [has been] argued that for some people previous attempts to influence health and social care services have proved so unsatisfactory that separation is less demoralising. (SCIE, 2004a, p. 21)

There is further unease about how service user groups in general address issues of 'race' and racism in line with social work guidance (SCIE, 2004a). It is clear that organizations need input from service users in order to improve services, but it is less clear whether service user groups should be influencing each other. BME service users are likely to feel that influencing other service user groups is beyond their current remit, knowledge and skills. Resources for raising their own capacity through training and development may be scarce or unavailable, and few may have the time and energy to engage with others. Most organizations support service user representatives through financial recompense, but may not wish to support wider training and development, even in areas such as anti-racist or anti-discriminatory practice.

How then to move towards realizable goals? Figure 5.1 suggests that anti-racist practice and service user developments are rooted in different places and the accrued knowledge is generally not shared between sectors. However, there is a need for a focus on anti-racist practice by service user groups, as well as by organizations serving these groups. There is also scope for a critical examination of service users from BME groups, and how they may seek representation. So a service user organization looking for institutional change also needs to consider its legal and moral responsibilities towards the development of anti-racist practice within its aims, objectives, processes and structures. The same legal and policy imperatives which steer formal social services agencies also apply to less formal, voluntary organizations such as those led by service users and carers.

Figure 5.1 places the service user organization at the heart of the process of change, which means that it contributes to anti-racist practice as well as gaining from it. Figure 5.1 assumes that service user organizations are motivated by principles of involvement and participation and should be seeking input on BME issues from BME members as well as training on 'race' and discrimination. Proactive commitment may need a respectful engagement with diversity and difference and an understanding of anti-discriminatory language and terminology. If the service user organization is actively engaging at these levels, it will be moving towards meeting its goals on anti-racist practice.

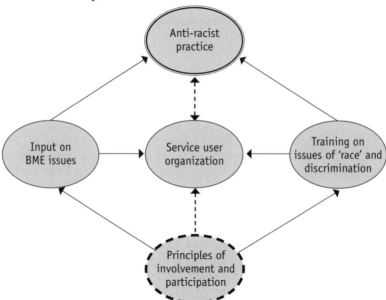

Figure 5.1 Anti-racist practice within a service user organization

Organizations wishing to incorporate anti-racist practice within their philosophy and ethos are likely to set in place training and development programmes which include areas of common concern, such as becoming or being seen as an expert on the needs of a particular group.

Critics (SCIE, 2004a) suggest that BME social workers who are seen to provide service user knowledge and experience may be undervalued, underpromoted and marginalized from other areas of more mainstream work. There is a danger that handing over responsibility of BME issues to

BME staff may result in a lack of obligation by white social workers to anti-racist practice. Also, in order to promote choice and self-determination, and avoid assumptions about matching BME service users and social workers on the basis of 'race' and ethnicity, BME service users should be offered services from professionals with a different ethnic background. BME service users may not necessarily wish to receive a service only from BME professionals, and some may actively vote against it.

The 'expert' label has been a problem not only for service users, but also for service users and BME individuals who are employed as social workers. A great many have struggled with promoting issues of real and immediate concern to their own communities within a professional context. They, like other marginalized groups, have looked for approaches which offer positive ways forward on best practice. Table 5.1 offers a solution-based model based on key issues at a number of levels, including how to deal with the expert/specialist label, how to progress within a system, how to seek organizational support, and how to deal with exploitative situations.

Table 5.1 Solution-based approach for developing good practice

Problem	Solution for black and ethnic minority individuals	Solution for service users
Becoming an expert or specialist	Take a lead within organizations and recommend that appropriate use of expert knowledge, based on personal and professional background, is properly used, not only on issues of 'race' but also in other areas. Encourage collaborative and collective approaches. Offer the lead to white colleagues who may not feel comfortable commenting on issues of 'race' and racism. Avoid the assumption that only BME individuals can speak on 'race' and racism	Ensure that knowledge is valued within the parameters stated by the individual or service user organization. A family or other group can bring a range of expertise which can, as a whole, be a powerful means to illustrate family, kinship and/or community ties. Examine the issue of expertise in relation to personal experience. Consider how a range of experiences from people with different backgrounds and perspectives can be brought together to form a collective response
Progression within the system	Knowledge and experience of the organization are likely to lead to an increase in confidence and fluency and an enhanced capacity to challenge structures and systems. This will enable progression driven by choice and control rather than the expectations of others	The early experiences of service user involvement and participation will result in the development of knowledge and experience. This will lead to an increase in confidence and fluency and an enhanced capacity to challenge structures and systems

Problem	Solution for black and ethnic minority individuals	Solution for service users
Lack of encouragement and support from organizations seeking participation	Support from like-minded colleagues and friends is invaluable, as are alliances with social workers and related professionals with similar experiences	Support from other service users and local, regional and national groups. Attendance at regional conferences where experiences can be shared and information exchanged
Exploitation	Understanding and use of legal and policy instruments such the Race Relations Act 2000, the Human Rights Act 1998 and the Protection from Harassment Act 1997	Look to national policy and other frameworks to support self-determination and independence. Relevant legal frameworks include the Carers (Recognition and Services) Act 1995, the Data Protection Act 1998 and the Human Rights Act 1998
Lack of understanding	The Race Relations (Amendment) Act 2000 and the Employment Equality (Religion or Belief) Regulations 2003 outlaw discrimination on grounds of religion and philosophical belief within employment. Race equality schemes produced by public sector organizations must include service user perspectives	The Equalities Act 2006 established the Equality and Human Rights Commission in 2007. This has the power to oversee equal treatment on the grounds of race, gender, disability, sexual orientation, religion/belief and age

Implementing equality within any context is an uphill struggle, but Thompson (2006) suggests that consideration of organizational and individual practice is an important first step towards recognition and action. However, this needs to work in both directions, that is, service user activists need to promote anti-racist practice, and anti-racist practitioners need to support service user participation. There is little doubt that combined energies will benefit both areas of practice. On the other hand, focusing on one area at the cost of another may result in one or both remaining at the rhetorical stage and accused of tokenism.

The potential to draw on experience which is common and shared remains untapped and needs to be encouraged at a number of levels including between and across the groups, as illustrated in Figure 5.2. The aim would be to locate the shared experiences of white service users and social workers as well as BME and white social workers. Also BME and white service users may have a great deal of understanding of how provision is received and be able to offer comment and feedback on improvements. The overlapping area offers a model of combined strength which can be utilized to change and enhance the work being undertaken by everyone involved.

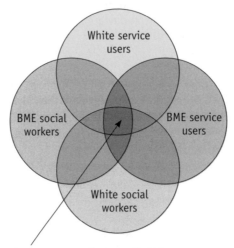

In order to communicate well, this common ground needs to be addressed by the key people involved

Figure 5.2 Communication between groups

Figure 5.2 offers a model which supports deeper engagement because tokenism and entrenched, simplified and negative practice continue to be areas of particular concern in anti-racist practice. For example, Thompson (2006) suggests that social work has simplified discrimination in relation to language (see Chapter 1) and that this has halted the development of critical and reflective practice. Anti-racist perspectives in particular have also been evaluated as negative, based on the word 'anti' rather than any other more helpful prefix.

Solution-based approaches (see Table 5.1) offer an opportunity to examine the common issues from parallel perspectives. They also provide a conceptual move towards positive thinking, particularly if they are aligned with new developments (Thompson, 2006). However, solutions are sought by those interested in sharing knowledge and skills with others or outsiders (Hayes, 2005). The territorial nature of organizations is explored further by Adams (2005). It is clear that even within a clear professional value base, those who control and administer welfare may find the implementation of egalitarian principles such as empowerment to be contradictory and complex. A simpler response may be to retain professional influence and avoid personal challenge:

> Empowerment can be too politically, financially and managerially dangerous. It is easier for the powerful to continue to manage the powerless in society. Empowerment could be about offering people informed choice, and thereby enabling exclusion to be challenged at the personal level. (Adams, 2002, p. 293)

Horner (2003) agrees that inclusive approaches should be controlled and determined by those receiving services, but equal participation is hard to achieve within structures which are inherently unequal. An important means by which structural and institutional control is maintained is by the setting of questionable strategic goals which are often based on operational rather than ethical standards. In order to develop good practice, organizations need to look beyond immediate service demands (Croft and Beresford, 1993).

Service users can also take a lead, individually or in groups, on how they can pre-plan, negotiate and agree a few simple rules, such as those set out below, when engaging with professionals. Assessing and stating needs may alleviate fear and anxiety about complex structures, ease communication and set in place processes which encourage institutional change:

- Clear guidance on anti-racist information, language, method and mode of delivery. For example, issues which relate to where a meeting will take place and how it may be conducted.
- Specification of the type, quality and quantity of information. For example, preference for electronically transmitted information which can be manipulated by the user.
- Formalized arrangements, such as the time and location set to meet service user needs, particularly those with health or other clinical needs.
- Car parking for those with mobility needs – other than disabled badges.

Consideration of practical issues such as these can make the difference between participation and non-participation. For example, many carers are only able to attend meetings in the middle of the day, after they have taken foster children to childcare/school and before the pick up at the end of the school day. Although this requirement is the same for any parent, carers have additional obligations and duties over and above those undertaken by a family member. In relation to anti-racist practice, additional consideration may need to be given to the needs of BME women with above average responsibilities as parents and carers, based on evidence that, for example, Muslim women particularly are underrepresented in the labour market, and more likely to be undertaking unpaid work from home (Brah, 1996). Of course, many administrative tasks such as these require a great deal of practical commitment from hard-pressed professionals. But where such systems work well, involvement is eased, and service users feel they have participated in actual as well as hypothetical terms.

Service users and social workers value established relationships bonded by common values. A model for practice which maximizes this is based on the idea of the service user as a consultant to any given project or intervention. This approach allows for an affiliation which may be medium or long term, based on mutual understanding and respect. It also ensures that the people involved can collaborate in a manner which is deep and meaningful. A key aim for the development of good anti-racist and any other practice is to provide an environment where discriminatory attitudes and behaviour can be appropriately challenged. Sustained contact can allow individuals to feel safe and confident enough to move away from what may have been entrenched positions. Approaches which promote understanding of different perspectives are more likely to lead to collective change.

Service user involvement is closely related to the provision of social care to BME communities. Evidence suggests that service users define good social work as responsive, holistic, long term and oriented towards the future (Cree and Davis, 2007). Approaches which promote service perspectives point towards principles, such as below, which can be developed to fit organizational needs (Payne, 2009):

- Community and family resources as well as formal services are recognized and utilized
- Social workers have long-term, continuing and trusting relationships with individuals and families
- Organizations consult service users and BME staff with local and/or specific cultural/religious knowledge about the locality and community
- Frequent contact with service users and representatives on particular and developing needs which require early interventions, such as work with the families and/or carers of young BME offenders
- Inspection and monitoring of existing services to ensure that BME service user needs are integrated, particularly for services which may be removed from immediate public scrutiny, such as women's aid refuges and voluntary/independent care homes.

Anti-racist and ethical practice promotes institutional change and values all the stakeholders involved in the process (Hugman, 2005). The overarching commitment to issues of social justice means that experience needs to be improved consistently and coherently in order to generate new knowledge on service user involvement.

Conclusions

This chapter has examined the involvement of service users from a range of perspectives, and provided ideas on how anti-racist practice can be developed by service users and organizations.

It is clear that seeking service user feedback is a recent and developing area of social work practice because prior work has focused more on how to deliver services, rather than how service users can contribute to change and development. The modernization of social work and social care has confused as well as clarified social work responsibilities towards service users, particularly in relation to consumer choice and self-determination in areas such as personalization. Social workers are keen to develop language and interpersonal skills, and this is an area which can build on existing knowledge and values. However, further discussions have to be inclusive, confident and well informed, and involve key stakeholders including service users, BME groups and professionals.

This chapter has evaluated the advantages, threats, power and influences created by service user participation in social work and linked it to the development of anti-racist practice. However, it is clear that processes which empower service users can challenge political and managerial power. There is also a widely held perception that social workers continue to use professional and institutional power to manage the powerless in society.

Power can also be owned and used by service users and BME individuals to change and enhance structures and systems. Service users and individuals seeking to take a lead may wish to consider where advantage as well as disadvantage is located and how it can support anti-racist and anti-discriminatory practice.

In summary, this chapter has raised many questions which may contribute to the ongoing debate on whether the lessons learned from anti-racist practice are pertinent or relevant, and how best they may inform future developments in both service user involvement and anti-racist practice. There appear to be many parallels between the experience of those advocating anti-racist practice and service user involvement, and understanding the perspective of both groups is undoubtedly valuable to organizational change and development. The potential to draw on this experience needs to be tapped at a number of levels including service user groups, black and white anti-racist practitioners and finally service users and BME social workers. Developing anti-racist practice requires an understanding of how services users can be drawn together to collectively inform change. Consideration of this separate and parallel experience is important for those involved, and for law and policy makers (SCIE, 2004a).

implications for practice

There is a great deal of work which needs to be done in order that social workers can fully incorporate service user perspectives into organizational structures and systems. In relation to BME service users, this work is more complex because the concern is with changing social work as well as service user organizations. In the first instance, providers can follow the ideas listed below to address service user concerns and develop anti-racist and anti-discriminatory practice. The implication is that attention is paid to information, guidance and support systems and that core values such as respect and self-determination inform policy and procedure:

- Service user knowledge on anti-racist practice should be valued implicitly and explicitly within specified service areas
- Service user needs are overtly addressed in processes where BME representation, consultation and/or feedback are sought
- Service users are offered anti-racist training, guidance, support and resources to enhance service-related knowledge, skills and values
- Service user organizations are asked to articulate individual and collective knowledge, skills and anti-racist values in relation to tasks and/or responsibilities
- Anti-racist and equalities law, policy and practice are adhered to by service user organizations
- Service users from BME groups should deploy their personal experiences more strategically when making representations
- Service user organizations should be encouraged to communicate with and learn about 'race' and racism from other local, regional, national and international groups
- Service user views should be sought, valued and acted on, but also challenged where appropriate and necessary.

main points

- The charitable origins of social work included the view that service users were a problem (SCIE, 2004a) and were deficient or desperate (Payne, 2005). It may be argued that this is reflected in the value placed on disadvantaged and discriminated against groups within public services today.

- The early experience in 'race' relations suggests that the process of change triggered by social unrest may not always result in the best possible or most effective law, policy and procedures, either for those seeking or those providing representation and consultation.

- Social work is struggling with the management of diminishing resources and such pressures fundamentally undermine core principles and values and tend to limit innovation, originality and improvement in relation to service user groups (Lloyd, 2002).

- The service user contribution has been undervalued within theoretical and practice knowledge.

- The NHS and Community Care Act 1990 placed a legal duty on public authorities to consult with the individual, rather than the family or group (Lawrence et al., 2003). What do you think of this development?
- Can 'nice people' such as social workers disempower service users?
- How do social workers reflect power and privilege in their work with service users (Thompson, 2006)?

taking it further

- Armstrong, F. and Barton, L. (eds) (1999) *Disability, Human Rights and Education: Cross Cultural Perspectives*, Open University Press, Buckingham.
  The editors offer an interesting collection of chapters written by a number of authors from many countries across the globe, with a primary focus on inclusive educational practices framed within human rights and disability. The overarching issue appears to hinge on understanding the 'wider structuring influences of economic conditions and political systems' (p. 1). The book provides an interesting range of perspectives on children and adults and an opportunity for a dialogue on the dominant sources of knowledge.
- Cree, V.E. and Davis, A. (2007) *Social Work: Voices from the Inside*, Routledge, London.
  Provides invaluable narrative data based on the accounts of 59 service users, carers and practitioners with direct experience of social work. The authors recommend it as essential reading for students and academics as it provides evidence of good practice in a range of contexts including work with older persons, children and families.
- Advocacy in Action (2007) Why bother? The truth about service user involvement, in Lymbery, M. and Postle, K. (eds) *Social Work: A Companion to Learning*, Sage, London.
  Advocacy in Action, a service user group, asks pertinent questions such as 'how can service users' partnerships be a cornerstone of professional learning' (p. 51)? It suggests that although service user contributions are likely to worry and unsettle students and others, the majority who participate in educational processes are fully aware of their impact. Therefore, service users who share personal accounts and perspectives actively demonstrate strength and spirit.

6 Developing anti-racist educational practice

Introduction

This chapter will examine social work educational standards for relevance and pertinence to 'race' and racism in relation to the following issues:

- equality in education
- teaching, learning and assessment in the workplace
- anti-racist practice in learning environments.

Educational practice is defined as work undertaken by the broad range of individuals based in university and practice settings who undertake and promote the teaching, learning and assessment of all learners. Continuous professional development is an overarching idea which applies to the career pathway followed by students, newly qualified and experienced social workers, and is defined as an: 'On-going and planned learning process that contributes to personal and professional development and can be applied or assessed against competences and organisational performance' (CWDC, 2007, Appendix G).

The 2009 report by the Social Work Task Force recommended major structural changes to social work education and practice leading to higher professional standards, better regulation and the creation of a national College of Social Work. It made a strong argument for greater alignment between entry requirements, initial and subsequent training, and for formalized partnerships between key stakeholders in social work education, for example universities and employers (Social Work Task Force, 2009). The report built on prior strategic thinking on how the government and employer organizations may best meet the knowledge, skills and support needs of current and future social workers. The 2009 government accepted its recommendations and put in place the Social Work Reform Board in January 2010, to act on the measures needed to raise professional standards, improve the public image of the profession, and involve service users and service providers more in social work education.

The report contained much discussion on better training, working conditions and professionalism, but said little on how core social work values and anti-discriminatory practice may be embedded in the emerging structures and processes. The need for a diverse workforce, particularly greater representation from BME and older or mature groups, was included in the report (Social Work Task Force, 2009) and also, presumably, in the Social Work Reform Board's long-term implementation plans.

The modernization of qualifying and post-qualifying programmes of study began in the early 1990s and led to the development of social work degree requirements (GSCC, 2002b), which emphasized the ethical components needed to practise in contemporary society. The degree replaced the Diploma in Social Work which demanded greater evidence of anti-discriminatory and anti-racist practice in the assessment of students' competence. The move towards universal ethical principles in the degree in social work requirements meant that programmes of study were no longer obliged to enhance or test a student's knowledge, understanding and strategies concerning issues relating to 'race' and racism (Singh, 2006). The change was not critiqued in any detail within the social work literature and so the lessons which may have been learned from the relationship between the old and new thinking were not fully utilized (Higham, 2009).

The 2009 reforms provide an opportunity to examine the relevance and applicability of 'race' and racism to contemporary thinking on social work training and education. For example, the recommended career structure for social workers is now better streamlined than before, and more closely aligned with post-qualifying training (Social Work Task Force, 2009). The job titles (see Figure 6.1 below) include expert responsibilities and advanced licensed status for managers and practice educators. This is particularly important for practice educators because, like practice teachers in the past, they hold important roles as gatekeepers to the profession.

It is clear that in future such people must have better job descriptions and tighter standards. However, the content of these documents is yet to be decided. From the perspective of anti-racist practice, the time may be right to recommend that the professional responsibilities of all relevant staff incorporate the legal and policy requirements of the Race Relations (Amendment) Act 2000 and the Equality Act 2006. This would enable all members of the organization to be able to contribute to, and be held responsible for, future developments in workplace education.

Section 58 of the Care Standards Act 2000 requires the registration of qualifying and post-qualifying students, as well as procedures on suitability for practice and terminating training (GSCC, 2007). Universities must put these in place and comply with the Race Relations (Amendment) Act 2000 and the Equalities Act 2006. Registration requirements and the protected title of 'social worker' guide students and professionals towards a lifelong learning ethos. This is evidenced in, and assessed through, practice portfolios. These begin in year one of programmes of study and are built upon annually thereafter within the assessed first and subsequent years of licensed practice.

Social work programmes of study have a history of collaboration and collective responsibility towards students on qualifying courses, and also for training those who directly lead and manage workplace education. Collaborative practice such as this is likely to be formalized into partnership arrangements within which key players, such as universities, employers and service users, are asked to engage at a number of levels to develop existing knowledge on, for example, how to assess anti-racist practice.

Social work education reforms and anti-racist practice

The comprehensive review of social work has influenced education in the UK for many years, culminating in the requirements in England and Wales for degrees in social work (DH, 2002). The qualifying degree is built on the National Occupational Standards (TOPSS, 2002), the social work subject benchmark statement (QAA, 2008), and the *Codes of Practice for Social Care Workers and Employers* (GSCC, 2002a). The standards produced since then for qualifying and post-qualifying training differ in the four countries of the UK, although prior and related requirements are better aligned to support coherence and efficiency. The report by the Social Work Task Force (2009, p. 16) supports many of the principles set out in these documents and seeks further government and employer commitment to 'clear, universal and binding standards'. This suggests that the Social Work Reform Board will be open to further developmental work on areas such as ethics, values and anti-racist practice.

The Social Work Task Force Report (2009) confirms that a career structure must be easy to follow, lead to well-defined roles, and match the requirements of other professional groups. The job structure set out in Figure 6.1, and developed in Table 6.1, includes criteria for entry and progression stages for graduates, newly qualified social workers and experienced/senior staff. There is an expectation that practice experience will be built upon and expert areas developed in child protection, mental health and safeguarding (Ruch, 2009; Higham, 2009). Graduates must complete their first assessed year in employment (AYE) in appropriate organizations, for example the NSPCC or CAFCASS, and gain the licence to practise before proceeding to full registration with the social work regulatory body. At the time of writing, there is less clarity on how newly qualified social workers will be supported to gain relevant employment, and how employer organizations will be made to comply with this demand. The emerging content of the AYE does, however, provide an excellent opportunity to further develop and test anti-racist knowledge and skills within the requirements for the licensed social worker.

Advanced professional/Practice educator/Social work manager

↑↑↑

Senior licensed social worker

↑

Licensed social worker

↑

Assessment

↑

Probationary social worker

↑

Graduation

↑

Social work student

↑

Entry into the profession

Figure 6.1 A social work career structure
Source: Adapted from Social Work Task Force, 2009, p. 43

The direct link between entry and progression through the different career stages suggests that staff will enhance expert knowledge and professional confidence, as well as consolidate experience, in order to develop knowledge of particular areas, such as anti-racist practice. There is an expectation that social workers will be closely supervised in the early years by more senior/licensed managers and practice educators. Those entering the profession will keep formal records of professional development in order to document upward progress through the different stages.

Additional responsibility for the development of anti-racist practice, or other areas of anti-discrimination, with students, probationary and early career staff will need to be considered by senior staff at all levels. For example, practice educators and managers will be responsible for input on the relevant knowledge and skills needed to work with BME individuals and groups. Table 6.1 takes the career structure set out in the Social Work Task Force Report and develops it to demonstrate possible areas of responsibility for each job grade, and this can be used and developed to ensure greater relevance and applicability.

Table 6.1 Anti-racist practice in workplace education

Title	Responsibility for anti-racist practice
Advanced professional	- Demonstrating leadership by gaining the advanced teaching organization status (recommended by the Social Work Task Force Report) - Creating a research ethos, gathering evidence and disseminating relevant findings to the wider organization - Building a resource library for students and learners - Ensuring that computer-based information includes links to research on anti-racist practice and related internet resources - Including anti-racist outputs in workforce and strategic planning within and across related organizations - Overseeing anti-racist standards in management, assessment and supervision - Developing services based on demographic data on BME groups - Taking positive account of the training/development needs of BME staff
Practice educator	- Managing teaching, supervision and assessment processes - Promoting methods based on anti-racist theories and laws - Developing policies, procedures and systems on approaches to teaching, learning and assessment in relation to 'race' and racism - Highlighting library and computer resources on teaching, learning and assessment - Ensuring that all performance management processes incorporate anti-racist practice - Taking account of the supervision and assessment needs of BME students
Social work manager	- Developing the ethos of the anti-racist learning organization and/or team - Monitoring and reviewing processes - Paying regular attention to anti-racist practice in team meetings and supervision sessions - Including anti-racist outputs in individual training and development plans
Senior licensed social worker	- Testing and challenging values in the supervision of all staff, students and learners - Promoting legal and policy responsibilities on 'race' and discrimination - Taking responsibility for anti-racist practice in day-to-day work
Licensed social worker	- Contributing to anti-racist policy and practice in the team, wider organization and wider interprofessional collaboration - Promoting anti-racist principles with service users and carers - Challenging colleagues, students and service users - Supporting BME staff and students
Probationary social work	- Seeking regular and in-depth input from trainers and supervisors on anti-racist practice in the workplace
Social work student	- Reading, researching and incorporating issues of 'race' and racism in academic and practice assessment - Seeking guidance, comment and support from lecturers, tutors and practice educators to develop ethical confidence
Entrant to a qualifying social work programme of study	- Evidencing knowledge of 'race' and racism in a written test and interview - Including anti-racist practice in the values and ethics section of the selection information

Credit-rated social work courses are based on professional standards for academic and professional education, and students are required to make direct links between continuous professional development needs and maintaining their own position on the social work register (GSCC, 2006). The reform programme is rooted in the need to regulate and categorize the profession through a generic degree qualification, and follow-up post-qualifying training which allows specialization.

The social work reforms are looking for greater professional certainty in the form of well-defined systems of accountability, such as performance management (Skills for Care, 2008) and effective supervision (CWDC, 2007) both for trainee and qualified social workers. In order to make concrete the commitment of employers to social work staff, the Social Work Task Force (2009) recommends that the Care Quality Commission and Ofsted inspect the measures in place for continuous professional training and support.

However, processes which focus on the internal workings of an organization are increasingly seen to threaten empowering and participatory practice. Hughes and Wearing (2007, p. 144) suggest that social work education in the UK is founded on European ideas, and that these feed into contemporary policies and practices which limit progress on anti-racist practice: 'the ethno-centric and mono-cultural content of this education is reflected in the hierarchies and power base within the social work profession'.

The push for competent practice is found within degree programmes as well as beyond and directly affects input on broader concerns, such as social justice and wellbeing. However, a comment from a service user in the Social Work Task Force Report (2009, p. 5) suggests that competent practice is likely to be based on well-founded knowledge of the situation and context: 'Good social workers provide clarity ... They tell you what can and can't be done, what's causing problems.'

The review into the death of 'Baby P', commissioned by the then government in November 2008, found the London borough of Haringey failing at a number of levels, including an overreliance on temporary staff. Early media scrutiny into the death of Baby P highlighted two significant indicators which required follow-up action from child protection workers. First, information held by the wider family and friends and, second, the undisclosed presence in the household of the partner of Baby P's mother.

This case holds important lessons for anti-racist practice, because professional understanding of the context within which families function is critical to the quality and quantity of intervention. The Baby P case suggests that there is a clear need for the gathering of meaningful assessment information on the links between the child and their surroundings. In relation to BME families and child protection, procedural responses need to be enhanced, rather than merely administered, by trained and experienced social workers working towards the long-term improvements.

Bureaucratic procedures have been blamed by many child protection enquiries and there is a need to continuously review some approaches, such as contracts with service users and other providers. Students and staff looking for anti-racist and anti-discriminatory models of working often find procedures extremely challenging because they epitomize an inhuman management response to human services:

> By forming contractual agreements and carrying out a plan of action which theoretically has the 'client's' consent, disparities in power between the client and the worker are overlooked. Such endeavours are incompatible with anti-oppressive practice. (Dominelli, 1996, p. 159)

Organizations which promote such working practices actively sustain their own power and position. When asked for comment, service users suggest that resource-led, monolithic institutions have an overall image as poor communicators, often lacking empathy and holistic identification with people who have particular needs, such as BME service users. Students and social workers based in overly bureaucratic organizations similarly struggle to demonstrate empathy with the complex sources of disadvantage facing vulnerable children such as Baby P.

People create the cultural environment, situation and atmosphere which makes them feel comfortable and relaxed but child protection enquiries evidence that the family setting can also be a place where children are secretly hurt and wounded, sometimes over years.

The question is, how will reforming structures, such as the national College of Social Work, promote understanding of what makes a safe family, community or neighbourhood? The Social Work Taskforce Report sees better education and greater university/employer/service user collaboration in applied research as a positive way forward. This is likely to lead to improved post-qualifying training in expert areas such as child wellbeing, with a particular focus on how to gather information from secretive and manipulative parents and carers.

Enquiries into child protection condemn social workers and add weight to the stereotype of a poorly educated and inadequately managed profession. At such times, it is easy to forget the significant contribution social workers make to work with children and families on an everyday basis, performing professionally in teams and organizations under considerable financial constraints and mounting societal expectations.

The modernization and reform agenda has changed the professional landscape, as, for example, social workers are seen to be more expert because they are better trained, regulated and controlled. Professional practice has improved and social work education is more able to meet service challenges through consultation with partner organizations on curriculum design and content. Service user involvement is developing, and individuals and groups are better informed about structures and systems of delivery.

Social work reforms have been paralleled by developments more widely across the world. The expressed commitment to interventions based on core values which utilize local communities and neighbourhoods is demonstrated by the significant and well-informed professional and academic thinking within international social work. The International Federation of Social Workers (IFSW) and the International Association of Schools of Social Work (IASSW) have agreed a definition of social work, which incorporates the following ethical principles:

> The social work profession promotes social change, problem solving in human relationships and the empowerment and liberation of people to enhance well-being. Utilising theories of human behaviour and social systems, social work intervenes at the points where people interact with their environments. Principles of human rights and social justice are fundamental to social work. (IFSW/IASSW, 2004)

Although overarching and general, the definition stresses that the key role of a social worker is to work directly with individuals and groups in a context-specific manner.

Social work is now a modernized profession located in a globalized world. It is, therefore, increasingly important for trainee and qualified social workers to confidently defend core values such as anti-racist practice within both educational and practice processes through a critical engagement with the following:

- understanding on the impact of 'race' and racism locally, nationally and internationally
- articulation of what works with BME children and families
- learning about family and kinship from other parts of the world.

This would enable practitioners and students to make better connections between theory, research and evidence-based practice within their everyday work. Within anti-racist education, this is likely to lead to a debate about the difficulties of using grand theories on 'race' and racism in teaching, learning and assessment.

Equality in qualifying education

Social work has an established history of university-based education in line with other professional qualifying programmes, such as teaching and nursing, which follow similar occupational standards and codes of ethical practice. Interprofessional learning is incorporated in structures, and there is a requirement that service users are formally involved in the selection and overall delivery of programmes.

Teachers involved in delivering education have a complex range of issues to balance when addressing issues of 'race', racism and discrimination within learning processes. One area of concern relates to the socio-economic disadvantages faced by students on the grounds of disability, gender, age, literacy, numeracy, low income and poor housing. Such students carry a load over and above that which is considered normal within learning environments, and universities are increasingly providing services to such individuals. University structures respond well to students' support needs, but a large percentage of social work education occurs in welfare organizations, and this area receives surprisingly little consideration by universities. However, disability discrimination is one area of law and policy which can be seen to lead the way for the rest, and is as relevant to anti-racist practice as any other area of discrimination.

Students in need of specialist support and funding with disabilities or physical or mental health are covered under the Disability Discrimination Act 1995. Guidance to support this provides unique information on access, barriers to practice, attitudes and assumptions and practicalities (Hull University, 2005) for students with disabilities in practice learning (Sapey et al., 2004). The guidance also sets out the roles and legal responsibilities of relevant academic, administrative and agency staff, such as practice teachers and assessors. This example suggests that legal frameworks can be translated into useful, accessible information supporting and guiding group needs in society.

Another area of concern centres on the relevance and applicability of the curriculum content of the social work degree. For example, there could be more on the context and history of migrant communities in the UK, a country which has uniquely benefited from the contribution of its ex-colonies. Augoustinos and Reynolds (2001, p. 267) suggest that: 'Teaching about the historical background and social circumstances of disadvantaged groups should ... counter the pernicious tendency to make dispositional rather than situational and historical attributions for their social disadvantages.' This may occur within any curriculum area which places social work within the wider welfare state, particularly in social policy, ethics, values and human rights.

The final area of concern relates to entry and progression within social work education. Selectors and others involved in the social work admission process are required to assess personal attributes, such as mental health, literacy and numeracy, within rigorous selection and interview processes and these can incorporate the applicant's understanding of 'race' and racism within the written and verbal criteria.

The literacy requirement has implications for BME students, particularly those who have recently arrived from other European countries and may have English as a second or third language. Categorized as home students, such individuals may not receive the additional support available to others from overseas. Often the onus is on the student to declare their individual needs, but programme providers are responsible for the design and implementation of systems and should include measures which meet the particular and specific needs of such students. The statement on values and ethics asks all providers to: 'ensure that the principles of valuing diversity and equalities awareness are integral to the teaching and learning of students' (DH, 2002, p. 3). There is an emphasis on students to provide supporting evidence of competence on, for example, anti-racist practice, in order that they can progress from year 1 to year 2 and onto year 3 (DH, 2002).

Providers of social work education have interpreted these requirements in a number of ways, supported by literature which translates occupational standards into curriculum content. Green and Statham (cited in Higham, 2006) offer an approach which assesses competence at the foundational, intermediate and final stages of student development. This is developed further in Table 6.2 to incorporate anti-racist practice within the three qualifying years and the first probationary year en route to a licence to practise. Students on undergraduate courses are required to provide documentary practice evidence of progress from safety to practise (year 1), capability to practise (year 2) and finally readiness for practice (final year).

Table 6.2 Progression on anti-racist practice

Year 1 Undergraduate social work student	Year 2 Undergraduate social work student	Year 3 Undergraduate social work student	AYE (probationary)
Academic and practice evidence on *safety to practise*, which demonstrates general understanding of local, regional and national profiles of BME individuals and communities	Academic and practice evidence on *capability to practise*, which demonstrates a working knowledge of anti-racist law, policy and practice in the context of social work practice	Academic and practice evidence on *readiness for practice*, which demonstrates an ability to intervene, assess and provide a service for BME service users within a practice placement opportunity	Training, support and supervision provided by employing bodies. This should evidence a capacity to assess, plan and review a complex case which demonstrates anti-racist practice within a work situation

The academic and practice-based evidence is collected by the student and quality assured by educational providers. The increasing thickness of the vertical lines in Table 6.2 suggests that the burden to provide the appropriate quality and quantity of material to progress to the next year gets greater. The Social Work Task Force recommends that the barriers to progression, graduation and the first AYE are set to assess an evermore complex engagement with service users. There is also an expectation that suitability for social work procedures on malpractice, wellbeing, illness, mental health and personality disorders are used in the entry and progression procedures.

Student experience on applied programmes such as social work is personally and professionally taxing and additional factors, such as cultural and linguistic difference, can only add to the existing inbuilt demands. Scrutiny of processes tends to highlight the means by which structures and systems pathologize and stereotype individuals, leading to feelings such as anger, passivity, loss of control and low self-esteem (Singh, 2006). Practitioners and academics committed to sound educational standards, human welfare and student wellbeing should be adapting structures and processes which promote success rather than failure for students disadvantaged by institutional discrimination. Greater understanding may lead to better policy and procedures based on an overarching responsibility for student needs. Everyone benefits from systems which are well thought out, proactive and responsive.

Anti-racist teaching and learning in the workplace

The greatest challenges to workplace practice educators lie in realistically including content on 'race' and racism within the practice curriculum. Educators are hindered by the limited theoretical literature on anti-racist dilemmas and the constraints of time and opportunity to develop methods and approaches. At the same time, codes of ethics as well as social work law, such as the Children Act 1989 which states that 'race', culture and religion must be addressed within an assessment of need (Jowitt and O'Loughlin, 2005), require that anti-racist practice be developed.

There is a view that in order to confidently develop anti-racist practice, social work managers need to provide a working environment which is safe, open and favourable to reflective and critical practice. At the same time, there is a lingering concern that the profession is wary of engaging with the subject because the supporting literature is unhelpful: 'many of the classic anti-racist social work texts seem to be written in a rather exhortatory, preaching, hectoring style which can leave the reader feeling guilty if they find themselves questioning anything' (Wilson et al., 2008, p. 89).

There is little doubt that a good learning environment enables critical reflection on personal attitudes and professional behaviour. The Social Work Task Force Report (2009) recommends institutional support and encouragement within the two (masters) or three (undergraduate) qualifying years and the AYE. This support is to ensure that early career social workers can progress from a rhetorical to substantive command of areas such as anti-racist practice.

The Social Care Institute of Excellence (SCIE, 2003b) defines a good learning environment as a situation which is open, flexible and amenable to the following:

- learning from innovative anti-racist practice
- feedback from BME students
- positive and constructive supervision and appraisal systems
- shared beliefs, values, goals and objectives
- use of research and evidence on 'race' and racism
- change and development
- leadership approaches which model anti-racist practice.

So for a student or a learner, a workplace should have good administrative systems, accessible and readily available information, people who value, understand and support educational processes, and a warm and welcoming ethos. People in charge of training and development should actively contribute to anti-racist policies on, for example, induction for new staff, good supervisory practice and assessment in the workplace. A combination of equality and social work laws should also be followed even though they may provide little force or compulsion to enable the development of anti-racist practice.

The National Occupational Standards (TOPSS, 2002) provide the foundation for assessing students and newly qualified social workers. The changes in the social work qualifying requirements expand the remit of social care organizations to provide learning opportunities which cater for all learners. As a result, many social work, health and related agencies are preparing to develop detailed policy and practice on workplace education, which has resulted in the examination of what constitutes a good learning environment. In order to promote this, the Social Work Task Force Report (2009) recommends that organizations consider gaining advanced teaching organization status, a move that is likely to encourage better practical support for social work staff in training.

The merger of social work children's departments with the education services, and the assimilation of health-based social workers into the NHS, has brought into focus the role and capacity of social work professionals in multi-professional settings (Higham, 2006). In this context, social workers are based within larger, more powerful organizations, such as hospitals and schools, where values and anti-racist practice may be conceived differently by professionals such as teachers, nurses and doctors. In situations where students and social workers are outnumbered, the dominant professional standards apply, and social workers struggle to maintain core values and develop professional identities while also sustaining engagement with service users:

> Social workers are ambivalent about distancing themselves from services users by claiming professional authority and expertise; at the same time, there has been considerable scepticism from elsewhere about the validity for social workers' claims for professional authority and expertise. (Smith, 2009, p. 146)

Students, practice educators and social workers committed to anti-racist practice require expertise as well as enhanced confidence to challenge racism and discrimination in multi-professional contexts. However, there is evidence to suggest that students are more likely to demonstrate broader ethical knowledge and understanding within practice assignments. A study undertaken by Heron (2006) compared assignments produced by two student groups in Britain and the USA on evidence of critical thinking on 'race'. Heron found that British students are more likely to confuse or replace 'race' with 'ethnicity', or even leave out references to anti-racist practice, and still pass assignments. This suggests that students may be wary of anti-racist practice and are instead using 'ethnicity' to evidence knowledge of 'race'. Practice educators clearly need to examine the depth of understanding in such work and seek training which enables them to provide teaching based on sound knowledge.

In relation to issues of 'race' and racism, the following principles may be usefully used to demonstrate general competence, knowledge and understanding:

- empathy with, and appreciation of, BME perspectives
- lessons learned from past experiences of racism and discrimination
- understanding of relevant organizational policies and procedures
- critical use of applicable research and evidence-based practice
- recognition, use and development of appropriate models of work
- understanding of the relationship between race, discrimination and oppression.

Such principles are echoed elsewhere in the world. For example, the Council on Social Work Education in the USA asks that attention be paid to 'race' and ethnicity within teaching, learning and assessment processes (King Pike, 2002). Students are required to reflect on their own experience, ethnicity and culture in relation to advantage/disadvantage, and educational providers are encouraged to create environmental conditions which promote understanding.

Principles of learning

Egalitarian adult education principles are largely based on the thinking of educators, such as Brazilian Paulo Freire, who defined learning as a broad facilitative and interactive process. According to Higham (2006, p. 137):

> Freire's pedagogy promotes a problem-solving style of learning – a method of participatory adult education that uses dialogue of mutual respect between the facilitator/teacher and the learner, where each participates equally in the learning process and learns from each other.

Explicit methods and approaches which are open to challenge and review are inherent within this thinking and have been used to inform social work education in Britain. An accurate and understandable exchange which is fair to all key stakeholders, but principally students and learners, has been acknowledged as the key to good practice. Assessment must be authentic and pitched at different levels and abilities depending on the type of course, for example undergraduate or postgraduate, past experience and stage of development.

Figure 6.2 illustrates the different elements which can inform the assessment of a social work student in relation to legal, procedural and theoretical understanding of issues of 'race' and racism. However, applied knowledge cannot be judged in isolation, it needs to be considered in relation to individual motivating influences relayed through actions, thoughts and emotions, that is, doing, thinking and feeling. Students are aware that educational experiences should be dynamic and flexible as well as allow concrete evidence of competence in the assessment processes.

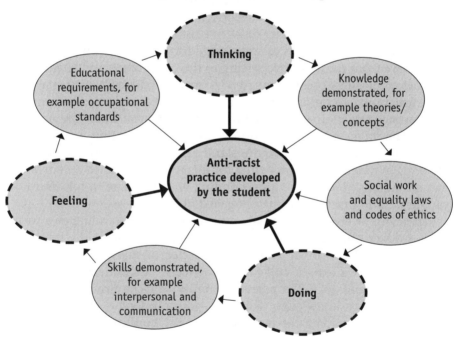

Figure 6.2 Assessment of anti-racist practice

Reflecting on the relationship between thoughts, emotions and actions is a good place to examine the impact any individual has on others. It also provides an opportunity to explore, for example, the difference between racist thoughts and racist deeds. This distinction is important because not all racist ideas are followed by racist activity. Racism occurs when action follows thought and/or attitude.

King Pike's (2002) examination of a range of studies on self-perception of prejudice revealed that the majority of BME individuals recognized discrimination at group rather than individual level. This suggests that the personal experience of racism is either being denied or downplayed by BME individuals. Assuming that white people are also likely to view prejudice at a group rather than individual level, analysis of personal and professional white identity may be a good point at which to evaluate self in relation to others. It may generate an interesting debate and lead to the early sharing of ideas on identity, ethnicity, culture and background within a practice placement.

Social work placements

One of the important challenges for social work students lies in maintaining control of their learning and development, while navigating their course of study. The early experiences of social work students are similar to those of other undergraduates/postgraduates who participate in all available activities in a rather exclusive, often safe, university environment. The pathway diverts at some stage for social work students when they move from the academic setting to the often harsh and challenging realities of a welfare organization led by operational needs. This change is both functional and psychological, as students move physically from one environment to another, that is, university to a social work/care organization. The move from one important role to another, that is, student to social worker-in-training, is more significant. The support provided for students in planning and preparing for this transfer is varied and dependent on the knowledge and understanding of the change in role and task (academic and practice) of those engaged in the process.

Measuring levels of conceptual and practical understanding of a social work student during the early stages of the placement, at the midpoint and at the end is normal assessment practice in the UK. However, the requirement to integrate anti-racist practice in assessment documentation is not mandatory. The assessor's ability to recognize and comment on the student's knowledge, skills and commitment is critical but the practice educator may not feel professionally confident in developing and using anti-racist methods of learning and assessment.

The focus on a positive outcome requires consideration of the power inherent in the relationship between the student and those around them. The practice educator is the person with the overall responsibility for ensuring that the student's learning is maximized and that all the documentation is completed by the relevant person at the right time. The practice educator, in conjunction with the supervisor and others involved in the assessment process, makes the final judgement on whether the student has met professional standards at the right level. As illustrated by Figure 6.3, the practice educator role is powerful and may impact substantially on the student's future career as an anti-racist practitioner. The student is at the core of the learning experience, supported by the practice teacher and the supervisor, but the link to the organization is through to the team and the line manager. The practice educator may work in the same organization as the student is placed or may be off site in another team or agency. Either way they hold the most important role (illustrated by the bolder box lines), while the supervisor provides day-to-day workload support (illustrated by the thinner box lines) and the line manager, within the team context, has a looser but important responsibility as a provider of the practice placement (illustrated by the dotted box lines).

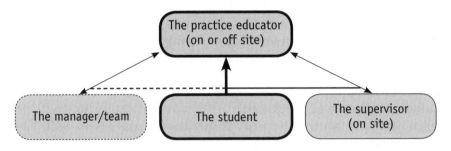

Figure 6.3 Precise assessment relationships

Although this model appears hierarchical, the thin and thick lines illustrate communication links and the clarity in the roles and responsibilities of those involved in judging the student's performance on issues of 'race' and racism. So the practice educator will oversee the practice placement and seek evidence of competent practice, which the student will be guided to generate at the right level and stage of development. The practice educator and the student have the strongest links, while the on-site supervisor will contribute to the learning outcomes, caseload management, supervision, observation of practice and feedback on the student's performance. The manager will hold organizational responsibilities in relation to the student's work and the team will contribute to the gathering of wider practice evidence.

Problems often occur when transparent lines of accountability are missing and the student is assessed on anti-racist practice in a messy, unfiltered or even nominal manner. Figure 6.4 offers a more egalitarian, inclusive approach, but it involves too many people offering the different levels of input on competence, although the practice educator, supported by the supervisor, still has the overall task of judging and reporting on the student's performance. The strongest link here should also be between the student and the practice educator but the relationship is likely to hindered by the number of people involved and poor lines of communication.

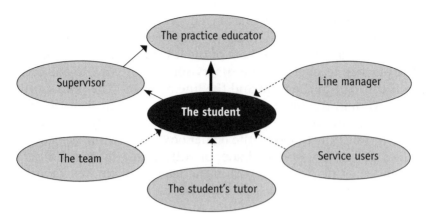

Figure 6.4 Imprecise assessment relationships

Evidence suggests that an insufficient examination of how students are supported leads to ill-formed methods and approaches to discrimination and oppression (Badwall et al., 2004). This is illustrated by Harjeet Badwall's candid account of her experiences as a woman of colour and a student on placement, working in a Canadian health agency with few policies and procedures. Her story shows how workers from BME backgrounds are sometimes viewed by such organizations. In her practice placement, Harjeet was assigned the role as a fixer of conflict between staff members, as well as being an expert and representative on issues of 'race' and class. This meant that although she was an inexperienced member of staff, she was given the responsibility of developing anti-racist practice because of her BME background. This experience highlighted a number of issues for Harjeet:

- the commitment of social care agencies, which identify as anti-racist, to issues of 'race' and racism
- the importance of knowledge and law
- the integration of anti-racist practice into everyday working
- the delegation of responsibility for anti-racist practice to junior staff
- the importance of critical reflection on the advantages and privileges of being white
- the dangers of overrelying on BME workers as 'race' experts.

Harjeet's conclusions also stress that anti-racist practice undertaken by BME professionals requires expert knowledge, high status and substantial training. For example, specific supervision, guidance and support is needed by people listening and responding to racist incidents and oppressive experiences because the process is stressful and can be exposing. Long-term work, such as policy development, can also be demanding and requires confident people able to utilize alliances with like-minded activists.

This experience of newly recruited workers in an agency with limited policy and procedure is no doubt being replicated throughout the world but, although generally complex and difficult, Badwall et al. (2004, p. 150) suggest that all staff must pursue anti-racism as an organizational goal: 'Even though white people cannot understand the "lived" experiences of racism, there must be in place a commitment from all involved, to finding points of connection. It is in this most challenging arena, we can attempt to create change.'

Methods of supervision

Supervision in social work organizations has been at the core of policy reform, for example in relation to standard setting, frequency and quality of supervision (Social Work Task Force, 2009).

Good supervisory practice is an important formalized means of communication between the supervisee (student) and the supervisor (practice teacher/assessor). Freire (1972) suggests that dialogue such as this enhances critical thinking, as long as supervisors do not simply impart information based on their own perspectives and realities. Methods must be based on an understanding of, and empathy with, individual requirements. Freire (1972, p. 66) further proposes that the lack of advanced consideration of, and attention to, individual needs is not only oppressive, but may lead to indoctrination:

> For the truly humanist educator, and the authentic revolutionary, the object of action is the reality to be transformed by them together with other men – not other men themselves. The oppressors are the ones who act upon men to indoctrinate them and adjust them to a reality which must remain untouched.

Supervision offers an opportunity to reflect on practice in its entirety and provides valuable time for exploration, reflection, learning and problem solving. The process should broadly benefit the worker, service users, the team and the agency, while focusing on accountability, case analysis and worker development. Social work has managed to develop a management process which readily encompasses a range of outcomes: 'Few work settings can claim a mechanism which at its best so smoothly combines the oversight of work undertaken, staff performance appraisal, staff development and staff care considerations' (Coulshed and Mullender, 2001, p. 163).

The supervision brief may incorporate many tasks and the supervisor may have a particular perspective which is constant or varies according to the job in hand. So a person may perform differently or the same depending on individual personality and professional context as a manager, administrator, educator and/or as someone who develops/supports/promotes natural ability (Coulshed and Mullender, 2001). Anti-racist practice, however, requires consistent commitment incorporated within all methods and approaches. Those engaged in the task may therefore need to critically reflect on their preferred way of working and then consider the following question: how can anti-racist practice be included in the tasks performed on a daily basis by me, by the student, by the team and by the organization?

The central purpose of supervision is to improve services and meet managerial, administrative, educational, developmental, support and advocacy needs (Coulshed and Mullender, 2001). Examples of good supervision suggest that the supervisor/supervisee assess and understand each other's adult learning styles. People who manage the relationship well are able to rely on the integrity of the other person, talk with ease, share tasks such as supervision notes, take time to understand the other person's perspective, manage time skilfully and deal with difficult situations. In relation to anti-racist practice, adult learning process should take into account issues such as a person's linguistic skills, culture, religion, faith and other forms of difference. Supervisors and supervisors who manage this sensitively are likely to build well-honed relationships based on sound understanding of theoretical approaches to adult learning.

Good supervisory practice requires individual as well as organizational commitment but despite guidance from social work care councils, supervisors struggle to safeguard the space to evaluate interventions with service users and reflect on the lessons learned. Fortunately, the days when supervision was seen as mere rumination have passed and it has gained greater credibility as a viable professional process within which a critical social worker can reflect on action (Schön, 1991).

In a bid to promote the development of good practice, it is useful to consider the principles for effective daily supervision offered by Caspi and Reid (2002, p. 55):

- Teach in small chunks
- Use direction and authority appropriately on racist dilemmas
- Prioritize and focus on work of greatest concern but allow time for anti-discriminatory practice
- Plan, prepare and structure supervision in an anti-racist and anti-discriminatory manner
- Provide ongoing, specific, useful and constructive feedback
- Incorporate adult learning principles
- Use a building block approach which maximizes personal knowledge and experiences
- Act as a role model on anti-racist practice
- Embed incremental and developmental learning
- Balance equity, fairness, autonomy and dependence
- Follow law, policy and good practice on human rights and equality.

These principles allow for the development of positive, confident approaches which avoid negative supervision styles that constrict and disempower through insufficient autonomy and control. Supervision based on the needs of the learner is likely to result in good, individualized practice.

Approaches that restrict opportunities for decision making tend to result in the development of untested basic skills, and so it is better to avoid the following:

- Reactive, unstructured or imprecise supervision which provides insufficient management responsibility, guidance and direction for the supervisee
- Therapeutic and counselling approaches which focus on individual pathology or failings
- Overwatchful supervision which lacks warmth, understanding and empathy.

Practice such as this is particularly problematic in relation to anti-racist practice, as a manager or supervisor who does not take full responsibility for the student or supervisee is unlikely to actively address discrimination or advocate on their behalf.

Brown and Bourne (1996) suggest that treating everyone equally without due allowance for style and perspective is discriminatory. Pathological approaches which contribute to oppressive practices rather than challenge structural and/or institutional barriers and constraints are also a problem.

Supervisors who micro-manage may also be criticized for primarily looking for problems. The inability to empathize or understand the perspective of others may be seen as a significant deficit in the personality of a practice teacher, supervisor or assessor.

In relation to the development of good practice, Boe (1996) suggests that supervisors and assessors are more likely to succeed in supporting students' development if they are skilful in:

- identifying and summarizing problems
- proposing a hypothesis
- reflecting, planning and evaluating.

They must also have an understanding of communicative competency, that is, establishing relationships and demonstrating respect, loyalty and empathy. There is a requirement to understand and assess the supervisee's technical competency, oral and written skills as well as their analytic competency. In order that this can be achieved, it is important to examine the factors which may either help or hinder learning and development (Boe, 1996). Table 6.3 sets out some of the areas which can enable those involved in educational processes to maximize anti-racist practice by setting some outcomes, approaches and principles used in day-to-day practice.

Table 6.3 Anti-racist responses to learning in the workplace

Areas	Responses
The organizational context	Development of appropriate images and representations
Vision, aims and objectives	Clear and explicit expression of anti-racist principles
Practice methods	Application of anti-racist theories and research evidence
Management and supervision	Performance management based on anti-racist ideas
Roles and responsibilities	Clearly defined anti-racist duties in student/worker learning agreements/contracts
Relationships	Anti-discriminatory attitudes and behaviour
Working arrangements	Rooted in ideas such as respect, fairness and justice
Daily activities/routines	Examined for inbuilt biases in supervision and assessment

Conclusions

Developing educational practice requires knowledge which tests and challenges all key stakeholders in the process. This chapter has focused on some of these areas and highlighted the importance of including anti-racist perspectives in broader institutional policy and procedures and programmes of study. In particular, social work reforms provide an opportunity for a new direction in post-qualifying education based on the needs of students and early career social workers, incorporating service user involvement. The need for learning environments which are safe and open as well as anti-racist in perspective is clearer than before.

The challenge is to address preconceived notions and ideas and replace them with knowledge which is practical and useful, as well as anti-racist. However, this requires a great deal of commitment which, if translated into qualifying and post-qualifying courses, will allow programme providers to expand the ethical content in curriculum design and delivery. But the demands on educators are likely to increase, and many will continue to prioritize immediate challenges and so will require regular reminders about the specific inclusion of 'race' and racism within educational processes.

Social workers are meeting exacting legal and policy demands on a daily basis and dealing with these by developing practice wisdom and intelligence. However, policy makers, leaders and managers need constant prompting to support approaches which allow a critical evaluation of uncertain situations or unique interventions.

Good educational practice, therefore, promotes a level of usefulness and coherence which learns from, and builds on, established individual and group practice and is framed within context and situation. Above all, scholarship in the workplace requires an advanced understanding of the complexity of human interaction in a manner which develops dynamic and confident ideas, values and principles and promotes inclusive and alternative perspectives.

implications for practice

Social workers wishing to develop policy and practice on workplace learning require planning and coordination as well as strategic management skills. In relation to 'race' and racism, practice educators are best placed to produce procedural guidance on what constitutes professional competence and what represents valid evidence. Attention needs to be paid to the quality, quantity and source of documentary information on which any learner is assessed, in order that occupational standards and operational knowledge can be judged alongside content on anti-racist practice.

Standardizing educational requirements is a key driver for social work reforms but documents such as the Social Work Task Force Report (2009) need to address the resource shortfall which results in the reduction of training and development budgets in recessionary times. Managers affected by short-term goals struggle to see the longer term workforce, quality and gatekeeping advantages of workplace education. In this scenario, practice education requires strong leadership to develop and maintain standards which inform anti-racist practice with students and other learners. Education also has to be sold better to operational staff; for example, good training should result in greater efficiency and better information in case records, reports, files and supervision discussion/notes particularly in relation to BME service users.

main points

- The 2009 report by the government-appointed Social Work Task Force recommends improved professional standards and better regulation by the proposed national College of Social Work. It also asks for greater alignment between entry requirements, initial and subsequent training, and formalized partnerships between key stakeholders in social work education, for example universities and employers.

- The IFSW/IASSW (2004) code of ethics defines the key roles and tasks of social workers as promoting problem solving, social change, empowerment, the liberation of people and the enhancement of society. Principles of human rights and social justice are fundamental to social work.

- The social work degree requirements ask for supporting evidence of competence in year 1, 2 and 3 (DH, 2002). Within this, students must demonstrate professional development in relation to anti-racist practice.

- Self-reflection needs to be introduced early to students in order that they can understand and define racism.
- Discrimination generally occurs when action follows thought and/or attitude.
- Workforce planning and continuous professional development are key organizational goals (Coulshed and Orme, 2006), but excessive workloads leave little supervision time to consider wider questions.

stop and think

- Do you agree with Neate's (2001) suggestion that social work is at a critical stage in its development?
- Social workers have an image as poor communicators, often lacking empathy and identification with service users. What do you think of this statement?
- Is it important for social workers to be able to work across national borders as decreed by the EU in the Bologna Declaration (Dominelli, 2004)?
- Social work students are encouraged to seek efficient, dynamic, flexible educational experiences. Has your experience reflected this?
- A significant concern about professional codes is that they are based on confused western thought and may be difficult to apply to the interests of BME groups. What do you think?
- Do professional codes of practice and conduct adequately guide and support moral positions and ethical practice on what is right as well as what is good?

taking it further

- Badwall, H., O'Connor, P. and Rossiter, A. (2004) Living out histories and identities in organisations: a case study from three perspectives, in Gould, N. and Baldwin, M. (eds) *Social Work, Critical Reflection and the Learning Organisation*, Ashgate, Aldershot.
  The authors explore a model of reflective practice within organizational change from the perspective of a team manager, a visiting professor and a newly employed social worker who was previously on placement as a student. This suggests that insufficient examination of organizational power and function is leading to ill-formed methods and approaches to discrimination and oppression. The authors conclude that, through this analysis, they learned to 'respect the complexity of competing agendas, power and historical subjectivities in reflective processes' (p. 160).
- Freire, P. (1972) *Pedagogy of the Oppressed*, Penguin Books, Harmondsworth.
  Freire suggests that education is key to liberation and that dialogue enhances critical thinking. Creative communication based on individual

perspective and reality moves beyond a simple exchange of information. Freire further proposes that poor consideration of individual needs is not only oppressive but may lead to indoctrination.

■ King Pike, C. (2002) Measuring racial climate in schools of social work: instrument development and validation, *Research in Social Work Practice*, **12**(1): 29–46.

An interesting example of a research project measuring the 'racial climate in programs and schools of social work' in the USA. Offers a sound analysis of a survey instrument derived from racial climate indicators defined as 'student's subjective perceptions of how both faculty and their peers generally responded to issues and people of diversity' (p. 33). The author suggests that anti-racist practice requires research assessment in order that educators can develop methods and tools to support evidence-based practice.

7 Conclusions

The overarching aim of this book has been to evaluate the relevance of anti-racist social work practice to contemporary public services. The book has brought together and introduced the relevant influences which have informed anti-racist practice within the UK and beyond (Chapters 1 and 2), set out the argument for knowledge-based professional practice within organizations (Chapters 3 and 4) and stressed the importance of incorporating service user perspectives (Chapter 5) in all areas of service delivery, including educational practice (Chapter 6).

In order to inform future developments, this chapter draws the general themes together and consolidates the key ideas on anti-racist practice for students, social workers, service users and BME people. The areas of focus relate to the social work duty to implement universal standards, promote knowledge-based practice and embrace change through education and training. If professionals see the relevance of anti-racist practice, they are likely to benefit from learning which is beyond their immediate experience. If social workers base their work on knowledge and evidence, they will be able to argue their case and make a difference to BME service users. If they are able to work positively with uncertainty, they will be able to inform learning on how professionals can be resilient in the face of change. If they contribute to social work education, the profession will be energized and have a bigger voice in welfare generally, and on anti-racism in particular. All this will be possible if social workers follow their duties as professionals and develop policies and procedures which promote anti-racist practice.

Universal influences

The analysis of national and international thinking suggests that social work is on the path to improve service standards, and along the way it is discovering new and efficient ways from other countries. Maintaining a professional identity on the national and international stage is also an emerging area for development, steered by organizations such as the British Association of Social Workers (BASW), the International Association of Schools of Social Work (IASSW) and the International Federation of Social Workers (IFSW). It is clear that professionals have to place themselves alongside others contributing to social justice and articulate ethical reasons for developing it further.

Understanding social work within a broader ethical context is particularly relevant to anti-racist practice. Practitioners with a sound, working knowledge of 'race' and racism are more likely to translate philosophical thinking into contemporary practice in an unencumbered and workable manner.

A great deal of law and policy in 'race' relations has been generated by social unrest and campaigning by BME individuals who have acted to improve service standards, representation and consultation. Community cohesion has been an area of particular concern for BME communities and poor integration remains a nagging issue for the government and bodies such as the Equality and Human Rights Commission (EHRC). Divisions based on colour, class, religion, culture and ethnic background (CRE, 2006) persistently contribute to group isolation.

There continues to be a divide between organizations promoting equality and those representing social workers, when it could be argued that welfare staff work on a daily basis with people facing discrimination and disadvantage. It is clear that organizations that embody professional interests, such BASW or the emerging national College of Social Work, need to have a stronger input into public policy on poverty and social exclusion. BME social workers and academics also have particular and specific experiences but have little voice on the national or global stage on anti-racist practice or social work more generally.

Tuhiwai Smith (2008) suggests that BME or indigenous perspectives are critical to the development of research-led social care because they are informed by important histories and traditions as well as struggles and ideals. White people in the UK have contributed a great deal to BME practice and research (Dominelli, 1988, 2008); this work has run in parallel with that done by BME activists (Sivanandan, 1991; Solomos and Back, 1995). The contribution made by all must be acknowledged in order that anti-racist practice continues to be seen as a concern of the majority as well as the minority.

The relationship between global imperatives and local need is being challenged as nation states respond to security threats such as terrorism. Held et al. (2001) suggest that external threats are leading countries to secularize society and eradicate cultural difference. On one hand, internationally understood notions of diversity are promoted as valuable and, on the other hand, there is a flattening of different cultural and religious perspectives by individual countries. For social workers and students, the messages are contradictory and complex but easier to access within an age where the World Wide Web has made the critical use of information more manageable as well as more unwieldy.

Knowledge-based practice

The principles set out in documents on modernizing social work are derived from international standards on civil, political and social rights, as well as the desire to regulate the profession. Anti-racist practice can build on historical knowledge but must be relevant to the time and place, because statements of intent are inclined to be broad and need to be translated into working policies and procedures. For example, the Social Work Task Force Report (2009) commented on the need for a diverse workforce and greater representation from BME groups. This requires further work in the first instance by the implementation body, the Social Work Reform Board, in order that anti-racist principles can be included and made concrete in professional regulation and registration systems. For example, standards have to be developed on:

- anti-racist practice within reporting, auditing and inspection systems
- training and support for BME staff and students
- teaching and research on 'race' and racism
- assessment of anti-racist practice for students and newly qualified social workers in the workplace
- curriculum on anti-racist practice in qualifying and post-qualifying programmes of study
- BME service user involvement in practice and education.

Terminology needs particular attention in all areas of ethical practice. Words have legal meaning in the UK and public sector workers are aware that poor use of language may appear discriminatory and abusive. Communication is at the heart of social work and so the profession is well placed to inform the development of skills and values in this area, particularly in assessment and reporting processes.

Social work agencies are in a good position to comment on all areas of welfare but particularly on anti-discriminatory practice within teams and organizations. Direct interventions are examined on a daily basis but there needs to be more discussion on how structures and systems, such as policies on effective communication, support professional values such as anti-racism.

Working with change

Social workers are generally able to work with change and uncertainty (Fook, 2000), but may not always have the necessary knowledge and skills to deal with ambiguity and doubt. This sometimes leads professionals to focus on practice skills rather than attempt an understanding of broader concepts and theories which offer explanations (Ford et al., 2004). Welfare resources and budgetary duties drive them further to prioritize service and workforce demands, and this leaves most practitioners too exhausted to pursue higher thinking and development.

The Social Work Task Force Report (2009) offers a structural solution in the form of continuous professional training which fits with career pathways and status on a par with other public sector workers. This offers employer-led guidance, support and training. Linked to registration and licensing requirements, this is a welcome move for social workers seeking to consolidate their professional standing. For BME staff, it offers additional opportunities for progression and advancement.

The commitment to the participation and involvement of service users from BME and other backgrounds is integrated into the modernization agenda. These developments have highlighted the commonalities between service users generally and BME groups, particularly in relation to strategies on challenging established systems and structures.

Social workers are dealing with many changes and are increasingly looking to understand and respond strategically, particularly in relation to:

- theorizing practice
- gaining confidence in specialist areas
- seeking service user views
- developing resilience and coping strategies.

Educating social workers

Students and newly qualified social workers are trained to understand the application of information and communication technology to welfare standards. Global influences have impacted on the development of common educational standards which allow students and employees to work within the EU (Soydan and Williams, 1998).

The IFSW/IASSW (2004) code of ethics suggests that human rights and social justice are key concerns for social work, and defines the key tasks as problem solving, enabling social change and liberating people. Social work students have to make sense of big ideological, theoretical concepts such as these and apply them to the local situation, taking account of the needs of the individual and family in a meaningful and useful way.

Social workers' programmes of study are complex and varied (Hawkins and Shohet, 2006) and include academic/practice components separated into three areas of development, that is, knowledge, skills and values. In addition, anti-racist practice requires students to evaluate their personal and professional identity in relation to discrimination and racism, which in turn may be assessed and challenged.

Lifelong learning and continuous professional development are important structures within which social workers can embed and enhance specialist expert knowledge. This is supported by the care councils of the UK, which offer mandatory guidance and underpinning rules in the codes of practice and conduct. The codes of practice support the progress of individuals and the codes of conduct oppose poor, incompetent work. The latter can be used particularly well to challenge discriminatory practices such as the unfair treatment of BME service users and staff.

Social workers generally believe in anti-racist practice, but find it difficult to reflect on their own power and privilege within the wider institution. Thompson (2006) suggests that professionals and academics need to critically examine the deep roots of hierarchical power as it can be used in an inconsistent and conflicting way, and allow practices which collude with group or institutional discrimination.

The anti-racist duty

The duty to be anti-racist is most compelling for social work professionals. The Equality Act 2006 and the EHRC regularly ask public authorities in Britain to produce race equality schemes in relation to general and specific performance. Regional autonomy, however, means that inconsistencies are common across the four countries of the UK and hinder the application of laws on racism and equality.

Social work laws are also problematic because they generally relate to specific duties to service user groups, but do little to directly address structural inequalities and discrimination. Students are taught a great deal about law in practice but are driven by assessment tasks which require applied knowledge of child protection, mental health and community care statute. Texts on social work law touch fleetingly on 'race', equality and discrimination. At the same time, the government, through bodies such as the EHRC, requires general adherence by all public service providers.

The argument for better knowledge informed by research is well made but public sector organizations need to address individual need as well as group disadvantage. BME people in general are as likely to face prejudice and discrimination collectively as individually. Building on the work of its predecessor, the Commission for Racial Equality, the EHRC defines the nature, source and act of racism and links to equal rights, poverty, low income and poor housing in its guidance.

King Pike (2002) found that BME groups are, however, more affected than BME individuals. Complexities such as this require some attention from social work research and literature, in order that more can be learned about how BME groups as well as individuals are seen by the profession and other service users. Social work also needs concrete evidence of the relationship between service provision, care giving, family and kinship (Ahmad and Atkin, 1996).

Adhering to procedure and guidance is something social workers do with ease but anti-racist practice requires additional policy development in, for example, the following areas:

- consistent national and regional application of anti-racist laws and policies
- knowledge and capacity building on the complex issues faced by BME service users
- ethical language which enables a better articulation of professional ideology.

The work undertaken on inequalities globally by the United Nations and nationally by the CRE and the EHRC has run parallel with the development of ethical principles by organizations such as the British Association of Social Workers. The foundations for anti-racist practice have been built on the premise that racial discrimination will continue to exist in the foreseeable future. This poses interesting questions for contemporary policy makers seeking to address the many-sided aspects of discrimination and understand the intersections between 'race', age, ethnicity, gender, age, sexuality and class (McGhee, 2008).

Identity is equally problematic for the majority white population who struggle to articulate the complexity of national values and sense of belonging (Modood, 2007).

There is little doubt that amalgamating groups has led to a better understanding of how multiple identities are constructed but there is a real danger that placing everyone in the same category will result in welfare winners and losers because resources and services will be targeted towards larger, more powerful population groups (Dominelli, 2004). In order to avoid this, categorization based on racial difference needs to be protected by governments within policies and laws (McGhee, 2008). However, this has to be informed by a clear, socially constructed definition of 'race' relations based on the sociological synthesis offered by Rex (2000):

- a situation of differentiation, inequality and pluralism as between groups
- clear distinction between such groups by their physical appearance, culture or ancestry
- the justification and explanation of this discrimination in terms of some kind of implicit or explicit theory.

Self-identification is important but anti-racist practitioners should be aware of and respond confidently to BME service users who use cultural difference as a smoke screen to avoid investigation. If social workers or other professionals had questioned, understood and justified the reasons for decision making in cases such as Victoria Climbié, the learning on how to work with families who use culture and kinship to manipulate the system would have been more comprehensively embedded in child protection procedures and other tragedies may have been averted.

Dominelli (1997, p. 148) suggests a campaigning, transformational approach to anti-racist practice and calls for concurrent change at the 'individual, institutional and cultural' levels within and across social work organizations. It may be that accepting and planning for the inevitability of change is not only liberating (Gilroy, 2000) but also more likely to lead to a redistribution of 'social power and resources' (Dominelli, 1997).

Glossary

Anti-discriminatory practice (see Discrimination below) – Aims to challenge structural, institutional and personal discrimination faced by individuals and groups on a number of grounds including 'race', age, gender and disability: 'an approach to social work practice which seeks to reduce, undermine or eliminate discrimination and oppression' (Thompson, 1993, p. 31).

It has a basis in all equal opportunities law and policy frameworks and aims to improve the circumstances of individuals and groups discriminated against on the grounds of 'race', sex, age, disability, religion, ethnic origin and cultural difference. It is derived from universal principles set out in professional codes such as the British Association of Social Workers code of ethics (BASW, 2002) and the codes of practice (covering both employees and employers) of the social care councils of the UK. These are incorporated in the social work degree requirements and the National Occupational Standards (DH, 2002).

Anti-oppressive practice – Within the UK anti-oppression is generally defined as a societal response to domination and suppression of one group over another (Thompson, 2003). It is a complex, overarching idea which can challenge structures as well as personal and psychological influences. In relation to the public sector, anti-oppressive practice asks the social work professional or student to change at three levels, that is, intellectual, emotional and practical

(Dominelli, 2004). Anti-oppressive practice seeks significant political and institutional change and is therefore hard to achieve. It is resource intensive and requires a significant shift in economic and political power for the social worker and the organization. Dominelli (2002, p. 5) suggests that defining anti-oppressive practice is key to understanding and achieving it:

Anti-oppressive practice, insofar as it is preoccupied with the implementation of social justice, is intimately bound up with notions of improving the quality of life or well being of individuals, groups and communities. This concern lends it a holistic mantle which encompasses all aspects of social life – culture, institutions, legal frameworks, political systems, socio-economic infrastructure and interpersonal relationships which both create and are created by social reality.

Anti-racist practice – Anti-racist practitioners challenge racist views, attitudes and behaviours in a methodical manner and maintain a focus on laws and policies. The legal duties of the public sector are set out in the Race Relations Act 1976, the Race Relations (Amendment) Act 2000 and the Equality Act 2006 and aim to improve the circumstances of BME groups in relation to goods, employment and (social) services. There is a statutory expectation that the service providers respond to disadvantage based on racial, cultural and religious difference.

Proponents of anti-racism ask that 'race' is seen as a social construct and suggest that social workers and students acquire a working knowledge of the processes which perpetuate racism within teams, organizations, structures and systems. Anti-racist advocates are more likely to challenge colleagues, employers and policy makers.

Anti-racist practice was commonly used in the 1980s by local government and, in particular, by the Greater London Council (GLC), which declared London as an 'anti-racist zone' and 1984 as anti-racist year (Gilroy, 1995, p. 138). Initiatives such as this allowed BME individuals, often peripheral in political systems, to gain greater access to the routines and conventions of public organizations. However, the influence gained by such thinkers was suppressed by the government, led by Margaret Thatcher, who subsequently abolished the GLC and many radical initiatives which promoted and empowered anti-racist community action.

Social care staff have been guided and trained to promote anti-racism, but some methods of training have been challenged. For example, during the 1980s, approaches to racism awareness training (RAT) became a focus for critics of social work because they were seen as oppressive towards white trainees (Solomos and Back, 1995). However, although the methods used within RAT raised questions about power and powerlessness, advocates of the approach legitimately challenged racist practices by social workers and other public sector staff (Dominelli, 1988). Poor practices such as RAT allowed critics to dismiss related (legally defined) concepts such as anti-discriminatory practice (Thompson, 2003) as politically correct.

Political correctness (PC) was derived from the experience of academics and students on university campuses in the USA where educational programmes sought to address past injustices such as slavery by linking them to 'race' and racism in contemporary multiracial societies (Solomos and Back, 1996). Political correctness was seen to overcompensate for the past, through affirmative or positive action, and was ridiculed both in the USA and the UK at the time. As a result, subsequent developments on anti-racist social work practice were hindered in Britain for a number of years. However, the debate that took place provided an important backdrop to contemporary thinking on the many complex and interesting questions about the nature, sources and acts of racism.

Assimilation – Assimilation suggests a cultural sucking in of the newly arrived immigrant into the host society. Sivanandan (2007, p. 49) proposes that this is 'absorption of the lesser into the greater', an idea which has been discussed since the 1970s, a time when the British were uneasy about influences from other countries but demonstrated charitable tolerance of new ideas. As Husband (1991a, p. 53) states, 'a tolerant society should not be confused with an equitable and just society'.

Black perspectives – The black perspectives movement promoted an engagement with issues of 'race' based on the lived and dynamic experiences rather than a purely theoretical understanding. The approach emerged during the 1980s and was advocated by Ely and Denney (1987), Ahmad (1990) and other writers who recommended that black workers and service users be actively consulted and their views incorporated in the provision of social and public services in order to promote sound values, moral principles and good interpersonal skills. Some of this thinking suggested that a practitioner could hold and apply anti-racist principles only if they were from a black and/or BME background.

Colour blind – The colour blind approach promotes a level playing field where everyone has the same advantages and where difference in relation to colour, 'race' and ethnicity is not recognized. Acknowledging the colour of an individual is seen to be discriminatory and therefore the approach is offered as a positive alternative. The term was traditionally linked to assimilation and integration as a means by which different perspectives could be absorbed into mainstream society. This suggests a limited and superficial understanding of the effects of racism and discrimination. Critics have concluded that it is only possible to address inequality if visible difference is acknowledged as an indicator of power in society (CCETSW, 1991a).

Culturally specific practice – This gained prominence within international and European thinking and focused on work with service users of different cultural and religious backgrounds with obligation and social responsibility at its core. Specificity suggests that professionals are trained to respond to the particular needs of the groups and communities they work with. This may involve a higher level of understanding in languages, traditions and customs. The approach is not widely used in British social work but is seen to promote understanding of specific groups in society (Augoustinos and Reynolds, 2001). The term omits analysis of political and power relations between groups and individuals.

Culture – This describes a system of meaning and custom (Cashmore, 1996) and extended to 'multicultural' suggests a recognition and approval of groups based on difference and diversity. Sivanandan (1991), Gilroy (1995), Ali and Barsamian (2005), Brah (1996) and Solomos and Back (1995) suggest that terms such as 'multicultural perspectives' create problems because they do not address institutional and structural discrimination. Culture is often simplified and related more to some newly arrived immigrant groups, such as

Indians, than others, such as those originating from Africa or the Caribbean. Also, during the 1970s and 80s, the cultural heritage of the white majority was largely underplayed, with little debate on the cuisine, customs and traditions of Scottish, English, Welsh and Irish peoples.

Discrimination – In essence, discrimination is neither a negative nor positive term, it is more an analysis and reaction to difference (Thompson, 2003). However, society responds overwhelmingly to individuals who discriminate negatively, acting out the belief that they are superior in intellect, behaviour, mental capacity and/or physique. Forsythe (1995) suggests that the superior/inferior idea is rooted in society's structures and systems. To counter this, unfair treatment on the grounds of 'race', sex, disability, age, sexual orientation and religious belief is unlawful in many countries of the world, including the UK. The Race Relations Act 1976 defined **direct** discrimination as overt and easy to define, and **indirect** discrimination as covert and difficult to pinpoint and challenge.

However, even with this distinction, a great deal of the challenge to discrimination depends, first, on some understanding of relevant the laws, and, second, on individuals having the confidence and resource to confront perpetrators. It requires an examination of the intention behind an action that is the subject of complaint. An obvious example may be a woman with an Indian or other foreign name who is not shortlisted for a vacant post but whose CV clearly matches the job description and person specification. A woman's right to equality is also covered by the Sex Discrimination Act 1975 and related equal pay laws.

The Race Relations Act 1976 and the Sex Discrimination Act 1975 have both been used to support workers in challenging organizational practice through employment tribunals and court proceedings, and so obvious and direct discrimination within employment practice is rare. However, it is still possible for skilful employers to subtly and discretely manipulate the system in a manner which means that the worker has to prove indirect discrimination, which, in the example, may be on the grounds of race and/or sex. In such a scenario, power and prejudice combine to oppress in a manner which abuses authority, influence and control. This is forbidden under the Equality Act 2006.

Diversity and difference – Diversity suggests that people can live parallel, separate lives and superficially share each others' cultures, religions and traditions without discussion or reflection. This is conceptually problematic, as it appears to lack a substantial analysis of legal, structural and institutional power based on social and economic difference. It also tends to promote the level playing field, that is, little difference in power between individuals, and focuses on personal and attitudinal change rather than legal, human and political rights.

Working with difference is also inclined to focus on the common cultural threads shared by individuals and groups but not on resolving the problems created by discrimination and racism.

Equal opportunities – This is based on the assumption that all members of society should have equal access to goods, services and employment. Equal opportunities policies aim to set in place positive measures to eliminate not only overt discrimination but also conditions, requirements and practices which are discriminatory in, for example, operational social work.

Ethnicity – This is derived from the Greek word *ethnikos* (Cashmore, 1996) and relates to a 'people or nation'. Modern-day usage suggests common origin, unity and awareness of shared characteristics, but ethnicity is seen to have limited relevance to white Britain.

The word is often used interchangeably with 'race' and aligned almost entirely to colour and difference.

Human rights – The Human Rights Act 1998 (see Chapter 2) is based on egalitarian, universal and humanitarian principles, further promoting equality of opportunity, social justice and fair treatment. The 1998 Act, however, often contradicts other laws, resulting in challenges to professional practice and the day-to-day responsibilities of social workers. The Human Rights Act 'always carries the concomitant duty to respect the rights of others … as professional social workers it is necessary to think in terms of duties (Beckett and Maynard, 2005, p. 33).

Integration – Integrated communities live together while maintaining their own special ways of living. This idea suggests that people can work well together and contribute equally to society. But it is problematic because equal access to goods and services is rare, and so it is difficult to achieve integration without consideration of the wider issues of equality and fairness.

Oppression – The word 'oppress' comes from the Latin *opprimere* 'to press on', 'to press against'. It suggests force, being flattened or squashed out of shape. Oppression is a complex term which concerns structural differences in power as well as the personal experience of oppressing or being oppressed. It relates to 'race', gender, sexual orientation, age and disability as separate domains and overlapping experiences.

Positive action – A more sophisticated kind of response than positive discrimination is to assess the discrepancies brought about by past discriminatory action and seek to bring about changes in the practices and assumptions that led to unjust and unequal outcomes. There are many possibilities here, none of which involve unfair treatment of any individual or group. This means that attention is paid to the many and varied obstacles to disadvantaged groups. Some obstacles can be removed, and others can be taken into account when assessing the worth of a person.

Instead of quotas, targets can be set. A target is an indicative plan to encourage a change in practices and produce a manifestly fairer result in the future. In order to be effective and successful, the process requires extensive recording of decisions and monitoring of practices and outcomes.

Positive action will often include special training arrangements, an effort to attract candidates from underrepresented groups, and a reassessment of the assumptions underlying decisions concerning suitability, qualifications and experience. Other positive action methods include offering facilities which meet different religious, dietary and holiday needs, as well as explicit encouragement to underrepresented groups to take up generally available opportunities, such as training to support continuous professional development.

Positive discrimination – The effects of past discrimination call for a specific policy response, such as a quota system for specific groups in society. Positive discrimination is legal in a few countries but it is illegal in the UK.

Prejudice – This may be defined as learned beliefs and values that lead an individual or a group of individuals to be prejudiced for or against members of particular groups. Prejudice usually refers to negative aspects that generate hostile views based on generalizations, invariably derived from inaccurate or incomplete information. People are often unwilling to change these views even when presented with clear evidence that they are factually wrong.

'Race' – The contemporary social definition of 'race' is commonly used to put together groups who share common origin or descent. Although 'race' as a concept is questionable at many levels (Dominelli, 2008), in relation to law and policy it is used to imply ethnicity, culture and ethnic difference. 'Race' has a range of meanings derived from history and science, complicated by the division of the human 'race' into subspecies of Negroid, Mongoloid and Caucasoid (Cashmore, 1996). Within social science literature, however, the term has changed over time from biological to social and cultural:

> Historically, the meaning of the term 'race' has varied. It once focused on a racialised hierarchy that encompassed the physical attributes of all races – identified by skin colour and depicted in popular parlance as white, yellow, red and black (Gobineau, 1953). Definitions of race propagated by Count Gobineau illustrate a biological theory on racialised skin colour. Later, it focused on allegedly different intelligence levels that favoured the 'white' race (Hernstein and Murray, 1994). (Dominelli, 2008, p. 8)

The questionable theories on the biological definition of 'race' have been enshrined in law and social policy and impact on individuals on an everyday basis. It may be argued that categorization such as this socially isolates individuals and groups from each other. For example, in contemporary Britain, where 4.6 million (or 7.9%) BME individuals reside (NSO, 2001), many second or third generation immigrants have a long-term vested interest in relating to one another, as well as the wider population, but many live in exclusive groups where religious and/or cultural practices are shared internally more than externally with wider society.

The literature on identity and identification particularly supports the right of the individual to see and be seen beyond colour or other personal features. Benjamin Zephaniah, poet, stated:

> Race is an important part of my identity, but I wish it wasn't. I'd like to identify myself as a martial artist, an Aston Villa

supporter, or a hip-hop reggae person but when the policeman stops me on the street it has nothing to do with that. (quoted in *The Guardian*, 21 March 2005, p. 5)

'Race' relations – This has been used widely since the 1960s within law and policy to promote greater understanding and cohesion between minority and majority communities. The term attempts to explain how groups work together. It is problematic because it implies that groups relate to each other purely on the basis of racial difference and so meaningful usage depends on whether racial difference is seen as a concrete idea.

Racial discrimination – Racial discrimination is used interchangeably with racism particularly in European and international conventions (Wrench and Solomos, 1993). The mixing of racism, racial discrimination and racial disadvantage does not address discrimination as the practical criminal result of racist ideology. For example, if acted out to the extreme, racism and discrimination may be harmful to those at the receiving end of racial violence. Confusing violent attack with disadvantage on the grounds of difference and diversity more generally suggests that extreme and moderate outcomes may be the same.

Racism – The Race Relations Act 1976 defined racism or racial discrimination as less favourable treatment of individuals and families on the grounds of colour, race, nationality (including citizenship), ethnic or national origins. According to the CRE (2007b, p. 3):

This wide definition was necessary because of the remarkable variety of unfair treatment ... on the grounds that a person was black (colour), Chinese (ethnic or national origins), Malaysian (nationality). It included discrimination against white people (colour) or against Europeans (national origin for example German people).

The word 'racism' generates a great deal of feeling and is difficult to define in one way only. It is an ideology or set of beliefs and its development may be explained by oppressive hostility between two sets of groups, nations or power blocs. For example, the slave trade was based on the notion that African people were racially inferior and thus open to justifiable exploitation. Cashmore (1996, p. 308) suggests that racism needs to be defined variously depending on the context and situation: 'Racism takes different empirical forms in different societies at different points in time.'

Social activism – This may relate to any group seeking to promote a particular concept or political view in a committed and passionate manner. In relation to anti-racist practice, activists developed many ideas on 'race' and racism during the 1970s and 80s, within both the public services and literature (Solomos and Back, 1996), but the intense conservatism of Margaret Thatcher's government curbed this important work.

While social activists were engaged in defending anti-racist practice in the 1970s, the government's legal and policy focus was on the management of newly arrived immigrants from Britain's ex-colonies. Concern with migration was reflected in other European countries and became increasingly linked to 'race' and racism:

A new politics of immigration has emerged in Europe as well as other parts of the globe. As Etienne Balibar notes in relation the situation in France ... immigration has become, par excellence, the name race, a new name ... this inter linkage between the politics of immigration and race has been evidence in the context of Britain for some time ... the impact of immigration on the politics of race is likely to grow over the coming decade. (Solomos and Back, 1996, p. 55)

The Commission for Racial Equality, the Institute of Race Relations and the

Central Council for Education and Training in Social Work (CCETSW, 1991a) hosted a number of important initiatives to counter punitive legal and policy measures which questioned the links between immigration and 'race' and provided important arguments to counter assumptions. CCETSW (1991a,1991b) developed much needed guidance for social work practitioners and students, which highlighted political, structural and institutional concerns from a range of perspectives, including important parallels between sectarianism in Northern Ireland for example and racism more generally.

However, the 1980s in particular was a difficult time for professionals wishing to work and think in a collective way. The premiership of Margaret Thatcher fuelled National Front activity and many liberals were faced with a hostile environment. In response to this scenario, a number of activists looked for positive strategies, including Husband (1991, p. 67) who appealed for greater 'humility' and openness: 'What is required is an honest recognition of the different histories and current social positions which inform individuals' personal and collective participation in the anti-racist struggle.'

Sivanandan (1991, p. 36) also asked for a re-examination of the past and called on black people to 'reclaim history' in the process of understanding and exercising power. However, the time and context meant that this appeared to be a call to arms across a black/white divide which stressed the 'fight' against racism at a time of heightened political and social activism in Britain.

Tolerance – Cultural tolerance and acceptance suggests forbearance, enduring or 'putting up with' others – a grudging acknowledgement of difference but generally inclined towards a colour blind approach. Augoustinos and Reynolds (2001, p. 73) suggest that this position is accepting and valuing but has its limits: 'freedom from bigotry may always be considered good. In contrast forbearance towards value systems that conflict with one's own is likely to have moral limits.'

References

Abrams, D. and Houston, D.M. (2006) *Equality, Diversity and Prejudice in Britain*, University of Kent.

Adams, R. (2002) Quality assurance, in Adams, R., Dominelli, L. and Payne, M. (eds) *Critical Practice in Social Work*, Palgrave Macmillan, Basingstoke.

Adams, R. (2005) Working with and across boundaries: tensions and dilemmas, in Adams, R., Dominelli, L. and Payne, M. (eds) *Social Work Futures: Crossing Boundaries, Transforming Practice*, Palgrave Macmillan, Basingstoke.

Advocacy in Action (2007) Why bother? The truth about service user involvement, in Lymbery, M. and Postle, K. (eds) *Social Work: A Companion to Learning*, Sage, London.

Ahmad, B. (1990) *Black Perspectives in Social Work*, Venture Press, Birmingham.

Ahmad, W.I. and Atkin, K. (1996) *'Race' and Community Care*, Open University Press, Buckingham.

Ali, T. and Barsamian, D. (2005) *Speaking of Empire and Resistance*, New Press, New York.

Anthias, F. and Yuval-Davis, N. (1995) *Racialized Boundaries: Race, Nation, Gender, Colour and Class and the Anti-racist Struggle*, Routledge, London.

Armstrong, F. and Barton, L. (eds) (1999) *Disability, Human Rights and Education: Cross Cultural Perspectives*, Open University Press, Buckingham.

Augoustinos, M. and Reynolds, K.J. (2001) *Understanding Prejudice, Racism, and Social Conflict*, Sage, London.

Badwall, H., O'Connor, P. and Rossiter, A. (2004) Living out histories and identities in organisations: a case study from three perspectives, in Gould, N. and Baldwin, M. (eds) *Social Work, Critical Reflection and the Learning Organisation*, Ashgate, Aldershot.

Baldwin, M. (2004) Critical reflection: opportunities and threats to professional learning and service development in social work organisations, in Gould, N. and Baldwin, M. (eds) *Social Work, Critical Reflection and the Learning Organisation*, Ashgate, Aldershot.

Banks, S. (1995) *Ethics and Values in Social Work*, BASW/Macmillan, Basingstoke.

Banks, S. (2004) *Ethics, Accountability and the Social Professions*, Palgrave Macmillan, Basingstoke.

BASW (British Association of Social Workers) (2002) *Code of Ethics for Social Work*, http://www.celticknot.org.uk/links/baswcode.html.

Beckett, C. and Maynard, A. (2005) *Values and Ethics in Social Work: An Introduction*, Sage, London.

Bhatti-Sinclair, K. (1994) Asian women and violence from male partners, in Lupton, C. and Gillespie, T. (eds) *Working with Violence*, BASW/Macmillan, Basingstoke.

Bhatti-Sinclair, K. (1999) Evaluating social work and medical practice with black and ethnic minority groups using the Clinical Audit Model, *British Journal of Social Work*, 29: 3003–320.

Blakemore, K. and Boneham, M. (1994) *Age, Race and Ethnicity: A Comparative Approach*, Open University Press, Buckingham.

Boe, S. (1996) The experiences of students and practice teachers: factors influencing students' practice learning, in Doel, M. and Shardlow, S. (eds) *Social Work in a Changing World: An International Perspective on Practice Learning*, Arena, Aldershot.

Brown, A. and Bourne, I. (1996) *The Social Work Supervisor*, Open University Press, Buckingham.

Brah, A. (1996) *Cartographies of Diaspora: Contesting Identities*, Routledge, London.

Braye, S. and Preston-Shoot, M. (1995) *Empowering Practice in Social Care*, Open University Press, Buckingham.

Braye, S. and Preston-Shoot, M. (2002) Social work and the law, in Adams, R., Dominelli, L. and Payne, M. (eds) *Social Work: Themes, Issues and Critical Debates,* Palgrave/Open University, Basingstoke.

British Council (2007) *Making a World of Difference: Cultural Relations in 2010*, British Council, London.

Burke, B. and Harrison, P. (2005) Black perspectives in social work, in Davies, M. (ed.) *The Blackwell Encyclopaedia of Social Work*, Blackwell, Oxford.

Calouste Gulbenkian Foundation (1968) *Community Work and Social Change: A Report on Training*, Longmans, London.

Carpenter, J. (2005) *Evaluating Outcomes in Social Work Education*, Social Care Institute for Excellence/Scottish Institute for Excellence in Social Work Education.

Cashmore, E. (1996) *Dictionary of Race and Ethnic Relations*, Routledge, London.

Caspi, J. and Reid, W.J. (2002) *Educational Supervision in Social Work*, Columbia University Press, New York.

CCETSW (Central Council for Education and Training in Social Work) (1991a) *Setting the Context for Change*, Northern Curriculum Development Project, CCTSW, London.

CCETSW (Central Council for Education and Training in Social Work) (1991b) *One Small Step Towards Racial Justice: The Teaching in the Diploma in Social Work Programmes*, CCTSW, London.

CEHR (Commission for Equality and Human Rights) (2006a) *Equality Act 2006: Overview*, www.cehr.org.uk.

CEHR (Commission for Equality and Human Rights) (2006b) *Easy Read Guide to the CEHR*, www.info.cehr.org.uk.

CERD (Committee on the Elimination of Racial Discrimination) (2003) *Concluding Observations of the Committee on the Elimination of Racial Discrimination: United Kingdom of Great Britain and Northern Ireland*, http://www.unhchr.ch/tbs/doc.nsf/(Symbol)/CERD.C.63.CO.11.En?Opendocument.

Chand, A. (2005) Do you speak English? Language barriers in child protection social work with minority ethnic families, *British Journal of Social Work*, **35**(6): 807–21.

Clark, C.L. (2000) *Social Work Ethics: Politics, Principles and Practice*, Palgrave – now Palgrave Macmillan, Basingstoke.

Commission on Integration and Cohesion (2007) *Our Shared Future*, www.integrationandcohesion.org.uk.

Community Care (2005) Individual needs are at the heart of Byrne's vision of adult social care, 14–20 July, www.communitycare.co.uk.

Coulshed, V. and Mullender, A. (2001) *Management in Social Work*, Palgrave – now Palgrave Macmillan, Basingstoke.

Coulshed, V. and Orme, J. (2006) *Social Work Practice*, Palgrave Macmillan, Basingstoke.

CRE (Commission for Racial Equality) (2002) *Statutory Code of Practice on the Duty to Promote Race Equality,* http://www.equalityhumanrights.com/uploaded_files/code_of_practice_on_the_duty_to_promote_race_equality.pdf

CRE (Commission for Racial Equality) (2006) *Meeting the Challenge of Community Relations in 21st century Britain*, CRE, www.cre.gov.uk/policy/newbody.html.

CRE (Commission for Racial Equality) (2007a) *Response to the Commission on Integration and Cohesion*, www.cre.gov.uk.

CRE (Commission for Racial Equality) (2007b) *Words and Meanings: Race, Ethnicity and National Origins*, www.cre.gov.uk.

Cree, V. and Davis, A. (2007) *Social Work: Voices from the Inside*, Routledge, London.

Croft, S. and Beresford, P. (1993) Neighbours, in Bornat, J., Pereira, C., Pilgrim, D. and Williams, F. (eds) *Community Care: A Reader*, Macmillan, Basingstoke.

CSCI (Commission for Social Care Inspection) (2006) *Equalities and Diversity Strategy*, www.csci.org.uk.

CWDC (Children's Workforce Development Council/Skills for Care) (2007) *Providing Effective Supervision: A Workforce Development Tool, Including a Unit of Competence and Supporting Guidance*, www.cwdcouncil.org.uk/assets/0000/2832/Providing_Effective_Supervision_unit.pdf.

Dalrymple, J. and Burke, B. (1995) *Anti-Oppressive Practice: Social Care and the Law*, Open University Press, Buckingham.

Davies, M. (ed.) (2005) *The Blackwell Encyclopaedia of Social Work*, Blackwell, Oxford.

DCLG (Department of Communities and Local Government) (2007) *REACH: An Independent Report to Government on Raising the Aspirations and Attainment of Black Boys and Young Black Men*, www.communities.gov.uk/publications/communities/reachreport.

DfES (Department for Education and Skills) (2004) *Every Child Matters: Change for Children*, London, TSO.

DH (Department of Health) (2000) *No Secrets*, www.dh.gov.uk/publications.

DH (Department of Health) (2002) *Requirements for Social Work Training*, DH, London.

DH (Department of Health) (2007) *Putting People First: A Shared Vision and Commitment to the Transformation of Adult Social Care*, www.dh.gov.uk/publications.

DH (Department of Health) (2008) *Human Rights in Healthcare: A Short Introduction*, www.dh.gov.uk/publications.

Doel, M. and Shardlow, S.M. (2005) *Modern Social Work Practice: Teaching and Learning in Practice Settings*, Ashgate.

Dominelli, L. (1988) *Anti-racist Social Work*, BASW/Macmillan, Basingstoke.

Dominelli, L. (1996) Deprofessionalising social work: anti-oppressive practice, competencies and postmodernism, *British Journal of Social Work*, 26: 153–75.

Dominelli, L. (1997) *Anti-Racist Social Work* (2nd edn), BASW/Palgrave, Basingstoke.

Dominelli, L. (2002) Anti-oppressive practice in context, in Adams, R., Dominelli, L. and Payne, M. (eds) *Social Work: Themes, Issues and Critical Debate*, Open University/Palgrave, Basingstoke.

Dominelli, L. (2004) *Social Work: Theory and Practice for a Changing Profession*, Polity Press, Cambridge.

Dominelli, L. (2008) *Anti-racist Social Work* (3rd edn), BASW/Palgrave Macmillan, Basingstoke.

Dominelli, L. and Thomas Bernard, W. (2003) *Broadening Horizons: International Exchanges in Social Work*, Ashgate, Southampton.

DTI (Department of Trade and Industry) (2006) *Fairness for All: A New Commission for Equality and Human Rights*, White Paper, Cm 6185, www.dti.gov.uk.

During, S. (1995) Postmodernism or postcolonialism today, in Ashcroft, B., Griffiths, G. and Tiffin, H. (eds) *The Postcolonial Studies Reader*, Routledge, London.

EHRC (Equality and Human Rights Commission) (2009) *Equality Bill: Parliamentary Briefing*, www.equalityhumanrights.com.

Ellis, R. and Whittington, D. (1998) *Quality Assurance in Social Care: An Introductory Workbook*, Arnold, London.

Ely, P. and Denney, D. (1987) *Social Work in a Multi-Racial Society*, Gower, Aldershot.

Equalities Review (2007a) *Interim Report for Consultation*, http://www.pfc.org.uk/files/Equalities_Review-Interim_Report.pdf.

Equalities Review (2007b) *Fairness and Freedom: The Final Report of the Equalities Review: A Summary*, www.theequalitiesreview.org.uk.

Fabian Society (2006) *Narrowing the Gap: The Final Report of the Fabian Commission on Life Chances and Child Poverty*, Fabian Society, London.

Fekete, L. (2006) Enlightened fundamentalism? Immigration, feminism and the Right, *Race and Class*, **48**(2): 1–22.

Fook, J. (2000) Deconstructing and reconstructing professional expertise, in Fawcett, B., Featherstone, B., Fook, J. and Rossiter, A. (eds) *Practice and Research in Social Work: Postmodern Feminist Perspectives*, Routledge, London.

Fook, J. (2002) *Social Work: Critical Theory and Practice*, Sage, London.

Fook, J. (2003) On the problem of difference, *Qualitative Social Work*, **2**(3): 359–63.

Fook, J. (2004) Some considerations on the potential contributions of intercultural social work, *Social Work and Society*, **2**(1): 83–6.

Forbat, L. (2004) The care and abuse of minoritized ethnic groups: the role of statutory services, *Critical Social Policy*, **24**(3): 312–31.

Forbes, I. and Mead, G. (1992) Measure for measure: a comparative analysis of measures to combat racial discrimination in the member countries of the European Community, University of Southampton.

Ford, P., Johnston, B., Mitchell, R. and Myles, F. (2004) Social work education and criticality: some thoughts from research, *Social Work Education*, **23**(2): 185–98.

Forsythe, B. (1995) Discrimination in social work: an historical note, *British Journal of Social Work*, 25: 1–16.

Frankenberg, R. (1993) *The Social Construction of Whiteness: White Women, Race Matters*, Routledge, London.

Freire, P. (1972) *Pedagogy of the Oppressed*, Penguin Books, Harmondsworth.

Gilligan, P. with Akhtar, S. (2006) Cultural barriers to the disclosure of child sexual abuse in Asian communities: listening to what women say, *British Journal of Social Work*, 36: 1361–77.

Gilligan, P. and Furness, S. (2006) The role of religion and spirituality in social work practice: views and experiences of social workers and students, *British Journal of Social Work*, 36: 617–37.

Gilroy, P. (1995) *There Ain't no Black in the Union Jack: The Cultural Politics of Race and Ration*, Routledge, London.

Gilroy, P. (2000) *Against Race: Imagining Political Culture Beyond the Color Line*, Belknap Press of Harvard University, Cambridge, MA.

Glastonbury, B. and LaMendola, W. (1992) *The Integrity of Intelligence*, Macmillan, Basingstoke.

GSCC (General Social Care Council) (2002a) *Codes of Practice for Social Care Workers and Employers*, GSCC, London.

GSCC (General Social Care Council) (2002b) *Accreditation of Universities to Grant Degrees in Social Work*, GSCC, London.

GSCC (General Social Care Council) (2005) *Specialist Standards and Requirements for Post-qualifying Social Work Education and Training: Leadership and Management*, GSCC, London.

GSCC (General Social Care Council) (2006) *Specialist Standards and Requirements for Post-qualifying Programmes: Practice Education*, GSCC, London.

GSCC (General Social Care Council) (2007) *Suitability for Social Work: Ensuring the Suitability of Social Work Students to Access and Continue their Training*, GSCC, London.

Guardian, The (2009) Unhappy return: fear and loathing await fugitives from Belfast racism, *The Guardian*, 27 June, pp. 16–17.

Guardian, The (2009) Meeting racism with humour: south pole joke raises loudest cheer of the night, *The Guardian*, 24 October.

Guardian, The (2009) We need to change mindsets, *The Guardian*, 25 November, p. 8.

Hall, S. (1996) Introduction: who needs identity, in Hall, S. and du Gay, P. (eds) *Questions of Cultural Identity*, Sage, London.

Hall, S. and du Gay, P. (eds) (1996) *Questions of Cultural Identity*, Sage, London.

Hawkins, P. and Shohet, R. (2006) *Supervision in the Helping Professions*, McGraw Hill/Open University Press, Maidenhead.

Hayes, D. (2005) Social work with asylum seekers and others subject to immigration control, in Adams, R., Dominelli, L. and Payne, M. (eds) *Social Work Futures: Crossing Boundaries, Transforming Practice*, Palgrave Macmillan, Basingstoke.

Healy, K. (2005) *Social Work Theories in Context: Creating Frameworks for Practice*, Palgrave Macmillan, Basingstoke.

Held, D. and McGrew, A. (2007) *Globalization and Anti-globalization: Beyond the Great Divide*, Polity Press, Cambridge.

Held, D., McGrew, A., Goldblatt, D. and Perraton, J. (2001) *Global Transformations: Politics, Economics and Culture*, Polity Press, Cambridge.

Heron, G. (2006) A cross cultural comparison on 'race' issues: is this the demise of a construct in higher education and social work practice, unpublished discussion paper, University of Strathclyde.

Herrnstein, R.J. and Murray, C. (1994) *The Bell Curve: Intelligence and Class Structure in American Life*, Free Press, London.

Higham, P. (2006) *Social Work: Introducing Professional Practice*, Sage, London.

Higham, P. (2009) *Post-Qualifying Social Work Practice*, Sage, London.

Home Office (2007) *Race Relations and the Police*, www.homeoffice.gov.uk.

Horner, N. (2003) *What is Social Work? Contexts and Perspectives*, Learning Matters, Exeter.

Hoyes, L. and Means, R. (1993) Markets, contracts and social care services: prospects and problems, in Bornat, J., Pereira, C., Pilgrim, D., and Williams, F. (eds) *Community Care: A Reader*, Macmillan/Open University, Basingstoke.

Hughes, M. and Wearing, M. (2007) *Organisations and Management in Social Work*, Sage, London.

Hugman, R. (2005) *New Approaches in Ethics for the Caring Professions*, Palgrave Macmillan, Basingstoke.

Hull University (2005) *Best Practice Guide: Disabled Students and Placements*, University of Hull.

Humphreys, C. (2005) Service user involvement in social work education, a case example, *Social Work Education*, 24(7): 797–803.

Husband, C. (1991) 'Race', conflictual politics, and anti-racist social work: lessons from the past for action in the 1990s, in *Setting the Context for Change*, CCETSW, London.

IFSW/IASSW (International Federation of Social Workers/International Association of Schools of Social Work (2004) *Ethics in Social Work, Statement of Principles*, http://www.ifsw.org/f38000032.html.

Johns, N. and Jordon, B. (2006) Social work, merit and ethnic diversity, *British Journal of Social Work*, 36: 1271–88.

Johns, R. (2005) *Using the Law in Social Work*, Learning Matters, Exeter.

Jones, C. (2000) Poverty, in Davies, M. (ed.) *The Blackwell Companion to Social Work*, Blackwell Publishing, Oxford.

Jordon, B. (1998) *The Politics of Welfare,* Sage, London.

Jowitt, M. and O'Loughlin, S. (2005) *Social Work with Children and Families*, Learning Matters, Exeter.

Kadushin, A. (1968) Games people play in supervision, *Social Work*, 13(3): 23–32.

Khan, P. and Dominelli, L. (2000) The impact of globalisation on social work in the UK, *European Journal of Social Work*, 3(2): 95–108.

Khan, S. (2008) Fairness not favours: how to reconnect with British Muslims, Fabian Society pamphlet (624).

King Pike, C. (2002) Measuring racial climate in schools of social work: instrument development and validation, *Research in Social Work Practice*, 12(1): 29–46.

Kirton, D. (2000) *'Race', Ethnicity and Adoption*, Open University Press, Buckingham.

Kohli, R.K. (2007) *Social Work with Unaccompanied Asylum Seeking Children*, Palgrave Macmillan, Basingstoke.

Kundnani, A. (2002) An unholy alliance? Racism, religion and communalism, *Race and Class*, **44**(2): 71–80.

Laird, S.E. (2003) Evaluating social work outcome in sub-Saharan Africa, *Qualitative Social Work*, Research in Practice, 2: 3.

Laming, H. (2003) *The Victoria Climbié Inquiry* (Laming Report), TSO, Norwich.

Lawrence, S., Dustin, D., Kasiram, M. and Partab, R. (2003) Exploring partnership: student evaluations of international exchanges in London and Durban, in Dominelli, L. and Thomas Bernard, W. (eds) *Broadening Horizons: International Exchanges in Social Work*, Ashgate, Aldershot.

Leach, B. (1996) Disabled people and the equal opportunities movement, in Hales, G. (ed.) *Beyond Disability: Towards an Enabling Society*, Sage, London.

Leaper, R.A. (1968) *Community Work*, Swale Press, London.

Lloyd, M. (2002) Care management, in Adams, R., Dominelli, L. and Payne, M. (eds) *Critical Practice in Social Work*, Palgrave Macmillan, Basingstoke.

Lyons, K. (2006) Globalisation and social work: international and local implications, *British Journal of Social Work*, 36: 365–80.

McGhee, D. (2005) *Intolerant Britain? Hate, Citizenship and Difference*, Open University Press, Buckingham.

McGhee, D. (2008) *The End of Multiculturalism: Terrorism, Integration and Human Rights*, Open University Press/McGraw-Hill, Maidenhead.

Macpherson, W. (1999) *The Stephen Lawrence Inquiry* (Macpherson Report), Cm 4262-I, TSO, Norwich.

Maxime, J.E. (1996) Some psychological models of black self concept, in Ahmed, S., Cheetham, J. and Small, J. (eds) *Social Work with Black Children and their Families*, Batsford/BAAF, London.

Means, R., Richards, S. and Smith, R. (2003) *Community Care: Policy and Practice*, Palgrave Macmillan, Basingstoke.

Midgley, J. (2000) Globalization, capitalism and social welfare: a social development perspective, in *Social Work and Globalization*, special issue.

Mishra, R. (1999) *Globalisation and the Welfare State*, Edward Elgar, Cheltenham.

Modood, T. (2007) *Multiculturalism: A Civic Idea*, Polity Press, Bristol.

Morris, K. (2002) Family based social work, in Adams, R., Dominelli, L. and Payne, M. (eds) *Critical Practice in Social Work*, Palgrave Macmillan, Basingstoke.

Neate, P. (2001) Questions to be asked, *Community Care*, 4–10 January.

Oakes, P.J. and Haslam, S.A. (2001) Distortion vs meaning: categorisation on trial for inciting intergroup hatred, in Augoustinos, M. and Reynolds, K.J. (eds) *Understanding Prejudice, Racism, and Social Conflict*, Sage, London.

ODPM (Office of the Deputy Prime Minister) (2006) *Executive Summary: ODPM Race Equality Scheme 2005–06*, ODPM Publications, London.

ONS (Office for National Statistics) (2001) *Census 2001*, http://www.statistics.gov.uk/census2001/census2001.asp.

Ouseley, H. (2007) The attack on multi-culturalism: a discussion , *Race and Class*, **48**(4): 77–81.

Owusu-Bempah, J. (2000) Race, in Davies, M. (ed.) *The Blackwell Companion to Social Work*, Blackwell Publishing, Oxford.

Parrott, B. (2001) Fatalism is the enemy of change, *Community Care*, 4–10 January.

Parton, N. (2002) Postmodern and constructionist approaches to social work, in Adams, R., Dominelli, L. and Payne, M. (eds) *Social Work: Themes, Issues and Critical Debate*, Open University/Palgrave, Basingstoke.

Patel, N. and Mertens, H. (eds) (1998) *Living and Ageing in Europe as a Minority: Profiles and Projects*, NIZW/CCETSW, Utrecht.

Payne, M. (2005) *The Origins of Social Work: Continuity and Change*, Palgrave Macmillan, Basingstoke.

Payne, M. (2009) *Social Care Practice in Context*, Palgrave Macmillan, Basingstoke.

Peirce, G. (2007) This historical context, *Race and Class*, **48**(4): 45–50.

Phillips, J., Ray, M. and Marshall, M. (2006) *Social Work with Older People* (4th edn), Palgrave Macmillan, Basingstoke.

Pinkerton, J. (2002) Child protection, in Adams, R., Dominelli, L. and Payne, M. (eds) *Critical Practice in Social Work*, Palgrave Macmillan, Basingstoke.

Powell, J. and Robison, J. (2007) The 'international dimension' in social work education: current developments in England, *European Journal of Social Work*, **19**(3): 383–99.

QAA (Quality Assurance Agency for Higher Education) (2008) *Subject Benchmark Statement for Social Work*, www.qaa.ac.uk/academicinfrastructure/benchmark/statements/socialwork08.pdf.

Race Equality Foundation (2008) *Response to the Discrimination Law Review*, www.equalities.gov.uk.

Rapley, M. (2001) How to do X without doing Y: accomplishing discrimination without being racist – doing equity, in Augoustinos, M. and Reynolds, K.J. (eds) *Understanding Prejudice, Racism, and Social Conflict*, Sage, London.

Rex, J. (2000) Race relations in sociological theory, in Back, L. and Solomos, J. *Theories of Race and Racism*, Routledge, London.

Robinson, L. (2001) A conceptual framework for social work practice with black children and adolescents in the United Kingdom: some first steps, *Journal of Social Work*, 1: 2.

Robinson, L. (2002) Social work through the life course, in Adams, R., Dominelli, L. and Payne, M. (eds) *Social Work: Themes, Issues and Critical Debate*, Open University/Palgrave, Basingstoke.

Rose, D. (2007) The politicisation of intelligence, *Race and Class*, **48**(4): 57–60.

Ruch, G. (ed.) (2009) *Post-Qualifying Child Care Social Work: Developing Reflective Practice*, Sage, London.

Sapey, B., Turner, R. and Orton, S. (2004) *Access to Practice: Overcoming the Barriers to Practice Learning for Disabled Social Work Students*, SWAPltsn, Southampton.

Scarman, L. (1982) *The Scarman Report: The Brixton Disorders, 10–12 April 1981*, Penguin Books, London.

Schön, D.A. (1991) *Reflective Practitioner: How Professionals Think in Action*, Ashgate, Aldershot.

Schwarz, B. (ed.) (1996) *The Expansion of England: Race, Ethnicity and Cultural History*, Routledge, London.

SCIE (Social Care Institute for Excellence) (2003a) *Users at the Heart: User Participation in the Governance and Operations of Social Care Regulatory Bodies*, SCIE, London.

SCIE (Social Care Institute for Excellence) (2003b) *A Framework for Supporting and Assessing Practice Learning*, Position Paper 2, SCIE, London.

SCIE (Social Care Institute for Excellence) (2004a) *Has Service User Participation Made a Difference to Social Care Services?* Position Paper 3, www.scie.org.uk/publications/positionpapers.pp03.asp.

SCIE (Social Care Institute for Excellence) (2004b) *Involving Service Users and Carers in Social Work Education*, Resource Guide 2, SCIE, London.

SCIE (Social Care Institute for Excellence) (2006) *Are We There Yet? Identifying the Characteristics of Social Care Organisations that Successfully Promote Diversity*, www.scie.org.uk/publications/raceequalitydiscussionpapers/redp03.pdf.

Seidler, V.J. (2010) *Embodying Identities: Culture, Differences and Social Theory*, Policy Press, Bristol.

Sewpaul, V. (2003) Reframing epistemologies and practice through international exchanges: global and local discourses in the development of critical consciousness, in Dominelli, L. and Thomas Bernard, W. (eds) *Broadening Horizons: International Exchanges in Social Work*, Ashgate, Southampton.

Sheppard, M. (2006) *Social Work and Social Exclusion: The Idea of Practice*, Ashgate, Aldershot.

Silove, D. and Ekblad, S. (2002) How well do refugees adapt after resettlement in Western countries?, *Acta Psychiatrica Scandinavica*, **106**(6): 401–2.

Simpson, L. (2007) *Population Forecasts for Birmingham, with an Ethnic Group Dimension*, Cathie Marsh Centre for Census and Survey Research, University of Manchester.

Singh, G. (2006) *Developing and Supporting Black and Minority Ethnic Practice Teachers and Assessors*, Practice Learning Taskforce, DH, London.

Sivanandan, A. (1991) Black struggles against racism, in *Setting the Context for Change*, CCETSW, Leeds.

Sivanandan, A. (2007) Racism, liberty and the war on terror: the global context, *Race and Class*, **48**(4): 45–50.

Smith, R. (2009) Inter-professional learning and multi-professional practice for PQ, in Higham, P. (ed.) *Post-qualifying Social Work Practice*, Sage, London.

Social Work Task Force (2009) *Building a Safe, Confident Future: The Final Report of the Social Work Task Force*, http://publications.education.gov.uk/default.aspx?PageFunction=productdetails&PageMode=publications&ProductId=DCSF-01114-2009.

Solomos, J. and Back, L. (1995) *Race, Politics and Social Change*, Routledge, London.

Solomos, J. and Back, L. (1996) *Racism and Society*, Macmillan, Basingstoke.

Soydan, H. and Williams, C. (1998) Exploring concepts, in Williams, C., Soydan, H. and Johnson, M.R. (eds) *Social Work and Minorities, European Perspectives*, Routledge, London.

Tew, J. (2006) Understanding power and powerlessness: towards a framework for emancipatory practice in social work, *Journal of Social Work*, **6**(1): 33–51.

Thompson, I.E. and Melia, K.M. (1988) *Nursing Ethics*, Churchill Livingstone, London.

Thompson, N. (1993) *Anti-discriminatory Practice*, BASW/Macmillan, Basingstoke.

Thompson, N. (2003) *Promoting Equality: Challenging Discrimination and Oppression*, Palgrave Macmillan, Basingstoke.

Thompson, N. (2006) *Anti-discriminatory Practice*, Palgrave Macmillan, Basingstoke.

Times, The (2007) From this … to this, *The Times*, 12 February, p. 4.

Times Higher Education (2009) Staff continue using terms deemed inappropriate by PC language advice, *Times Higher Education*, 6–12 August, p. 9.

TOPSS (Training Organisation for Personal Social Services) (2002) *National Occupational Standards for Social Work*, TOPSS, Leeds.

Tuhiwai Smith, L. (2008) *Decolonizing Methodologies: Research and Indigenous Peoples*, Zed Books, London.

UNICEF (2007) *Child Poverty in Perspective: An Overview of Child Well-being in Rich Countries*, Report Card 7, UNICEF Innocenti Research Centre, Florence, http://www.unicef.org/media/files/ChildPovertyReport.pdf.

US Department of Justice (2010) *Annual Survey of Jails 2004: Jurisdiction-level Data*, www.data.gov/raw/2183.

Waters, M. (1995) *Globalization*, Routledge, London.

Watson, D. (ed.) (1985) *A Code of Ethics for Social Work: The Second Step*, Routledge & Kegan Paul, London.

Willcocks, L. and Harrow, J. (1992) *Rediscovering Public Services Management*, McGraw-Hill, London.

Williams, C. and Soydan, H. (2005) When and how does ethnicity matter? A cross-national study of social work responses to ethnicity in child protection cases, *British Journal of Social Work*, 35: 901–20.

Wilson, K., Ruch, G., Lymbery, M. and Cooper, A. (2008) *Social Work: An Introduction to Contemporary Practice*, Pearson/Longman, Harlow.

Wrench, J. and Solomos, J. (eds) (1993) *Racism and Migration in Western Europe*, Berg, Oxford.

Yeates, N. (2001) *Globalization and Social Policy*, Sage, London.

Younghusband, E. (1967) *Social Work and Social Values, Readings in Social Work, 3*, NISW/George Allen & Unwin, London.

Author index

Subject index

empowerment xix, 2, 13, 31, 59, 66, 86, 93, 98, 101–3, 108, 115, 118, 120, 123, 130–3, 141
equalities impact 10, 38, 87
Equality Act 2006 xvii, 2–5, 7, 11, 13, 24, 56, 98, 109, 112, 137, 164, 167, 170
Equality and Human Rights Commission (EHRC) xvii, 3–4, 44, 89, 101, 129, 161, 165
Equal Opportunities Commission 3, 59
ethnicity xiv, 10, 19, 21, 32, 38, 69, 75, 78–80, 85, 87–8, 90, 98, 104, 108–9, 128, 148, 150, 165, 169, 170
European Association of Schools of Social Work 48
European Convention for the Protection of Human and Fundamental Rights 57
Every Child Matters 11, 42
evidence-based practice 8, 65, 69, 90, 98, 108, 111, 116, 143

feminist perspectives 85–6, 121

General Social Care Council xvii, 33, 86, 90, 125
globalization 28, 35
Gypsies xv, 45

Human Rights Act 1998 14, 56, 58, 72, 129, 170

identification 18, 20, 23, 49
identity xii, xvii–xviii, 3, 12–13, 19, 20, 23–4, 42, 58–9, 62, 71, 73–7, 81, 87–8, 117, 121, 150, 165, 171
International Association of Schools of Social Work 48, 143, 161, 163
International Convention on the Elimination of all forms of Racial Discrimination 44, 58
interprofessional working 49, 68–72, 76, 92–3, 140, 143

kinship xvi, 20, 32, 42–43, 51, 70, 88, 128, 143, 164–5

labelling and stereotyping 98, 105
Laming Report 11, 92, 95
language xvi, 2, 14, 16, 19, 20–1, 24, 30–2, 34, 36, 38, 41, 43, 57, 74, 77, 88–9, 106, 117, 123, 127, 130–3, 144, 162, 165, 169
literacy 38, 89, 144

Macpherson Report 11
management 68, 99, 100
management in research 107
modernization xviii, 4, 9, 86
modernization agenda 87, 120–2, 133, 137, 142, 162–3

National College of Social Work xviii, 136, 142, 157, 161
National Health Service and Community Care Act 1990 11
National Occupational Standards 44, 49, 86, 100, 138, 147, 167
No Secrets 92, 94

Paulo Freire 148
positive discrimination 170–1
poverty xiii, 7–8, 17, 24, 29, 38–42, 51, 63, 85, 161, 164
power 11, 14, 17, 30, 35, 37, 45, 78–80, 97, 100, 102–3, 108, 110, 122, 142, 150–1, 164, 168–73
practice placements 91, 145, 150, 151–2
practice teachers/educators 84, 137, 139–40, 144, 151
prejudice 35, 40, 45, 59, 62–63, 67–8, 71, 104, 117, 121–3, 150, 164, 170–1
professional standards xviii, 97, 136, 141, 147, 150, 157
Putting People First 116–17

quasi-markets 120

race equality impact 10, 12
Race Relations Act 1965 2–3, 9
Race Relations Act 1976 2–3, 9–10, 24, 118, 167, 172
Race Relations (Amendment) Act 2000 2–3, 9, 24, 97, 129, 167, 169
racial discrimination 2, 24, 44–5, 50, 58, 165, 172
reflective practice 65–7, 105
research in practice 107, 111
Roma xv–xvi, 45

service users 4–5, 23, 27, 34–5, 40–1, 46, 50, 58–9, 63, 70, 76, 85–9, 91, 93, 96, 102, 107, 111, 115–35, 140, 143, 145, 152–4, 157, 160, 163–9
Sex Discrimination Act 1975 169
social cohesion 19, 50, 120
social justice 5–6, 19, 39, 44, 54, 71, 108, 132, 141, 161, 163, 167, 170